OUT OF THE
THIRD WORLD

ASHOK SHARMA

MEADOW GROVE PUBLISHING

OUT OF THE THIRD WORLD

By Ashok Sharma

While all events in this book truly occured, I have relied on memory to fill in the gaps. Thus, names, places, incidents, and events may not be entirely accurate.

Meadow Grove Publishing
P.O. Box 284
La Canada, CA 91012-0284, USA
www.meadowgrovepublishing.com
Contact: ashok@meadowgrovepublishing.com
Tel. 818.408.6437

Printed in the United States of America
Published by Meadow Grove Publishing

Cover design by Alex Melone
Interior by Nick May
Edited by Alex Melone at TypeRight

ISBN 978-1-7336912-0-8 (hc.)
ISBN 978-1-7336912-1-5 (pbk.)
ISBN 978-1-7336912-2-2 (ebk.)

FIRST EDITION

Dedicated to my beloved late parents,
Balkrishan and Radharani,
who made inordinate sacrifices for me.

Contents

BOOK ONE

Chapter 1

Out of the Third World

Over a half-century ago, just past midnight, I landed at the Gatwick International Airport near London, England with the ambition to become a medical doctor.

Past the immigration control, I searched for my older brother, Sham, who was to pick me up, but he was a no-show. As the crowds thinned and then disappeared, I exited the terminal with my suitcase in hand. At the curbside, I grew despondent as I paced back and forth, searching for him. The flight from my home country, Tanzania, a third-world country in East Africa, was delayed by a day after it departed late and then stopped overnight in Cairo to refuel. However, Sham, with no phone at home, didn't know that, as the communication and information technology was underdeveloped in those days.

An hour after I landed, the passenger pick-up and drop-off curb was also deserted, except for an Indian man standing a stone's throw away from me. He lit a cigarette, started smoking, and looked around like a sleuth. After another puff, he looked at me casually, as if waiting for me to make the first move, and then his eyes moved past me toward a small black car parked down the curb. With no money and out of options, I hesitantly approached him. When I got closer, he turned toward me and asked if I needed a ride. *Wow.* My savior had appeared from nowhere.

I took out the piece of paper from my pocket that had Sham's address at Fredrick Road in Woolwich, London, and handed it to him. He read it and said he would take me there. He threw the smoking cigarette to the ground and crushed it with his foot. I placed my faith in a total stranger in the hopes he'd have empathy for a fellow Indian in a foreign land.

He led me to the car parked along the curb and dumped my bag in the car's trunk as I took a seat in the passenger's side. Seated in the driver's seat, he browsed through a thick map book for a few minutes, flipping several pages rapidly back and forth as the light from the outside airport illuminated the inside of the car. He shoved the map in the side of his seat, then suddenly took off and sped out of the airport.

It was all surreal, like I'd landed on an alien planet, but it was actually the first world. The car raced through the narrow, deserted streets of London lined with adjoining red-brick homes with tall, wooden-trimmed windows lit only by dim yellow fluorescent lights. He drove for miles and miles—sped up, slowed down, stopped at street signs, checked the map book, and took off again, repeating the same cycle multiple times. After an hour of aimless driving, I realized he was lost and didn't know where he was going. We passed by some shops, and one had a side clock hanging that displayed three o'clock.

After another two hours of erratic driving, I was worried about how much he would charge my brother for all this extra driving. Eventually, at five o'clock in the morning, he drove up a sloping street, and at the top left corner, I read the street sign: *Fredrick Road*. I took a sigh of relief that, finally, we were near my destination. He stopped at the curb near the house address on the piece of paper.

It was like the typical London red-brick houses I had passed earlier, with tall windows and adjoined houses on either side. The man got out, climbed a few steps to the white entry door, and knocked. After a minute, he impatiently knocked harder. A light flicked on inside, visible through the rectangular glazed-glass pane of the door, and a sleepy, skinny Indian in pajamas opened the door and yawned.

By now, I had exited the car and was standing at the front door near the man and told the drowsy guy that I was Sham's brother. He nodded and went back in to fetch him.

The house had a second set of stairs, left to the main entry stair-case, close to the sidewalk that led to a second entry door to the base-ment, typical of many English homes. A window to the left of the base-ment door lit up, and Sham called out my name. I called him back excitedly as he opened the basement door. As I turned to descend the front stairs, my "cabbie" rushed in front of me down the basement stairs and demanded six pounds from Sham for his fare. That shocked me as it was a lot of money in those days, and I would later discover it was worth a week of Sham's hard-earned salary.

I followed Sham through the door into a narrow hallway that ran along his room in the basement. In his room, he opened one of the two doors of a yellow armoire near the front window, and from the top shelf, he took out a small bundle of half-folded currency bills and counted six one-pound bills. Only a few bills were left after he handed the six pounds to the man pacing impatiently in the hallway for his money. He bolted after counting the money, probably headed back to the airport to fleece another lost Indian.

It was after many years that I came to appreciate and realize this initial sacrifice, and many later, that Sham had made for me. I learned that in your teenage years, a brother was the closest friend you could have and trust. It would be a rare nefarious man who betrayed his own brother, and the saying, "Blood is thicker than water," couldn't relate more to us.

Chapter 2

Woolwich College

My brother, Sham, who was barely a year older than me, was a handsome guy with thick black hair, like a famous Bollywood movie star. Someone had actually likened him, with fair accuracy, to a popular Indian movie star of those days, Dharmendra, as his face and hair matched the actor's. Dharmendra was a village boy from the north Indian state of Punjab. He was a Punjabi Sikh who had forsaken his turban, shaved off his beard and long hair, and changed his name from Dharminder Singh to his screen name Dharmendra. He learned Hindi and moved to Bombay, now called Mumbai, the hub for Bollywood films and became famous. Ostensibly, Sham had inherited his hair genes from my mom because our dad had male pattern baldness. The rest of my brothers and I had full heads of hair, but not as thick as my brother's as we were young. Sham was a jovial person, and I loved his sense of humor and ability to lighten a tense situation with his jokes.

It was early Saturday morning when I arrived at my new home. I began familiarizing myself with its quirks and intricacies. Our room was a small one-bedroom one-bath private flat in the basement. The room door opened into the hallway, close to stairs leading to the ground floor, and our bathroom was to the left of those stairs.

I was nervous about sharing this cozy room with another adult, even though he was my brother, as I always had a separate room at our rented home in Tanzania; however, I was just grateful that I had a place to stay in this new country. The room's prominent feature was an expansive window facing the street as you looked up over the small basement courtyard wall in front of the room dressed in thin satin-like curtains. The sun streaming in from the window illuminated the room's light-yellow wallpaper and gray vinyl-like floor, making it look spacious during the daytime. When the window was open, you could simply hop into the room from the outside courtyard.

Later that morning, Sham said we should get some groceries. As we left the basement exit door and headed up the outside stairs, the same man who had opened the door when I had arrived was also leaving the house from the main ground-floor door. He picked up two milk bottles in front of the door and placed them inside the house.

Milk came in glass bottles then, each with a wide opening at the top that was sealed with golden or silver foil, depending on the richness of the cream that floated on the surface of the milk inside. It was delivered by a milkman, sprouting many milkman jokes— some true, especially about adultery, as the milkman arrived in the morning when a husband had left for work, leaving only the housewife who left the empty bottles out and picked up the fresh bottles. Many years later, I read a story about a lady visiting friends who wondered why her son had deep red hair when neither she nor her husband had a trace of red hair. "It is a genetic mutation," the lady insisted. Soon, the milkman arrived with his delivery, wearing a broad smile as he greeted the lady cheerfully. Everyone became quiet as they noticed the prominent deep red of the milkman's hair. Another tale was told of a husband, seated on a tall bar stool at an old bar. He told the barman he wanted to give a toast to his wife because she loved him more than any woman could love a man.

When the skeptical barman asked what made him so sure, he responded, "I was homesick for six days, and whenever she heard the milk truck coming, she would rush out yelling excitedly at the milkman, 'My husband is home! My husband is home!'"

Sham called out to the man, "Rafi *sahib*, this is my younger brother, Ashok." *Sahib* was added to a person's name for respect in the Punjabi language. We shook hands. He was a quiet guy as we spoke in our native tongue, not saying much. After our brief encounter, Rafi headed to his small black car parked near the curb. After we parted, Sham told me that Rafi was the owner of the five-bedroom house we lived in. He rented out the rooms; Sham was the only tenant so far, now joined by me. Rafi was a Punjabi-Muslim Pakistani immigrant who had lived in London for many years and worked in a factory. His younger brother, Alam, who was single, also lived there. Rafi, his wife, and their two young daughters occupied the rooms in the main ground floor of the house.

We went to a market where there were fresh vegetable and fruit stalls. It was Saturday, so the market was crowded. It was my first experience of culture shock as I came from a country where most of the people were black, and here I was, where most—almost all—the people were Caucasian. We were two brown faces in a sea of white. Not only that, England was a crowded but organized country—which took some getting used to—unlike the sparsely populated Tanzania, where you could drive a hundred miles without sight of a person. We mostly looked around and bought some vegetables and then headed to a small Indian-owned grocery store to buy some Indian groceries. In those days, you stood in a line at a store, and when your turn came, you asked the shop owner for the items you wanted. Supermarkets didn't exist yet.

All this was new to me. At home in Tanzania, my mom did the grocery shopping and went to the local fruit and vegetable market. Occasionally, I tagged along when I was in junior high but never after I went to high school. I realized we were two single guys and would have to fend for ourselves; Sham had already been doing that, which would ease my transition.

We took the groceries back home and put them in the kitchen closet reserved for Sham. Then Sham told me that we should bathe at a public bathhouse. Our bathroom had a bathtub, but we could not access the hot water unless we inserted some coins in a small metal box-like control valve that triggered a burner that heated water. However, it produced hot water only for a short time unless we kept putting more coins in the box, which would cost a lot, per Sham, if we tried to fill the tub partially for a bath. There were no showers, so the low-cost option was a public bath.

The public bath was an old government-subsidized building in the center of Woolwich. Sham paid four pence coins at the front window, and the man gave each of us a large folded bath towel and a thick slab of soap. I saw only men patrons there. There were rows of rooms along a long hallway, each with a thick black wooden door. I went to one empty bathroom, and Sham went to the adjacent one.

The room had a large bathtub stretching along its far side wall opposite the door and took most of the room's space that I would find out later was typical of bathrooms in England. I turned on the large hot and cold water faucets and adjusted them to get the water to the right temperature and sealed the drain at the bottom with a plastic cork attached to a thin chain, filling the bathtub halfway. I took off my clothes and placed them next to the fresh towel and slowly entered the water. This was my first shower since I had left Tanzania, and it felt good to enter the warm water. In Tanzania, there was no piped hot water, and we had to heat water in a bucker over a fire pit and then pour the hot water into a bathtub. I felt relaxed, and as the water cooled, I turned the hot water tap on just enough to keep the water at the right temperature, steam coming off the surface that nearly touched the lip of the tub. I scrubbed my body with the thick soap.

After the bath, I unplugged the tub to drain it while I used the large towel to dry myself and dressed up. Sham was done before me and was waiting at the entrance when I dumped the towel in a container. My body felt fresh after the bath as we headed back home.

I would realize that a bath was a luxury, and we would have to limit our visits to two times a week, sometimes once a week, to save money.

The next day, I asked Sham if he knew where Norwood College was located and if we could go there to see it. I had received an acceptance letter when I was in Tanzania but had no idea how to follow up or register there. We left late that Sunday morning to find Norwood College. I was excited about this new experience, especially in an advanced first-world country.

London was divided into about thirty-three administrative areas called boroughs. Woolwich, where we lived, was a town in southeast London in the Royal Borough of Greenwich. We were far from central London, the hub of all the excitement and activity. We walked down Fredrick Road where we lived and went down several streets until reaching the main road of town where we waited for a bus. The bus stop had a list of the bus numbers that served that stop, the bus schedule, and their respective destinations on a piece of paper located in a glass-covered container.

The iconic red double-decker buses, called the Routemaster buses, came at frequent regular intervals. They were introduced in 1956 and were truly the national symbol of the United Kingdom until they were retired in 2005 from general service because of the difficulty in accommodating disabled passengers. On the front top of the second deck was the bus number in large letters and under it was the name of the town the bus terminated its journey. We passed the giant reflective windows of the bus before stepping onto the platform at its rear.

After stepping onto a platform upon entering, there was a metal pole to grab onto. Passengers would wait there, grabbing the bar, as the bus neared their destination and disembark quickly, exchanging seamlessly with those waiting on the curb outside. It all happened so fast, like a drill, and the bus did not stop for long.

It was entertaining for me to watch all this as we waited, and it wasn't long before Sham pointed to an approaching bus and said that it was ours. When it stopped, a few passengers got off, and we boarded.

Once inside, the bus driver ignored us, as he did every passenger, and we grabbed onto cold metal poles. The engine, disguised by a red hood, was loud, and I wondered how the driver could spend all day beside it, listening to its groans and wails.

The bus conductor stood close to the pole, and when those entering were onboard, he pressed a nearby bell to inform the driver it was safe to drive. There were stairs leading to the second deck next to the pole for those who wanted to sit on the second deck. Many, especially older people, took the first deck.

I followed Sham up the stairs to the second deck and soon realized why he had decided to go up. It gave us a fantastic view of the city. He said the best seats for view were right in the front, facing the two large front windows. Each seat had space for two passengers, and the seats were lined up in two rows on each side of the aisle. We were able to find seats in the front easily because most locals preferred not to take them since you would have the longest walk to disembark. We were halfway through the second deck aisle when the bus took off—another reason why many avoided the front seats. We grabbed the side seats as the bus's momentum pulled us back and slowly progressed forward, finally reaching the seats above the driver's cubicle. This unprecedented view exhilarated me, and I felt like I was sitting on a flying carpet. The traffic, the people walking on the sidewalks, the stores, and the passing homes rushed through my mind.

The bus conductor carried a small cylindrical ticket machine near his flank that hung from his neck with a strap. He came up after the bus had been traveling for a while and collected fares from the newly seated passengers after they told him their destinations. He issued them a small ticket from his machine, which made a clicking sound as it issued the ticket. I was impressed as he came after every stop and knew the passengers who had tickets and only went to those newly seated. Sham told me that conductors also remembered your destination, as he had once gone past his accidentally and soon the conductor came to demand more fare. He told me you could request the conductor to call out when you reached your destination, and he would do so before the bus stopped. We could periodically hear him shouting the next stop's name and then the relevant passengers would dart out. I thought that the bus conductors must have had great memories to remember who had paid and where they should get off before incurring more fare.

The bus stopped at many stops, and I had no idea where we were heading. I thought Sham knew the whereabouts of Norwood College. After about an hour, he said that he was lost and that the college was difficult to find. This was surprising as we changed a few buses, but he never asked anyone in the town where the college was located. Later, I found out that he wasn't serious about finding this college and had another plan that worked out better for me anyway. He revealed that there was a new college that had opened near his work in walking distance from where we lived. Why go to a college like Norwood College that was so far from our home, taking into account the travel time?

I told him that I had an acceptance letter from Norwood College, and my student visa was given based on that. I might not have gotten into this new college he was talking about. He told me not to worry, as there were many colleges in London, at least one in every town. This was not Tanzania, where there was only one college in the whole country located in the capital city. The colleges started in early September, so I had at least two more months to apply personally. While I was still somewhat worried about whether my British student visa was issued based on my admission letter from Norwood College, Sham reassured me it would be no problem, especially because this new college near his work would need new students to enroll.

Sham said our stop was approaching, so we vacated our seats and went to the back of the second deck to the stairs, grabbing one of the two ceiling bars for stability. When the bus came to a stop, we were in the middle of Oxford Street, one of the busiest shopping streets in London, where some gargantuan department stores were located.

The sidewalk was crowded with girls, often in pairs. The English girls were the sexiest girls I had ever seen, skimpily dressed in short hot pants and boots. The few men I noticed were overdressed, with long pants, boots, and jackets, a sort of mismatch—like the men were dressed for both of them. As we strolled down the pavement, I told Sham, "You know grandpa told me long ago when I was six learning Urdu from him to not look at a girl's face because you may get tempted and it will distract you from your studies. Only look at her legs, and you will be okay. I'm not sure that advice applies to England."

"Grandpa was talking about Africa and India where girls' legs are covered with clothes. He would have given the opposite advice had he ever come here. Poor grandpa is dead now," Sham said. We both laughed while we admired the girls.

We went into a huge store called Selfridges with many long pillars in front like the Colosseum. I was awestruck by its size as I had never seen such a large store. There were all sorts of items like fancy clothes, shoes, and apparel in small sections. It was a major tourist attraction as well. We walked around, admiring and window shopping. Interestingly, for such a luxurious store in a prime area, the items seemed relatively cheap and within the affordability of the average person. I guess they used economies of scale to profit. The store had six stories, and we went to each one of them. Of course, we didn't have any money to buy anything.

We walked down Oxford Street until we reached an underground station sign called Marble Arch. Past that, there was a large expansive park called Hyde Park, which had a small lake. There were groups of people gathered around speakers scattered at various spots, like islands over a sea of green grass. We listened to a few speeches. It was an exercise in free speech, where anyone wanting to express their views in public could speak and attract a small crowd of listeners and curious tourists. There was a young guy with shoulder-length hair wearing a t-shirt with the words "Socialists United," who was berating the United States about its involvement in Vietnam and the bombing of North Vietnam.

There was also an African giving an impassioned speech about the alleged atrocities by Nigerian troops in the civil war in Biafra, a part of Nigeria in West Africa. I was not sure if anyone knew where this place was and what he was talking about. It was fun, like free entertainment, to watch these people speaking so passionately about the causes they were expounding. Some had full loudspeaker setups, attracting bigger crowds. It was apparent to me that they were really practicing public speaking, and this was a great forum to hone their skills, like an outdoor toastmasters' club. It took guts and courage to speak to a crowd, especially for a newbie.

After wandering around Hyde Park for an hour, we decided to return as we were far from home. We changed several buses and returned to Woolwich late in the afternoon. Sham told me that when he left for work the next day, I could come with him, and he could show me the college. He worked for a large motorcycle store and was one of the salesmen for motorcycle parts. He showed me an advertisement in a local paper about job openings at some factories, including one at a Pepsi Cola factory in a nearby town and told me which bus to take to go there after visiting my college. I had a few months to kill before the college commenced and sitting at home would be boring, so it seemed like a good idea to explore. At this stage, it hadn't occurred to me how I would pay for college or how much it would cost.

We left in the morning around seven thirty and walked down several streets for twenty minutes and reached the new college that had a sign that read, *WOOLWICH COLLEGE FOR FURTHER EDUCATION.* Sham said that there used to be small shops in the area that were demolished to make space to build the college. It was a nice, spacious modern brick building with expansive windows along its walls. We walked along its long walls and turned to its front where there was a bus stop. Sham took one bus and told me the number of the bus to take to reach the Pepsi factory and to ask the conductor to notify me when the bus reached there.

The buses came at regular intervals. Soon my bus came, and I hopped on, taking a lower deck seat near the exit to get out quickly when my destination arrived. When the conductor came around to collect the fare, I asked him to inform me when we arrived at my destination in front of the Pepsi Cola factory. The bus was filled with people rushing to work, and when the bus arrived at the factory, the conductor called out to me, and I hopped off the bus after thanking him. The stop was right in front of the tall Pepsi factory.

I went to the administrative offices and talked to a girl at the entrance of the offices, asking her if they had a job for me. She entered my name and address in a book and gave me a small timecard with my name and took me down several stairs to a door that opened directly into the factory floor.

"Aren't you going to take off your jacket?" she asked. I was wearing a tie and a jacket, thinking I was going to work in an office. The sprawling factory floor had rows of different types of soda bottles coming down long lines of flat, narrow rollercoasters. My job was to remove the bottles from one of the horizontal rollercoasters before they reached the end of the line, where there was a stopper. It was repetitive manual work, and it took a while getting used to. Every day, bottles of different types of soda came down. Some days it was the famous Pepsi Cola bottles, other days were carbonated bottles of water in various sizes used in bars to make specialty alcoholic drinks. All the bottles were made of glass in those days.

It was a lonely job, and that was fine with me as I was a shy person anyhow. During the half-hour lunch break in the factory cafeteria a floor above, I had to look for items I could eat as a vegetarian, and that was always a problem. Most days, I ended up filling my plate with boiled peas that were available every day. I sat on my own and saw there was not much talking among other workers who were English, as the break was short and everyone wanted to finish eating and go down. My work ended at about four-thirty in the afternoon, and all the workers headed to the bus stop but took different buses depending on where they lived.

We were paid every Friday with cash inside small brown envelopes. I was paid six pounds in two bills, one five-pound and one one-pound note. I realized the value of hard-earned money and understood the amount the man who drove me home from the airport had charged Sham.

The work was exhausting because I'd never done manual labor before. I had to get the bottles out of the moving rollers fast, or they would jam and backup at the stopper and were then harder to remove. I was exhausted by the end of the day and went to sleep by eight at night. One night, I had a nightmare that the bottles were coming fast and jammed. They were falling over the roller and crashing on the ground as I tried to catch them. Sham woke me up and calmed me, as I was yelling in sleep, "The bottles are falling." I worked at the factory for over two months and had earned about sixty pounds over that period. I deposited most of my money in a savings account I had opened at the Midland Bank. They gave me a small passbook in which the teller entered the deposit amount and signed it. As an earner, I started contributing to buying our groceries on Saturday as Sham paid our rent.

Around August 1967, I went to register at Woolwich College at the administrative office with forty British pounds in my pocket, my total annual academic fee for the first year, my savings account virtually drained. That was a lot of money in those days. I asked the girl at the front desk if there was any discount for Commonwealth citizens. She called the administrator, a tall, balding guy wearing a scruffy black suit and tie, who told me tersely, "There is no discount even if you are a citizen of London," before turning around to head back to his office in the rear. I reluctantly handed the two crispy twenty-pound bills to the girl as it had taken me almost two months of hard factory labor to save it. Her eyeballs widened as she took the money, perhaps because it was equivalent to months of her wages. You earned more on the factory floor than as an office clerk. While I felt content that my first year's fees for the two-year college were paid,

I was certain my dad would send me money to pay for my share of living expenses and the second year's tuition when it came time. Dad and I corresponded regularly, and he sent me money in the form of a bank draft from Moscow Narodny Bank, a Russian bank.

Several years after independence, the Tanzanian government had promulgated a policy of "African socialism" with widespread nationalization of institutions, factories, and banks. The previous British bank, Barclays Bank, which had branches in most towns, had left and were replaced by Moscow Narodny, which handled foreign transactions, especially with Britain, because it had an office near central London. To cash the bank draft, I had to take and change several trains to reach Moscow Narodny and show my passport to the teller. He checked that the name on the draft matched the on my passport and gave me the check amount in cash. The check was for fifty pounds, and Dad had sent it to me after I was in England for about three months. The amount he could send was now limited, not that he had much to spare for me anyway. There were new controls on sending money overseas by the Tanzanian government to conserve foreign exchange that had dwindled fast under socialism. On my return to Woolwich, I deposited most of the cash in my Midland Bank savings account and kept some for groceries and other personal expenses. In a few weeks, I would commence my first year of college.

Chapter 3

The Adopted Sister-In-Law

The lady of the house, our landlord Rafi's wife, was short and chubby with round cheeks. She wore a loose, baggy *salwar kameez*, also called a Punjabi suit or dress, the traditional dress worn by Punjabi women. The *salwar* consisted of pajama-like pants with narrow hems above the ankles to look like cuffs. Ironically, the baggy ones made women look fatter and less sexy than they actually were. The *kameez* was a loose-fitting tunic with long sleeves that reached down to the knees. Some also wore a *dupatta,* or long headscarf, the third piece of the dress that covered the hair like many traditional Muslim women of those days. Younger Punjabi girls wore tighter and sexier versions of the *salwar kameez.*

I met Rafi's wife a few days after my arrival when she waddled into the kitchen as Sham and I were preparing to cook our dinner, a totally new experience for me. When she entered, Sham told her in Punjabi, "*Bhabhiji,* this is my younger brother, Ashok." She responded that her husband had told her of my arrival. *Bhabhiji* was the Punjabi word for a sister-in-law. *Bhabhiji* was respectful and implied that Sham thought of Rafi as his brother, even though we were Punjabi Hindus and they were Punjabi Muslims and we were not related in any way. Conforming to what Sham called her, I also addressed her as *Bhabhiji.*

Our daily routine after work was the same. When we reached home from a full day's work at about five o'clock in the evening, we headed to the kitchen located at the rear of the ground floor, with a large window overlooking a small backyard with grass. Cooking was a tedious task for the two of us, but a necessary evil for survival. No one had ever taught us how to cook since all the cooking at home in Tanzania was done by my mom. Sham had taught himself rudimentary cooking in the year he'd been in England.

It was a division of labor: I cut the vegetables, like cabbage and potatoes, in weird shapes, and he made the dough from *atta,* or wheat flour, in a small steel bowl. He put a handful of *atta* into the bowl and sprinkled a spoonful of *ghee,* or clarified butter, from a glass jar onto it. This gave the final product a better taste, enabled it to puff up, and decreased the chances of it sticking to the pan. He poured a small amount of water into the bowl and mixed it thoroughly with a hand. It had to be fine-tuned—too much water and the dough would be watery, not fit to make the round, flat *rotis,* or tortilla-shaped pancakes that formed the staple of Punjabi food. The dough, once at a firm consistency, was kneaded using the flat front part of his fist to make it firmer. A properly made dough was firm and easy to piece off.

After making the roti, he sliced half an onion and a tomato. If I was done with cutting the vegetables, and he was still busy with the dough or getting stuff ready to cook the vegetables, then I cut the tomato and onion also. Chilies that gave the food a better taste were hard to find at the Indian grocery store on our weekend shopping trips and most times had to do without. He heated a few tablespoonfuls of *ghee* in a pot with a handle on the gas stove and poured the onions and the tomatoes into brown the onions. They sometimes got burnt if the burner flame was too high or we were not watching. After that, he put in some curry powder, cumin seeds, turmeric, and coriander seeds, and let the onions and the tomatoes soak up their flavor by stirring with a wooden spatula. Into the resulting thick paste, he dumped the raw vegetables I had cut and stirred them until they were soaked with the curry mixture. He poured a cup or more of water into the resulting mixture and increased the heat to let it boil to cook the vegetables and get them to soak in the diluted curry paste.

On another burner, we placed a concave disc-shaped *tava*, or Indian saucepan, and started warming it. Pinching off a small piece of dough the size of a golf ball with his hand, Sham compressed and rolled it between palms of his two hands to convert it into a small, thick flat circular disc. Then he sprinkled some dry wheat flour onto a round wooden board and placed the circular dough in its middle. Using a wooden rolling pin and rolling it back and forth with gentle pressure, he flattened the dough like a thick tortilla. This required skill to get it right, like sprinkling some dry flour if it started to stick to the wooden board and roll areas of the dough jutting to one side to try to make the whole thing circular. Our *rotis* were often not nicely rounded, but the appearance didn't bother us.

By then, the concave pan was warm, and he stripped the *roti* from the wooden board onto the palms of his two hands and slapped it onto the pan. If the pan was too hot, the *roti* would cook too fast and burn. After one side warmed up, he turned it over by holding one side with two long flat-bladed metal prongs. Once both sides were semi-cooked, he moved the pan and applied each side of the *roti* directly to the flame for a short time, holding its edge with the prongs to keep his hand away from the flame. This enabled the *roti* to puff up, like a discus, as the trapped air and water inside steamed and expanded, splitting the *roti* into a thin, layered bread that made it softer and taste better than if it were heated on the concave pan, which would have ended in a one-layered *roti*. After he placed it on a plate, I applied a little *ghee* to it so it wouldn't be dry when we ate it.

Often, *Bhabhiji* would waddle in, pretending to do something else, like polishing her dishes, and offer Sham some tips on his cooking. Rafi didn't come home from his factory job until later, around seven or eight o'clock in the evening, and I never saw him or his younger brother, Alam, in the kitchen, assuming *Bhabhiji* took their food to them in the living room. At this point, I didn't realize that her visits were excuses to see Sham, but I could tell she was somewhat attracted to him. This would cause a problem later. However, I was certain that Sham only thought of her as B*habhiji*.

By the time we finished cooking, eating, and washing and putting away the dishes, it was almost eight in the evening. We went back to our room and turned on our portable paraffin heater as it was cold. Sometimes, that was the first thing I did on returning from college, or if the tank was low, I would go down to a small local mom and pop store to buy a gallon of paraffin. In the room, I tried to study, but when two people live in one room, talking is inevitable. Plus, there was nothing else for Sham to do, and he wanted to talk about things that happened at his work. By nine o'clock at night, we were asleep.

Chapter 4

The Nigerian

My first day at this newly minted Woolwich College was inauspicious. The first classroom I attended was a large, well-lit room with rows of new wooden tables and benches. A large blackboard hung on the front wall behind a long wooden table and stool for the tutor. I always came to class early—an old habit from my high school days—so I have time to get the textbook and writing material out of my leather briefcase and can get some studying done.

The class makeup was eclectic: Most of the students were English, but the second largest contingent was Indian—mostly kids of Indian immigrants—one Australian, two Greeks, two Chinese, one Romanian girl, and one Turkish boy. However, students changed with classes as not all of them studied the same subjects.

Some days later, as usual, I came about thirty minutes early for my morning class. Twenty minutes had passed as I looked at the round clock on the back wall, yet I was the only student in the class. It was just past the start time when I looked back again, wondering if I had made a mistake in going to the wrong class or if it was a day off, but we had just started college. It was eerily silent. I turned back again to look at the clock when I saw a girl looking through the backdoor window.

She was a fellow student, Miss Christine Betts, a pretty, tall English girl who wore a miniskirt and black high-heeled shoes. She opened the door.

"Mr. Sharma, you know we have a field trip today?" she said.

I looked puzzled. It seemed I had not understood that announcement when it was made previously.

"No. I did not know," I replied, without asking what a field trip was, not wanting to sound stupid.

"Come with me. The coach is waiting."

As I tried to put my stuff in my briefcase quickly, she said, "Leave that here. The coach will return to college. You can pick it then."

I followed her down the stairs, and we reached the front of the college where a coach full of students was waiting. It seemed like everyone else knew about the trip except me, and I wondered how I could have missed the announcement. It was not completely surprising as I had difficulty understanding English people, and that worried me. The front door of the coach was open, and we boarded. I walked past the driver who had the engine on and took a seat near a window at the back of the full coach. Miss Betts took her original seat near the front of the bus next to another female student.

The driver closed the entry door, and the coach soon departed. It was an exhilarating, long ride in a coach with soft seats. I looked out of the window at the bustling city life and people waiting at bus stops and rushing to work, though I'd no idea where we were headed. After almost two hours of winding through the bustling streets of London, the coach stopped in front of a massive building with a large sign, stating, *VICTORIA AND ALBERT MUSEUM.*

All the students disembarked, and we were met by some guides who took us in groups. There were two other museums in close vicinity that we also toured that day, the science museum and the natural history museum. The science museum had a German V2 rocket—the type that was used to bomb London in the waning days of WWII, killing over 10,000 people as the Nazis made a desperate attempt to turn the tide of war they were losing—with half of its cover removed to display its complex internal engines and parts. The natural history museum had fascinating species of preserved animals and skeletons of dinosaurs. We had lunch in a cafeteria there. By the time we returned to college, it was past five o'clock in the evening, and I went to pick up my stuff in the class. It was a surreal experience for a person like me from the third world who had never seen such things. I had learned a lot in one day. When I walked back home, I realized that I owed it to the kindness of Christine, whom I would call Miss Betts thereafter, and she would call me Mr. Sharma.

Here was an English student, who didn't know me as I had not talked with her before but had made the coach driver wait as she hadn't seen me on the coach and came to fetch me. I wondered how many other students, sitting comfortably in the coach, would have taken such an initiative; I guessed none. The adage, of remembering people not by the big things they did for you but the simple things, couldn't be truer in this case. The gratitude I owed her for this simple gesture and consideration became etched in my brain for the rest of my life onwards.

Lunch hour was a busy time at Woolwich College. All classes broke at noon, and everyone—students, tutors, and janitors—rushed to the cafeteria. I was standing in a long winding line next to the gray wall of the cafeteria, far from the actual food serving counters, when I noticed an older man, ostensibly in the early thirties, standing in line before me. He was a new student in our class who had appeared a few weeks after classes began. Interesting that, when you are eighteen years old, a person in his early thirties looks much older, like from a different generation. It was particularly unusual because he was about twice the age of the average student at the college.

He was a black African wearing a neatly pressed black suit, a waist-coat, a white shirt, and a dark tie. He was somewhat beefy, slightly shorter than me, and balding at the crown of his head. In front of his scalp, a thin fuzzy hairline started in the middle near the forehead and widened toward the back to merge into the hair on both sides of his temples, leaving triangular bald areas on either side in front. He was dressed more like someone going to a formal dinner than a college. Of course, I was curious as this was the first time I saw a fellow countryman from Africa at the college. At first, he momentarily turned his head around to look at the line behind him and our glances met, but nothing was said. The line moved a little. He then turned his head back again, like he wanted to talk to me.

"What country in Africa are you from?" I asked, like a reflex, as our glances met again, and my curiosity took the better of me.

"I'm from Biafra." He smiled.

"Oh, you are Nigerian. Biafra is in Nigeria."

"We are fighting for independence from Nigeria."

"I'm from Tanzania, the largest country in East Africa." I extended my hand, and he gave me a firm handshake.

Biafra was a breakaway state in the southeast of Nigeria, the largest country in West Africa. It had declared independence from Nigeria in 1967, leading to a vicious civil war. Nigeria itself had gained independence from Great Britain in 1962. When the European colonial powers, especially the British, French, and Germans, divvied up the African continent south of the Sahara Desert in the nineteenth century, it was called the Dark Continent because most of it was unexplored. The divisions, created by artificial boundaries on a map in Europe, ignored the harsh reality of splitting tribes into separate countries. Over a century and a half later, when these artificially created countries became independent, the tribal rivalries for political power, dominance, and resources led to bloodshed, and, in case of Nigeria, a civil war. Religion played an added divisive role: the majority of the tribes in Nigeria were Muslim, while the Ibos, who formed the majority in Biafra, were Christians. The colonialists, being small in numbers, ruled the countries by the "divide-and-rule" policy. Often, members of a minority tribe were promoted overwhelmingly in privileged administrative positions and in the local police and army led by colonial officers. This ensured their loyalty and kept the majority under control. The resentful majority often led the fight for independence. After independence, the minority, placed in a subordinate role and sidelined, especially as a retaliatory move by the majority against their collusion with the colonialists, felt aggrieved. In Nigeria, it led to a civil war.

To strike a longer conversation, I asked, "Why did Biafra split off?

"Our people, the Ibos, were massacred in the north and discriminated against. Biafra declared independence last year."

"Isn't there a lot of oil in Nigeria?"

"Yes. Biafra controls most of it near the Niger Delta. The Nigerian government wants it."

"I hope they will come to some solution acceptable to both sides."

"Nigerians are determined to exterminate us. Biafra is fighting back."

I felt uncomfortable continuing with this topic because the other non-Biafran Nigerians probably had a different story, so I changed the topic and asked, "By the way, what's your name?"

"Norbert Eliumelu."

"I'm Ashok Sharma. Call me Sharma. Ashok is hard to pronounce, even for some Indians."

"You were born in India and moved to Tanzania?"

"No. I was born in Tanzania. I've never been to India. My father came to East Africa from India as a kid in 1922. Tanzania was called Tanganyika then."

The line was moving, and we were around the corner where the metal food containers of different types of unfamiliar meats and boiled vegetables like green peas and Brussel sprouts were served by friendly old English ladies. Norbert had his plate filled with some meat and peas. I filled mine with peas and Brussel sprouts.

I was deeply impressed with Norbert's persona, aura of self-confidence, and ease in moving and conversing with everyone, including the old English ladies serving the food behind the counters. He beamed enthusiasm that made you feel like life was great and should be lived to the fullest. We sat down to eat at a table in the sprawling cafeteria.

"I did not see you when college started. When did you enroll here?"

"I registered late."

"What did you do before coming here?" I asked since he looked much older to have just finished high school.

"I was the chief anatomy lab technician at Middlesex Hospital Medical School."

"How long?" I was now curious.

"Eight years."

"When did you come to England?"

"In 1953."

"It must have been different then."

"Yes. A small English kid walking with his mother asked me, 'Do you have a tail?' The mom tried to hush him up. I smiled and stooped forward, lifting my jacket on the back. 'Look, I don't have a tail.'"

"Why did you leave your job?"

"I worked for the professor of anatomy. He is the dean of the medical school. I helped and taught medical students anatomy. I decided to go into medicine to become a doctor."

I was now really interested. I had hit a gold mine. Here was a person who worked at a medical school for the dean of the medical school teaching medical students anatomy! What could be a better resource of insider information for me to find out how to gain admission into a medical school.

"The dean could not take you directly into medicine?"

"He wants me to do A-levels first as it is a requirement for admission. He will take me with lower grades. I'm here to do my A-levels."

"Oh, I see."

"And Sharma, what about you? What are your plans?"

"I also want to study medicine."

He looked around and shook his head. "It is impossible to get into a medical school."

What? I looked puzzled because here the dean had promised to take him, but it was impossible for me to get into a medical school. He looked around to see that no one was listening, and then leaned forward and said softly, "They take only British students."

It was like an insider divulging a secret to me. "It can't be impossible."

"The healthcare is totally free here. There is a severe shortage of doctors in the British national health system. So why would they take you, a foreigner, instead of one of their own?"

It definitely made sense to me. Why would they take a fresh off the boat foreigner with an accent and no knowledge of British culture over a native-born British student?

"Are you a British citizen?"

"Yes."

"So, what is the best thing for me to do?"

"Go to a medical school in India. They teach tropical medicine there. You need that to work back home in Tanzania."

"Before I came here, that was my plan, but in my last year in high school, my father decided to send me here because my older brother migrated here from India last year and my dad told me that Indian students from Africa were beaten badly as an initiation ritual in India's medical schools. Some had suffered bad injuries and even death. That really scared me."

"You are wasting your time here. Go to India." Norbert looked serious and looked at me in the eyes. He was very convincing.

The rest of the day, I felt despondent. When I went home that evening, I cursed myself for coming to England and wished I had stuck to my original plan to go to India to study medicine because all the medical doctors I had come across in Tanzania were Indians. Here, I had even failed to understand an announcement about a field trip.

I decided I should go to India and wrote to my dad about what Norbert had told me—that I was wasting my time here as I would never get admission into a medical school, and if he could find out from an Indian doctor he knew how I could get into an Indian medical school. I would rather take my chances with their hazing problem. In the meantime, I wrote letters to some medical schools in India located in Bombay, requesting information about admission requirements and how to apply. They never replied. Dad wrote back that he did not know any Indian doctor in a personal capacity, as they were usually rich, haughty, and aloof as if they were some superior gods.

I wanted to be rich like them. That's precisely why I wanted to be a medical doctor, but I also wanted to be humble. Poor Dad made an appointment to see one for a minor medical ailment that he was treating himself with an over the counter balm to save money so he could ask them about the information I needed. The doctor charged him his usual hefty fee for the medical condition but was vague and testy about Dad's questions I needed answered. Dad wrote about what little he could gather. I would have to go to a college in India to take advanced-level science courses, and it was very difficult to get into medical schools there unless you had some connections. The same went for the premedical colleges, as you were competing against a large pool of smart local students.

Another problem was that under India's suffocating socialistic bureaucracy, Dad had helped me procure, fill out, and submit a thick application package to the Indian High Commission in Tanzania to get a student visa for India after I completed high school. In the typical inefficiency of the third world, the High Commission people never responded despite the fact I was the top student in my high school in Tanga, where we lived. So, I stayed put, with the India plan going nowhere. I wrote to Dad that I also needed connections in England and told him of Norbert's favorable admission prospects because he worked for the dean of the medical school and that that begged the question of how many friends of the medical school professors got in by the same connection route. A few weeks later, Norbert asked me when I was going to India, and I told him not any time soon. He shook his head with the same negative warning.

My acquaintance with Norbert evolved into a deep friendship over the succeeding months. We were often together during breaks, walked together in the college halls, and ate lunch together. Often, Miss Betts sat with us at lunch. I was amazed at Norbert's ability to carry on conversations with her and others that were mature and in-depth, while I had difficulty figuring out what to say beyond basic niceties and greetings. He was always formally dressed like when I first met him, friendly, highly intelligent, and mature. Everyone liked him because of his communication skills and ability to make them feel good. His confidence was catching. I wanted some of his stardust to fall on me. This was the first time in my life since middle school that I had a real close friend. However, I had serious other problems in those early weeks that I was afraid to divulge to him or anyone else.

Chapter 5

Study Difficulties

Every weekday, our college broke at four o'clock in the afternoon, and I would begin the twenty-minute walk home. After Sham returned at five o'clock and we did our routine of cooking, eating, cleaning, and returning to our room at about eight, we usually talked some more. I started to feel that the evenings were being wasted as far as my studies went. It had been okay before I started college when we had nothing else to do, but now it was becoming a serious impediment to solving the serious difficulties I faced in my studies.

My study difficulties began with the first day of the first semester's chemistry class in September of 1967. Entering through the single wooden door with its two ominous vertical glass panes, I knew I was in trouble. The blackboard was the first thing I saw, filled with the foreign language of diagrams and calculations jumping out at me, mocking my intelligence. Starting a few feet in front of the board were sturdy long wooden countertop tables in regular intervals, typical of labs, with a sink on one side and next to it a Bunsen burner and a small pipe outlet with a tap. The burner had a round metal base with a brass tube stuck in the middle. A flexible rubber hose was attached to an opening on the side of the metal tube for ingress of natural gas.

The burner produced an open gas flame, which was used for heating chemicals, sterilization, and combustion during chemistry experiments.

I sat on a high chair, much like a bar stool, at the first countertop facing the chemistry tutor, Mr. Hill, whose table was propped up higher than the students'. He was a young man, like someone who had just graduated from university, with slightly wavy hair that was flattened on his head. His hairline had a horseshoe-shaped protuberance that receded on the sides, and his wide, prominent eyes looked directly into ours. As he taught the first chapter in our chemistry textbook on atomic theory at the sub-atomic particle level, I had difficulty understanding him, partly because of my difficulty understanding British English and partly because the subject matter was difficult. I copied down what he had drawn on the board in my notes, but the lecture didn't make sense; I didn't understand a thing. The rest of the students gave away no inkling of confusion when they left the class, which worried me even more. Was I the only one who didn't understand a thing about the lecture?

While I was always at the top of my class in chemistry in my high school in Tanzania, college chemistry was a huge leap in difficulty. It was like my high school chemistry class was equivalent to the difficulty of getting to the first base camp at Mount Everest, and my college class was like getting to the top of Everest. I was rattled and deeply worried at this inauspicious start to a subject I thought I was good at—and this was only the first chapter in our thick chemistry textbook.

As days progressed at the college, my worries intensified with my inability to grasp the chapters that were piling on top of each other. I needed time to study on my own. Various ideas were gushing through my head, but I was already studying in the library during my lunch break. I had to find a way to study in the evening after school. With the specter of failure looming on my mind, eventually, I'd have to do something radical out of desperation.

I decided to stay back after the last class at four in the afternoon and study at the college library on the third floor. This caused a conundrum for me: If I stayed back, Sham would have to do the tedious cooking on his own. It was a real hard chore for both of us. I reasoned that he was doing it anyhow before I came to live with him, but then he was doing it only for himself. However, I realized it would be unfair for me not to contribute to the effort as it was for both of us. It was difficult and embarrassing for me to bring this plan up to Sham, but days went by and my panic intensified. I told him that I was badly behind in my studies and needed to stay back at the library to complete my homework assignments. When I told him that he should not cook for me as I would eat at the college, he shrugged, because unlike him, I was a vegetarian. He wondered what I would eat at the college. I felt deeply guilty because it would take even longer for him to cook as he felt obligated to cook for me.

My new routine was to go to the college library after my last class and study there until the college cafeteria on the ground floor opened at five-thirty. All the fulltime students left by four, but at six, part-time students, mostly doing vocational studies, filled the evening classes. Many had their dinner at the cafeteria before they headed to their classes. They were older and many were working and learning new skills. The evening classes were not that busy. The only thing I could eat from the evening menu was baked beans and toast, a common combination sold in English cafeterias. The baked beans came in cans labeled Heinz that were heated, and the toast had a thin layer of butter. The beans were then spread onto the toast. I would cut a small piece of the toast and beans with the knife, holding the toast steady with the fork to eat it in pieces. I was done eating in about ten minutes and would head back to the library to study until the library closed. Usually, I was the only student. When seven rolled around, I'd leave when the volunteer librarian got up from her desk, turned off the lights, and locked the library.

I needed more time to study, so after a few days, I went to see the college headmaster and head of the math and science department, Mr. John Cooper, at his office. He seemed to be in his late thirties with red cheeks typical of English people and had nice thick hair combed back. I told him that I needed more time to study, but the library closed at seven. I asked if he would allow me to use one of the many empty classrooms to study in after the library closed. He thought for a while, trying to find a solution, and said that he would tell the evening janitor to allow me to use one designated empty classroom till nine o'clock when the evening classes ended, and all the rooms were locked for the night. I was grateful to him because this entailed using all the lights in an empty classroom for just one student.

After the library closed at seven o'clock in the evening, I went to the designated classroom till nine o'clock, when the evening classes ended, and I saw the janitor arrive at the windowpane of the door of my classroom. He came to my room last after he had turned off all the other lights. I was the last student to leave the dark college, and it was eerily quiet outside when I walked back along sidewalks only illuminated by street lights.

One evening, the cafeteria didn't have any baked beans and toast, and I was starving when I reached home. Even when they had baked beans and toast, I was usually ravenous when I stepped into the flat. The house was dark and quiet, and everyone was asleep. I went to the kitchen to eat what Sham had left for me. It was vegetable curry, but very watery, like it hadn't been boiled enough to let the water evaporate. The vegetables were not well cooked either. The tortilla-like *roti* left was an oblong pear shape instead of round, and it was somewhat hard and burnt. I was so hungry that I gobbled down all of it. It seemed poor Sham had lost interest in cooking as I wasn't there to help or give him company. I felt deep contrition, but Sham still cooked for me since he had to cook for himself. However, I was making headway in my studies.

Chapter 6

Focus on Exams

The lesson I'd learned from my high school days was that you could study as much as you liked, but it wouldn't amount to anything at all if you could not concentrate and apply the knowledge in the exams. The facts you learned were like pieces of a jigsaw puzzle. The secret was to fit the pieces together to build a picture, the answer to the exam question.

My comprehension of British English had improved, as I listened carefully to their speech and attempted to decipher every word. For that, I had to partially thank the English phonetics class that all foreign students at the college were encouraged to attend. The tutor was an older Englishman who taught us how native English speakers pronounced letters, syllables, and words. One lesson involved him over-enunciating the "p" sound to demonstrate how it was pronounced by native speakers. I would later regret not taking the class as seriously as I should have.

In physics, chemistry, and biology classes, I practiced multi-tasking. I looked at the tutor speaking or at what he was drawing on the blackboard and glanced quickly at my notebook to jot down the gist of what he said. As my notes were written hurriedly, the writing was of poor quality, and most of the notes were in outline form because it was impossible and inadvisable to attempt to write down every word or sentence the tutor spoke without compromising my comprehension of the tutor.

When a class ended, all the students left, but I usually had some time before the next class, so I stayed back to fine tune and edit my notes. My aim was to comprehend the subject matter and not memorize it like a parrot. By comprehending the subject matter, it stayed in my long-term memory. Taking time to go over my notes after class was my first attempt to consolidate the lecture data in my brain; I called it my first memory consolidation step.

The typical student who wrote notes did not review them until close to the exam or many days after the lecture, if at all. The outline notes would be virtually useless and incomprehensible, and trying to study from the textbook chapter took much longer to comprehend.

If there was a longer break between the classes, I headed to the library for my second consolidation step. To keep out distractions and concentrate, I closed my eyes for a few minutes to recall in my brain whatever I could remember about the last lecture, with a mental picture of the tutor lecturing and drawing on the board.

After that, I drew a line below my rough class notes and wrote the notes for the lecture line by line, slowly in my nice handwriting so I could read and understand them easily the next time I reviewed them. This was my third consolidation step.

I had six consolidation steps in total. The fourth was reading and taking notes out of the chapter in the book and comparing them to my lecture notes, and the fifth was mentally answering the end-of-chapter questions. While this was time consuming, by my fifth revision, I had a much better comprehension of the subject matter taught in the last class, and this consolidation into my long-term memory was a powerful tool that would pay rich dividends by exam time.

The last revision step was answering questions at the end of the chapter by writing down the answers on my note pad, just like I was taking a real test, while I timed myself. I was always thinking like an examiner. Interestingly, we had no homework assignments to do, so all studying had to be done by our own volition, and I repeated this six-revision step process after every lecture.

I had discovered in eighth grade that studying was an active, focused process where the mental faculties had to be alert, and it was important to sit at a desk and take notes. If my mind wandered and my eyes began to get heavy studying in bed or if I kept myself awake with cups of coffee late at night, mediocre results would ensue.

Distraction was a big enemy of knowledge retention. A student studying seriously in the quietness of a library outperformed one studying at home with a myriad of disturbances like talking siblings or breaks for snacks and tea.

During my twenty-minute walk back home from the college at nine o'clock at night, my brain was active, reviewing some aspect of what I had studied that evening that needed extra stress to consolidate further the facts in my permanent memory. I especially reviewed any unusual or tricky facts likely to be asked in an exam. I did the same on my walk to college in the morning. In fact, I lived, breathed, and reviewed at all times except when I was asleep. It was my full-time obsession.

Students in my class didn't talk about the exams. They went about their classroom business in a nonchalant way, as if they understood perfectly what the tutors taught. They closed their books at the end of the class and bolted out. I had no idea how much the other students had prepared for the exams, what their capabilities were, and what competition I was up against. In fact, I feared I would be the last in exams with the difficulties I had at the beginning with chemistry. I had no idea what type of questions the tutors would ask, but I'd prepared hard, including completing those simulated mock tests. By the exam dates, I felt that I'd fulfilled my old mantra: "Be prepared for an exam any day," like an efficient army ready to go into battle on short notice.

Our first exams were held in December of 1967, almost four months after our classes started and before the Christmas break that would mark the end of our term. After all the exams, I felt I'd done well, but how the papers would be graded was a wild card. I was curious how the other students had performed; no one said anything and went their own ways after each exam as if it were taboo to talk about it. You didn't want to discuss with the next person any difficulty you had had or what you had answered in case you found out you had made a mistake, which led to post-test depression.

After the last exam, I walked down an open, broad balcony on the second floor where various classrooms and the library opened up to. At the landing near the stairs, I saw a classmate, a very good-looking Indian girl, Farida, with thick hair falling against her upper neck, talking animatedly with another classmate, an Australian male student. I increased my pace to sneak past them and headed down the stairs. I assumed they were discussing the exam, and I didn't want to divulge anything about my performance. However, as I went around them, they weren't talking about the exam but instead something fun.

I had just passed them when Farida quickly turned around and pointed to me. "Oh, Sharma, party!" As I stopped, she gave me a piece of paper with an address and directions to her home for a party that Friday evening to celebrate the end of the first-term exams. She told me the time and the bus number and route to take to reach her home. I accepted the paper and left, leaving them to continue chatting. It worried me somewhat that if she was having a party, they all must have done well on the exams. Heading back home, I had no intention of going to this party because my primary focus was on my studies. I had never been to a young people's party and was deeply worried about temptations and entanglements—all distractions to my studies that I could not afford. Lurking behind my mind was another fear.

The young Indians enjoyed the freedoms here that were denied in their home countries, like partying and dating. Farida's family had migrated from East Africa, where I came from. She belonged to an insular community called the Khojas, or Shia Ismailis, who had converted to a moderate and modern form of Shia Islam from Hinduism in the past one hundred years and whose spiritual leader was the Aga Khan. Khojas only married or dated other Khojas. My imagination stretched to the remote possibility of getting involved with her, which would be disastrous if her parents found out I was a Hindu or if my parents found out she was a Muslim. It was too complicated for me even to contemplate, so I shut the idea out of my mind. To stop the whole process in its embryonic stage, I tore up the paper on my return home and threw it away to guarantee my absence. Also, I couldn't tell Sham I was going partying and he was not invited as no one at college knew I lived with my brother. Knowing him, he would have loved to go. With the college closed for Christmas break, I thought I need not worry about this party anyway because it would be forgotten in the intervening weeks when we returned. Plus, who would remember or care I was a no-show?

My daily routine was different now as I had time in the morning and afternoons when Sham was at work. I continued to study like the exam was simply a step in a longer journey. I started to study new chapters that would be taught when the college resumed and always reviewed the previous ones later in the afternoon.

In the evenings when Sham returned from work, we cooked like we did before college had started. I was relaxed and chatted with Sham after we had eaten and cleaned up our kitchen mess. On Saturdays, we left home, took various trains and subways to Shepherd's Bush where our cousin Naresh, a tall skinny fellow, lived. His parents had gone back to India after living in Tanzania for decades. We knew Naresh from Tanzania, and he had migrated from India, like Sham, to look for work. Naresh worked for British Railways and lived in a single rented room in a house.

The three of us had a good time visiting central London, Hyde Park, and other places. Naresh was a great cook, and we all did some shopping for vegetables at the Shepherd's Bush open market. Naresh cooked a delicious homemade Indian meal. I loved his *parathas*, or Indian flatbread that looked like the traditional *naan* with two layers and a gap in between cooked with butter or ghee on a frying pan. We stayed with him all Saturday, slept there, and returned on Sunday.

English winter came, and the snow began. I was miserable from the cold as I came from the tropics. I wore a long gray coat over my clothes when I went out but was never warm enough as I never learned how to wear proper warm clothing, like thermals and neck scarfs. To keep warm in our room, I would walk down to a small store to buy a gallon of paraffin for the heater to keep its blue flame burning. Often, it had to be done twice a day because otherwise the fuel ran out late at night when the shop was closed, and we would freeze. I usually got another gallon before the store closed at five o'clock in the evening.

One day after a real cold weekend at Naresh's, I felt sick with a sore throat, running nose, and cough. I'd never experienced such symptoms in warm Tanzania. I went up to the kitchen to make some tea, as I often did at noon. *Bhabhiji* was in the kitchen. On a far corner of the kitchen was a glass cabinet with a lot of small bottles of pink liquid medicine, all almost full. I asked *Bhabhiji* what she did when her kids or anyone else in the family got sick. She gave me name and address of a local Pakistani doctor, Doctor Sarin, and told me there was a medicine shop close by.

I went to a small office where a lady doctor, Doctor Sarin, sat across a table, wearing a loose-fitting, pink traditional Punjabi dress, or the *kurta pajama,* but not the *dupatta* that *Bhabhiji* usually wore to cover her hair. She had a pen in one hand next to a prescription pad. I sat on a chair across from her and told her my woes. She looked at me for a few seconds as I continued but started writing on the pad. Before I had finished, she tore a page from the pad and gave it to me to take it to the nearby pharmacy. It was a prescription. Throughout the whole visit, she never spoke a word.

I took the prescription to the nearby pharmacist *Bhabhiji* had told me about who gave me a clear glass bottle filled with the same pink liquid as the ones gathering dust in *Bhabhiji's* kitchen cabinet.

Filling a tablespoon, I took the medicine regularly and recovered over the next few days. On further discussion with *Bhabhiji* in the kitchen in the following days, it was apparent that whenever her kids got sick, mostly from a weather-related flu, they went to Doctor Sarin who wrote another prescription for another bottle of the syrup, instead of using the one they had used previously for the same problem. The full bottles piled up as the kids stopped taking the medicine as soon as they got better, just as I did.

I later thought this created a tremendous waste in the government-owned British national health system because the patient didn't have to pay a penny for the doctor's visit or the prescriptions, unlike in Tanzania where we only saw a doctor when we really had to. Here, if *Bhabhiji* had to pay a few pennies for the medical services or the prescriptions, she would have used the same medication left over from the last time she saw the doctor.

As the day before our Christmas and New Year's break ended, in early January of 1968, many thoughts crossed my mind about the exams we had taken and how I had fared, especially compared to rest of the students. After the holidays, as I headed to our college on the morning of the first day of the spring term in early January of 1968, my mind shifted to Farida's party, contemplating what excuse I should give her for not showing up if the topic came up. It had to be a credible lie because I dared not to tell her the real reason. By the time I reached college, I had settled on the excuse that I had lost the paper she had given me with the directions to her home, but I reassured myself that as several weeks had passed the party was long forgotten and this topic would not come up.

Chapter 7

The Aftermath

As usual, I was early to the first class of my second semester. This new classroom was smaller, with pairs of two adjoining desks and chairs in several rows.

Students started trickling in close to nine o'clock. Farida walked in, smiling and talking animatedly to another student, apparently about the party. Both stopped inside the classroom just past the entry door. Another student passed by and thanked her for the party. She acknowledged that with, "Glad you enjoyed it." Now I knew I had to step up as the party was not forgotten. However, her good mood seemed like a good omen.

I seized the opportunity to tell her my excuse when she was alone. As she walked past me, I greeted her and waved. Suddenly, all her smiles vanished, and she walked past me, ignoring me without responding as if I weren't there and sat at the back, far from me. I turned around and saw her glaring at me. I'd seen that look before somewhere, and I knew it meant she was mad as hell. I got up and headed toward her. When I reached her and tried to speak, she took her stuff and walked past the next rows of desks and chairs, pushing two chairs in to go to the last far row next to the large window across the room's entry. It was now obvious she was furious at me for not attending the party and did not want anything to do with me.

Feeling deeply humiliated, I was in a semi-panic mode and went back to my desk. I looked around to see that no other student had noticed. At least they wouldn't think I'd done something terribly wrong. I decided my only option was to apologize profusely to her because I should have given her an excuse when I was invited. Accepting the invitation and not showing up had triggered Farida's raw nerve and wrath.

The tutor was late, and the students chatted to each other happily while I looked down at my desk quietly and despondent. Norbert was a no-show. I hoped with his diplomatic skills, I could ask him to calm her anger against me. I turned my head back to my left to look at Farida, and she was now chatting happily with another English female student. I heard her say something like, "Some individuals think they are too good to party," as our gazes met. I wanted to apologize, but I didn't know when to do it. She didn't even want to talk to me, and I was afraid she would make a scene if I tried again. I also didn't want to apologize with so many students around. I decided I would follow her out after the class and try again when she was alone.

A new worry gripped my mind. It was based on how my past experiences molded my present behavior and fears. In years past, I had learned a hard lesson—that when one female classmate turned against a male classmate, she worked on her other female classmates to do the same, a horrible experience for the poor underdog male. Here I was in a different country, but it seemed like Farida was determined to turn all the girls in class against me. I couldn't afford this serious distraction if it came to pass. However, a surprising, unexpected event upended all my fears and cleared my slate, and the party would get buried deep in the event's rubble when the tutor arrived.

The tutor was a lean Englishman who wore black plastic-rimmed glasses on his slightly pointed nose. He parted his hair on the left, with the hair on the right of the crease falling toward the front of his right temple. I recognized him right away as he had taught the electricity subsection of our physics class. He entered the class carrying a bundle of papers, slammed them on the table, and waited for the class to quiet down. He got to the point. "Your physics exam results." There was pin-drop silence.

He started stating the scores of the students alphabetically, beginning with the first letter of their surnames. One of the first ones was Miss Betts. The first few scores were low, below fifty percent. As he continued, no one had passed. Then came the highest score at that point, a Chinese student from Hong Kong with fifty-four percent. I wondered if the papers had been graded harshly. It didn't make sense because I believed that the tutors wanted their students to succeed. Because my last name started with S, I was the last grade called. I wondered if I had also failed. I looked down at the book, afraid to look at the tutor massacring everyone. I felt like the last one in a row of victims of a firing squad, awaiting my turn with horror. Then came the bombshell.

"Mr. Sharma, ninety-four."

Someone gasped, "What?"

I felt it was too good to be true. The class was incredulous.

At first, I questioned how only two students passed, and how my score was forty points higher than my nearest competitor. *Did I mishear?* I needed to see my exam answer papers with the scores.

"I'll hand your papers to you after class." A heavy English student, who always wore a black suit and liked to give his frank opinion to teachers, blurted, "The exam was difficult. Unfair."

"But Mr. Sharma. Back to work."

The tutor was blunt and started teaching the first section of electricity by drawing an electric circuit on the board. I started writing my notes as usual.

When the class ended, I was afraid to look around. Everyone's face was sullen and quiet as if they were shell-shocked. I assumed Farida now got the message why I skipped her party. The tutor called out names and handed students their marked exam papers, and they left hurriedly. Near the stairs, I saw the Chinese student looking pensively at his paper with two outstretched arms. We had never spoken in class. As I passed a few feet away, he looked at me, and our gazes met; no words were exchanged, and I went to my next class.

The same scenario repeated in chemistry and biology. I scored over ninety in both the subjects while almost the whole class flunked again. I had overestimated the capabilities of my classmates, or they thought it was the beginning of the first year, so why study at all? They had no idea how hard I studied or the effort I put in specifically targeted at scoring high on the exams.

I felt no exhilaration. This wasn't a unique experience for me as I always got high scores in my high school class and was always the top student. The study techniques I used now were developed and refined during those four years when I studied most of the time. However, I didn't rest on my laurels. This was just the first term, and I had no idea how it could relate to my admission to a medical school that Norbert had convinced me was impossible to get into. Norbert had not shown up, but no one noticed as he failed just as miserably as the rest of them and were deeply worried about themselves.

For me, nothing had changed—it was back to books, and the library, preparing for the next exams, and the same daily routine, including studying five hours after our classes ended. Sham was now more understanding, and the quality of the food he cooked had improved when I returned home. I didn't tell him, nor did he ask, about my performance at college. It had been the same with my dad in high school. He had found out once when I had been in twelfth grade. I had heard him tell my mom that one of my classmate's dad had told him, "Your son is very good at his studies." He had trusted me because he had always seen me studying when I had been at home.

Over the following months, the rest of my classmates were now more serious with their studies, took notes, paid attention to the tutors, and attended classes regularly. Some furtively looked at me during the class lectures. Mercifully, no one congratulated me because they all had pride and ego. They knew the problem; they could improve their performance and reach the top if they put in the required effort, focused, and reduced distractions. These were difficult tasks for young adults with surging hormones.

Farida was back to her normal friendly style, with smiles as if nothing had happened between us. I was no longer her pariah, although she was more subdued. The reality had hit her that her exam results did not portend well for her dream of gaining admission to a British medical school. The only person I'd heard of who had gotten admission from our college to a medical school was a second-year red-haired English girl, conditional on her getting a grade B and a grade C in the final university administered A-level exams, but ostensibly she had done well in her college exams in the first year.

While I was in class, I liked listening in to what other students were talking about before the tutor came in for the class. One day, I was sitting at a desk behind Farida who was sitting next to an English girl who had acne scars, which made her look older than she was. This was in the same smaller classroom where the physics exam results had been announced. It was apparent from the conversation that Farida was throwing in the towel and was going to study at a medical school in Pakistan where she felt she would fit in better compared to India.

This was understandable to me. Pakistan was founded by her co-religionist, Mohammed Ali Jinnah, who was also Khoja or Shia Ismaili like her, even though most of the Khojas lived in India, especially in Bombay, where Jinnah had built a palatial home in 1932 near the beach and where India's top medical schools were, like Grant Medical School. However, it made me worry again that I was in the same boat as her from what Norbert had impressed on me. I thought Farida might have that problem with the few Pakistani medical schools. It was a third-world inefficiency problem of that time period. This discussion gave me the impetus to write to some more Indian medical schools, but I never heard anything back that time either.

The Australian student in my class sought my help in chemistry. Like in my high school years, I didn't patronize him but gave him hints to solve the steps of the problem. I forwent solving it outright as that could be easily forgotten. I had solved the same problem that my colleague had through travails and diligence. I knew why and where the difficulty lay and how to explain it in the simple "student language" instead of the "tutor language." It was a most gratifying experience and made me a better student.

That students talked behind my back became evident when I headed to the cafeteria one day and noticed two English students, who were not my classmates, chatting. A girl with short blondish hair and a short skirt had her back against the large hallway window, and a boy was facing her. I had seen her around in the past. After I had passed them, I heard the girl tell the boy in hushed tones, "He got a hundred percent on all his exams." It was the old story of how a rumor changed as it spread. I concluded if the news had spread to students in other classes, then my own classmates were the source. However, there was a fall out from my performance that I'd not expected or ever experienced in high school.

All the students had their own lockers on a lower floor where they stored books or supplies during breaks or overnight. I had just opened my locker door when two Indian girls, whom I had never seen before, approached me. One talked while the other just listened.

"Where are you from?"

"Tanzania."

"Tazmania?"

"No, Tanzania."

"Where is that?"

"In East Africa. And you are from?"

They did not seem to be from India because all the girls from India and Pakistan whom I had seen so far were Punjabis and wore the traditional Punjabi dress; these girls wore pants.

"British Guyana." It was a country in South America, north of Brazil, where in the nineteenth century, many Indians were taken by the British as indentured laborers to work in the sugar plantations.

"In South America?"

"Yes. Can you help me with some chemistry problems?"

"I know. I had problems with it at the start."

"Can we come to your home?"

"Your parents will not like that."

"Don't worry. We'll tell them we are visiting a girlfriend."

"I don't have a home."

"You have a room?"

"No room."

They looked surprised.

"Let's study in the library."

"Where do you live?"

"Here, most of the time."

They looked at each other, confused.

"Actually, I'm going to the library. Follow me."

"Oh, not right now. We have a class soon."

A few days later, I was studying alone in the library at a table far from the entrance as I had an hour's break before the next class. The same girl came and sat next to me. She wore a skirt and high heels but also makeup and lipstick like someone going to a party. She took a seat next to me and moved her seat closer so it was in contact with mine. I could smell her perfume.

She didn't have any books with her and asked me some questions about a chapter, so I started explaining on my note pad. I felt she was not paying attention because instead of looking at what I was writing, she was looking intently at me. She pushed her body closer so we were in direct contact along the thighs and trunk. I felt embarrassed as I had never been in physical contact with a girl before. She then tilted her upper body almost pushing me to the side. I had to steady myself as she continued to press against me.

She did not say anything, and I was worried if someone came by, they would think we were lovers. Being confused at how to extricate myself from the situation, I closed the book. Behind us someone entered the library and cleared his throat. She pulled herself upright, but we were still in contact. I continued with my explanation of the subject matter I was teaching.

The person who entered took a seat in front of us; it was Norbert. I felt relief—a close friend would not tell anyone what he had seen. With folded hands on the desk, he looked at the girl and said, "Cozy here. You look beautiful." The girl blushed and looked at her watch. "I am late for my class." She got up, bolted, and never bothered me again.

It was then I realized it was not a fluke when an Indian Sikh girl whom I had seen in our English phonetics class, often wandered into the library when I was studying, staring at me as she walked past. She was skinny, like the providence had placed a good-looking face on a bamboo stick. She had braided hair made into a ponytail and wore a tight silk Punjabi dress. My fears were soon confirmed.

I was seated at a table facing the entry door of the library after a lunch break at the college cafeteria when Norbert, who usually socialized with others after I left him after lunch, came and sat across from me. I had my textbook open. The Sikh girl, as she often did, walked in with her arms folded, looking at me. Norbert greeted her and started chatting with her. However, I kept studying, looking down at the open textbook, ignoring both. It was obvious that she was looking at me while talking to Norbert. She attempted to elicit a reaction from me while Norbert flattered her, as he did to all girls, telling her how pretty she looked.

"Your friend here, does he have any other interests?" she asked Norbert, but kept gazing at me.

"Yes. He has."

"I mean not just study."

"He likes chemistry experiments."

"That's study. What about girls?"

"I love girls."

"I'm asking about your friend."

I continued ignoring her.

"May I kiss you?" Norbert blurted out suddenly.

I was surprised at his audacity.

"You must be kidding." She looked upset.

"I never kid."

As Norbert tried to stand for the act, the girl bolted, deeply offended by his asinine behavior. Norbert, with his over-confidence, mistook her interest in me as an invitation to take liberties with her. After that, she left me alone and never spoke with Norbert. It was then I concluded that it took two willing partners to tango, and if one was not interested, it was a non-starter.

When I went home that evening, I wondered if being an A student was an aphrodisiac because these things didn't happen during my first term. Some days later, I walked down a hallway alone when I passed two English girls with miniskirts. As I walked past them, one turned to me, looked me up and down, and whistled. That surprised me because I thought only boys whistled at girls—it was rude! I felt embarrassed but also somewhat flattered.

Occasionally, I had fantasies about girls but immediately blanked them out as a serious distraction with a hefty price tag. I had observed in high school that boys who were sexually precocious performed poorly in their studies and were often at the bottom of the class. In our class, this phenomenon was epitomized by two Greek students, Charalambu and Demetrio. Charalambu had wavy hair in front and was a real fucker. It was common whispered talk in the class that he had sex with girls from vocational classes in the large gym hall above the cafeteria. One day, I was sitting in the front desk of the physics class, and I heard a pretty Romanian classmate repeatedly say, "I'm a good girl," at the rear of the class. Lo and behold, Charalambu was standing close in front of her, holding both of her hands firmly, cajoling. As she tried to extricate herself from his clutches, he persistently and bluntly proposed her for sex, refusing to take no for an answer. He didn't care that his classmates were around, listening.

Like a Greek Norbert, his approach was direct and blunt. Ostensibly, he was in college mainly for sex. His close friend Demetrio was a quieter guy but just as deadly, his flat black hair falling in front of his brow. They were both dunces at their studies, a confirmation of my theory that an inordinate obsession with sex in college seriously compromised study performance—a real path to failure.

One day I heard that Mr. John Cooper, the head of the math and science department, had suffered a heart attack and was admitted to a hospital. I'd no idea what a heart attack was except something to do with the heart. I saw an opportunity; I could win some kudos from him by visiting him.

I had little idea how the mechanics of the admission process to a medical school worked except what Norbert had told me, that the application needed the college's principal's recommendation and that it was submitted directly by the headmaster to the medical school. Mr. Cooper was also the acting principal. I was deeply indebted to him as he had authorized a room to be available for me to study after the library closed.

One college admissions office staff person told me where Mr. Cooper was. I took a bus during a few-hour break in the morning and reached the hospital. It was a nice, cozy hospital and looked more like a country cottage. I had never been to a hospital before. The nurse at the front desk gave me directions to Mr. Cooper's room, which was easy to find as the hospital was small. I knocked on the door of the private room and entered and greeted Mr. Cooper, who was sitting on the bed upright. There was a portable table in front of him with a pitcher of water. He looked restful and somewhat serious and worried. However, he never really smiled when I had seen him before. I shook his hand and took a chair close to the bed.

The room had a large window close to the bed, and the bright sunlight filtered in. There was a nice flower pot on the window-sill and a beautiful small garden outside with colorful plants and flowers. Mr. Cooper told me that he was in one of the better hospitals.

His heart attack had started with chest pain, which was treated with pain medication on admittance to the hospital. Treatment was mainly bed rest for five days and avoiding raising his arms. He said he was instructed to follow a low-fat diet, lose weight, and start a gradual exercise program after recovery. I was not a good conversationalist and so mainly asked questions. He told me that he was pain free now and looked forward to returning to work. He seemed cheered by my visit, and I told him that we missed him at the college, wished him a speedy recovery, and then departed. When I returned to college, I did not tell anyone, including Norbert, of my visit. I felt this was a good investment and time worth spent because someday I could be asking Mr. Cooper to write my recommendation for my medical school application.

Chapter 8

Outside of the Box Solution

My worries about admission to a medical school had mounted since I'd heard Farida express her fears and reservations to the English classmate. While no Indian medical school I had written to replied to my letters requesting information about the application process, the premedical school requirements, or if they would accept A-level results from exams given by the British universities, it reminded me of what Albert Einstein had once said: "The definition of insanity is doing the same thing over and over again and expecting a different result." Here, I was writing to Indian medical schools repeatedly and expecting different results, expecting a response that never came. I stopped this insanity and decided my only hope lay in getting into a medical school in Great Britain.

It was like I was stuck in the middle of a swinging bridge with hostile people on both sides. I began to think of an outside of the box solution, just as I had done to solve the conundrum of helping Sham cook dinner.

I did a thought experiment, with many hypotheses, to see what my chances were of getting into a medical school, imaging all the scenarios and their possible results. Norbert told me that the first difficult step was to get an interview at a medical school, though that did not guarantee a conditional acceptance because medical schools interviewed many applicants for the same spot to pick the best.

To get an interview at a medical school, I assumed that you needed a strong recommendation from the college headmaster. To get a strong recommendation, I assumed you had to do well in your first-year studies, and the main gauge of that for the headmaster was your exam results. With my stellar performance on my first-term exams, I could replicate that in the second and third term, thereby making it very likely that our acting headmaster, Mr. Cooper, whom I had visited in the hospital, would give me a strong recommendation and that would likely get me a medical school interview or at least a foot in the door.

But here was the catch.

In my thought experiments, I further hypothesized that the medical school interviewed five applicants for one spot—all with stellar recommendations—but most were British students. At the interview, I would be at a disadvantage with my poorer command of spoken English, accent, and lack of communication skills. Why would they take me when the others had a better command of spoken English, no accent, and knowledge of local culture as they were born into it and likely to be a better fit in the health system here?

The conundrum then for me was how I could negate the advantages the British interviewees had over me by offering something they did not have or something the medical school coveted. And what did the medical schools covet? I thought for a while.

Presto! They coveted the top A-level grades. Since all, or most, of the applicants had not taken their A-level exams, as the interviews were offered after the first year had just ended, and the A-level exams were taken at the end of the second college year, the medical school could only give a conditional offer, if they decided to accept one applicant after the interview.

I had to achieve something that was objective to stand out among the applicants. I got the idea from hearing about the second-year red-haired English girl who had gotten a conditional offer to a London medical school. Maybe the adage that a bird in the hand was better than two in the bush was applicable here. The medical school might favor the one who had the grade already than one without a firm guarantee the student would get it. I occasionally crossed paths with this girl when walking around college with Norbert, who carried out extensive conversations with her. She was a smart student, confident, a good conversationalist like Norbert, and walked straight. I could see that if she was my competitor for an interview, she would leave me in the dust.

I had to do something radical. I envisioned that if I got a grade A in advanced-level biology in an exam given by a British university at the end of my first college year before I went for the interview, it would be a game changer and improve my chances of a conditional acceptance, perhaps conditional on getting further good grades in physics and chemistry. This was my outside of the box solution. Excited about this plan I'd conjectured, like the excitement of making a new discovery, I decided to present it to Norbert. I needed confirmation about the soundness of the idea.

When I told Norbert about this idea, he laughed and shot it down and advised me not to waste my time on it. He insisted it was impossible to get a grade A in biology, even at the end of the usual two years of college. He claimed that he hadn't come across, or heard about, any medical student who got an A in biology when he worked at the Middlesex Medical School. That was precisely the point, I told him. If no one got it but I got it, then that would give me an edge over others, even as a foreign student. However, Norbert was right about the difficulty in scoring a grade A from what I knew about advanced-level biology.

Advanced-level biology was an exceedingly difficult subject for several reasons. Not only was it an amalgam of two major subjects, zoology and botany, but both the components had separate lab parts, effectively making biology a subject comprising of four sub-subjects.

All this made it the most challenging subject to get a grade A in. The exam was administered by an association of several universities called the Associated Examining Board.

The exam consisted of a written part that was worth sixty percent of the total score and a lab portion that was worth forty percent. To get an A, or over eighty percent, one would have to score high in both the written and lab portions. Since the questions were essay-type, it was impossible to get the perfect sixty percent score in the written part. If I did well and got fifty percent in the written portion, I would still need to score thirty percent in the lab portion to get A.

The examining boards also used some secret rubric to ensure that there was a minimum score in the lab or the practical portion even to pass. So, if I got fifty-five percent in the written portion, but got a low fifteen percent in the practical or lab portion, I might not get a B.

I decided to get an A in biology by the end of my first year, despite an ostensibly impossible task, but unless I tried and gave it my best, I wouldn't know what could be achieved. It would also give me valuable practice and insight into taking a real A-level exam as otherwise, I would have to take it at the end of my second year anyhow. I could do all the studying and preparing for exams that I was already doing, and the only weak link in the chain would be the lab portion. I had to find a way to strengthen animal dissections for zoology and plant dissections for botany.

Our first dissection classes had actually started in the first term after several weeks. All the dissection animals were preserved with formalin, a mixture of formaldehyde and alcohol, which had an odious smell and occasionally caused my eyes to tear. For the animal dissection, our first dissection was a dogfish, which belonged to the shark family. Sharks are the most successful ocean predators and have survived for over 400 million years in the oceans. As it was postulated in biology textbooks, life originated in the oceans in what was called the "primordial soup," and then some fish gradually migrated on to land, ostensibly from increased competition. It seemed logical to start with the study of the anatomy of an existing ocean creature descended from a species of those days and compare it to mammals like humans. Our mammal dissection specimen was a rat.

Our biology tutor dissected the first specimen on a large square wooden board, with all of us surrounding him, to demonstrate the various layers and steps we would take. First, he identified the external features like the eyes, nostrils, gills, fins, and reproductive organs with a small metal probe. The fish had the two large pectoral fins, like fans, near its head, which became the upper limbs in mammals several hundred million years down the evolutionary pathway, and two smaller ventral fins toward the tail that evolved into the lower limbs. Then he placed the fish on its back, or dorsum, and made two deep vertical incisions like a surgeon on either edge of its belly, or the ventral surface, using a scalpel. A horizontal incision was made at the lower end of the abdomen across to connect with the two vertical incisions. Like skinning an animal, he used a small pair of forceps to peel the thick rectangular abdominal wall upwards and used a small pair of scissors to cut any fascia or fibers that were not cut by the scalpel. He excised the peeled ventral wall near the head end using a scalpel. We could now see inside the fish's abdomen and the thorax. The organs were neatly and tightly packed, a marvel of nature.

Most of the organs were covered by the large liver lobes. He pulled one lobe up with the forceps and poked with the probe the large stomach underneath that led to the duodenum and the intestine, with its prominent spiral valves visible on the surface of the intestinal wall that increased the surface area for the absorption of digested food. In the more advanced species like the mammals, including humans, the valves were replaced during evolution by the more efficient microscopic finger-like projections called the villi, like the technological advancement from the early model of the Ford car to the new Tesla one hundred years later.

He continued with the most important and difficult dissection, the exposure and demonstration of the cranial nerves that originated from different parts of the brain and emerged through holes in the skull. There were twelve cranial nerves on each side of the head in a dogfish, just like in humans, and served the same functions in both species. By careful dissection, he exposed the brain, which was centrally located in the head and looked like a whitish, bulbous tube. The brain continued below as the spinal cord, a thinner tube that went to the tail-end of the fish.

From the top of the brain, he exposed the two olfactory nerves, resembling two prongs that supplied the organs of smell, the olfactory lobes, then the thicker optic nerves that connected the brain to the eyes and so on. The dissection seemed tedious as the nerves, whitish to gray in color, were buried in other tissues and could be mistaken as surrounding tissues and easily cut by mistake. He cautioned that we would lose points in an exam if a nerve was cut or nicked.

We were instructed to read about the animal's anatomy from our dissection guide before the next lab session the following week. In the next lab class, we were given one dogfish each to dissect, and we used our dissection guides to help us. The tutor was also around to help and guide us. I'd never dissected an animal before, and it was not easy to for a beginner. I made mistakes, as expected, like cutting a cranial nerve by mistake, and I was unable to identify the smaller third and fourth cranial nerves that supplied and controlled the eye muscles. I sketched the completed dissection, with annotations, on a blank paper.

The dogfish's heart was much simpler than the mammalian heart: it had a thin-walled atrium with two lateral bulges leading to a thick-walled bulging chamber, the ventricle that led to a thickened artery that took the deoxygenated blood to the gills for oxygenation. There were valves separating the respective segments. As fish evolved into amphibians, the two bulges became separate chambers, the atria, like in mammals. I found it fascinating when the tutor told us that the dogfish also had a gall bladder similar to humans. Each student's specimen was stored by the lab technician for the next session, usually a week later.

Our next project was a dissection of a frog, a cold-blooded amphibian, because it spent part of its early life in water and adult life mostly on land. It was the intermediate step in evolution when the fish migrated to land. In its early stage, the frog laid its eggs in the water, which hatched to produce tadpoles that resembled tiny fish; later, they developed into frogs that migrated to land but stayed close to water to reproduce.

The adult frog specimen was spread out like an X with pins stuck to the ends of its four outstretched legs and the body in the center. The abdominal layer was dissected to expose the dominant organ, the liver, with its three lobes covering most of the other organs. The liver was pulled up to expose a small gall bladder underneath, the gastro-intestinal tract, and the rudimentary lungs as most of the breathing in a frog is done by the skin. The gastrointestinal tract ended in a pouch called the cloaca, where all waste, including urine and repro-ductive material, was expelled. In mammals, this pouch developed a partition wall to split it into the rectum and the bladder, so they didn't have to evacuate the bowels every time they urinated. Above the liver was the three-chambered heart, with two atria and one ventricle as the oxygenated and deoxygenated blood mixed in the ventricle. With evolutionary advance, the ventricle was also split into two chambers by a septum, separating oxygenated and deoxygenated blood, enabling mammals to be more agile.

The third animal we dissected was a rat to learn the mammalian anatomy. The rat was spread out in a similar fashion. The abdominal layers like the skin, fascia, and peritoneum were dissected with a knife, forceps, and scissors to expose the internal organs. I followed the dissection guide with the tutor's help when needed, to display the liver and various other abdominal organs like the stomach, ileum, jejunum, rectum, liver, pancreas, spleen, and kidneys. We also dissected the heart and the main arteries originating from the heart in the chest and the abdomen.

During the dissection sessions, I asked the tutor for advice and help, but my primary aim was to gain as much information from him about the exam: what questions could be asked and how the examiners would know what we dissected, as it seemed like a tedious and messy task to send them all the dissected specimens that could be damaged on route. I learned that the questions could be framed like this: "Dissect the cranial nerves of a dogfish on one side and sketch your dissection with a labeled diagram or dissect the second to ninth cranial nerves." In case of a frog or a rat, it could be a dissection to display the gastrointestinal tract or the heart and the great vessels. It could be any combination. Usually, only one animal specimen was given. When I inquired how to do a complex dissection in the limited time given for the exam as there was also the botany part, he said to do the best I could. As to the completed work, he said the tutor supervising the exam, usually one of the tutors who taught us, would look at the annotated diagram drawn by the student and carefully compare it to the dissected specimen. He would certify by signature at the bottom of the page that it was an accurate drawing of the dissection. For example, if a cranial nerve was bisected and the student drew it intact, he would not sign or accept the paper until the student corrected the false information. There was no cheating. The exam pages would be taken away by the tutor once he signed it.

When I'd firmly decided by the early second term to take the A-level exam at the end of the first year, ending in June of 1968, I concluded that to get a high score in the lab portion, I had to do a nice clear dissection at a reasonably rapid pace and then make a clear sketch of it on the drawing paper and label it accurately. That required a lot of practice dissecting several animals to achieve this goal. This was not feasible because the college gave each student only one animal per year for dissection as this was a community college, like most colleges in England, supported by the government or the taxpayers. The annual fees we paid would not cover all they spent on the students. No wonder it was difficult to get an A in biology. I had asked the tutor how we could be expected to remember dissections done in the first year for an exam held at the end of the second year. He responded we would be given a second specimen during the second year when everyone took their A-level biology exam. *That will still not be enough to do well in the exam*, I thought. Now it made sense when Norbert said that he had not come across any student who had gotten an A in biology when he worked at Middlesex Medical School.

The lab technician, a blond-haired, medium-built guy, ran all the labs—biology, chemistry, and physics—and set up the lab materials for the students before a class started. I talked to him at the end of a biology lab session when everyone had left. He was collecting the specimens for storage, and I asked him where he had gotten the lab animals for dissection. He gave me the name and address of a lab located in the town of Croydon that was far from Woolwich and gave me a set of dissecting instruments like scalpels, scissors, and forceps for my own use after I told him I needed to improve my dissection. I promised to return them after I was done with my dissection practice. This was another example of how the English people helped me.

Bingo! I decided to go to the lab in Croydon on Saturdays to buy animals to practice dissection. I felt guilty in informing Sham about my new plan because Saturday was our only fun day when we went to visit our cousin, Naresh. It was a double whammy for Sham; first I had stopped helping him with the daily evening cooking, and now Sham would have to go alone to see Naresh. I explained the reason why I had to do this. Sham, in his usual fashion, was sympathetic, but I knew he was disappointed.

Every Saturday, I left home early and took various buses to reach Croydon. At a small lab, I met a man wearing a white lab coat. He did not say much or ask questions like why the hell I bought a formalin-preserved animal every Saturday. He looked Indian but spoke like English people, so I assumed he had lived in England for a long time. He gave me the preserved animal specimen in a sealed plastic bag, and I paid him the reasonable price given to me because I was a student. He told me no students ever came there and that all his customers were institutions.

Back home, I opened the bag with dissection scissors and placed the specimen on a wooden board on our table. Immediately, the room was filled with the odious smell of formalin. Sham had already left by then. One time, he had been there but left quickly, repelled by the smell. I didn't care about the smell or the occasional tearing of the eyes; I was after the ultimate prize. Most of my day was spent dissecting the animal carefully, following the dissection guide and drawing an annotated diagram, just as if I were taking an exam. I rotated animals every week from a dogfish to a rat to a frog.

Like the judge, the jury, and the executioner, I set my exam questions for each Saturday, like, "Display the cardiovascular system of the rat and draw a labeled diagram," or, "Display the gastrointestinal tract of a rat," and I would get a rat specimen, dissect and display the gastrointestinal system, and then move it to the side to display the cardiovascular system, draw it, and then time myself and give myself a score. To make full use of the animal, I would make various combinations of questions that could be asked, especially trick questions.

Meanwhile, our college was now in full swing as the second term forged ahead and gathered steam after a slow, depressing start from those atrocious exam results. One day, before a biology class, the English lab technician was clearing the blackboard for our class and arranging some demonstrations for the tutor. I was sitting at the long front bench a few feet from Miss Betts. Suddenly, Norbert arrived and proceeded to the front of the board where the tutor usually stood and gave a powerful rhetorical impromptu speech. Usually, it would be odd and out of place for someone else to do that, but everyone was conversant with his theatrics. It went something like this:

"I have to tell you the truth that has been on my mind for a long time. It must be told, and I will say it. I have lived in England for fourteen years, and I will say that the British are the best and the noblest people in the world. They will always help you when you need help."

As his speech progressed, Norbert heaped more praise about the largess and the amiability of the British people. During some statements, mesmerized, I nodded in agreement as I recalled how Miss Betts had delayed the coach to fetch me from the same spot where I sat now during the first week of college for the field trip. The lab technician was amused, standing on the side, and seemed flattered. Miss Betts listened pensively. Spoken like a true sycophant, Norbert convinced every one of his impeccable pro-British credentials as if he needed to rub them in or dispel any doubts. After this histrionic performance, as expected in a small college, the word spread among students and the staff about Norbert's pro-British stance, just as he wanted. His stature, respect, and awe he commanded had reached its zenith. I was his best friend and felt more of his stardust sprinkle on me. It was like walking in the shadow of a great guy and a great public speaker, and I'd become his true sycophant.

Our second term ended around mid-April of 1968. We took our exams again, in physics, chemistry, and biology. Every exam given was important in some way, and this second exam was more important because the subject matter was more difficult. When the college headmaster wrote his recommendations, he would be guided mainly by the student's exam results as the exams placed all the students on the same footing. With my motto of, "Ready for an exam any day," I knew I did well to get all A grades. After the final exam, there were a few days left before the college closed for the Easter break. There was the annual college party that everyone talked about as they were more cheerful after the exams and felt they had done much better. The failures of the first-term exams were a distant memory. But I was studying just as hard, especially in biology, to implement my new secret plan.

On the party day, the college closed at seven o'clock so all the students could go. It was held in a large banquet hall in the front part of the college. There were no late evening classes so I could not stay till nine at night in my designated empty classroom. I packed my stuff and left the library to head home as I had no intention of going to the party.

I walked down the hallway from the library to the stairs leading to the ground-floor courtyard to exit the college from the rear. The college was brightened by its outdoor lights when I reached the bottom of the stairs, and I could see the party in full swing through the large glass windows of the banquet hall located about fifty yards away, with a lot of students dancing. The patio in front of the stairs led to a series of wide semicircular steps to another lower patio that lead to the banquet hall entrance.

As I turned around away from the party hall at the bottom of the stairs, I remembered I wanted to check some notes and turned around and walked a few yards to the steps facing the banquet hall, sat down, and opened my briefcase to review the notes. After I reviewed the notes, I was about to put the notebook back into my briefcase when I saw Norbert heading toward me. He said he had seen me from the banquet hall and sat down next to me with our feet on the step below.

"Coming to the party?"

"No. Going home." With Norbert, I could speak my mind freely.

"I danced with Christine." Christine was Miss Betts' first name.

"What happened?"

"I felt really hot. I was really charged up." He shook both fists toward his chest, like grabbing and pulling another body toward himself. "I asked her to come to my house with me."

"What?" I looked surprised.

"My penis was really hard. She said no and stopped dancing. She pulled away."

"Good for her."

"I asked why. And she said, 'You want to fuck me.'"

"Smart girl. She read your filthy dirty mind."

"But you know what, she said I would go with Mr. Sharma if he asked me."

"No. I don't want to go with her. I live with my brother."

"You have a real problem with your head in the books."

"All you think about is sex." I was upset at his sexual peccadillos, especially after his faux pas with the Sikh girl.

"Do the real thing instead of rubbing yourself."

"What? Rubbing yourself?"

"Then you have wet dreams like high school boys get."

"Your head is like a penis. Always thinking about sex."

"You like boys?"

"Goodbye. Miss Betts has a boyfriend."

I left hurriedly, red-faced and angry, though I had just conjectured Miss Betts had a boyfriend to irritate Norbert. I had never actually seen her with one, and why would she be at a party without him? As I hurried home, my mind was confused about my sexuality. I was nineteen yet did not know what "rubbing yourself" was, or how to do it. I got wet dreams once or twice a week but during deep sleep and only wondered why I had leaked thick whitish fluid from my penis when I woke up. It was an uncomfortable feeling, and I felt deeply guilty. I was too ashamed to tell this to anyone, and Sham never mentioned any such thing.

The next day, Norbert came earlier to class, and I apologized to him. We made up as I was worried about the fall out if we stopped talking, often being together and eating lunch together. Everyone would ask what had happened to our comradery. I could not afford any distraction, and with Norbert's endearment to the rest of the students, he could toast me, or that was my fear.

A day later, the college would close for Easter break. I was walking down a hallway with a large window along its upper half and saw Miss Betts sitting at a small desk with her elbows and hands resting on it across from a young English man wearing a black business suit and a tie. He was a little old to be a student, and I had never seen him before. As I walked past them, they both turned to look at me, and our gazes met. No words were exchanged, and I was not sure if Miss Betts wanted me to greet her this time as I usually did. I assumed he was her boyfriend. I felt relieved because I had told Norbert that she had a boyfriend, though I felt something else—a tinge of fleeting jealousy. Jealousy was quickly replaced with happiness; she was a beautiful, elegant girl who deserved this handsome guy. The next day in class, we were back to being friends as usual, and she never mentioned him nor did I ask, as it was none of my business.

Our classes broke for Easter break and the college closed. While most of the students talked about how they would spend their Easter vacation, I was forging ahead full blast with my secret plan to take the university advanced-level biology exam in June 1968.

Chapter 9

Norbert Drops Out

The summer term started after the Easter holidays. When we returned, the exam results were announced. For me, it was a knockout again, with scores over 90% in all the three subjects, physics, chemistry, and biology. My score in chemistry was in the high nineties, which would have an implication later. The closest to me was a Turkish student, Ali Unal, and a Chinese student from Singapore. They got mainly B and C grades. The rest of the students fared much better than the first-term exams. The memory of the first-term exam massacre was obliterated, and all passed with smiles on their faces, except for one student.

Norbert enjoyed the college ambiance. He was riding high, suave, always impeccably dressed in his suit, tie, and waistcoat over a crisp white shirt. He was respected because of his confidence and great social prowess and always flattered girls on how beautiful they looked. Here was the perfect African, or specifically Nigerian, gentleman, or Biafran as he liked me to think of him. But highs can precede lows. Norbert fared miserably in the exams and flunked them all with ludicrous, laughable scores. If below fifty percent was a fail grade, they should have invented one especially for him to gauge how low one could go. His scores were in the low twenties. It seemed he should have gotten zeros, except that would be too impolite. With this total humiliation, he disappeared from the college without telling anyone and was a no-show after the first day when the results were announced. Even the two Greek Don Juans passed, though right at the fence, where pass grade glared at its fail counterpart.

During the ensuing days, some students asked me where Norbert was and when he would return, but I had no idea where he was as he had never told me where he lived. However, unbeknownst to others, I knew the reason for his disappearing act—his miserable performance in exams had shattered his ego. A great know-it-all talker and an orator, the congenial "college politician" and social butterfly had flopped when it came to studies and exams. The chicken had come home to roost; I never saw him studying or writing notes during lectures, not to mention his frequent absenteeism from the college. Some days later, our last class for the day ended, and I was heading down deserted stairs on the back side of the hallway, as I always did after class, to my locker in a lower hallway when I felt someone snooping around, following me down the stairs stealthily. I turned around, and it was Norbert. I wasn't surprised, as only he knew my daily routine.

"My God, Norbert! Where have you been? They've been asking about you."

He shushed me with a finger in front of his mouth and told me in a hushed voice to follow him to a deserted side of the college; he didn't want anyone to see him. He was carrying a black briefcase made of leather. We stood along a tall brick wall.

"What happened?" I asked him.

He looked around to see that no student was around. "Can't stay here. They failed me in all the exams. Even biology, my best subject."

"What do you mean they failed you? They only grade you on your answers."

"You don't understand. I'm a black man."

"They failed you because of your color?"

"I worry about my future. They did not want me to pass."

This paranoia baffled me. "Look, you say you are a black man. I'm a brown man and an East-African Indian. You are West African Nigerian, or Biafran as you like to be called. What is the common factor?"

He tried to change the subject by fiddling with his briefcase.

"African," I said. "That is the common factor. We are both Africans because we are both born in Africa. So, the tutors failed one African, but not the other just because of difference in the shade of their colors?"

Norbert pulled out a note pad from his briefcase and showed me some notes written in clear and nice handwriting. "I'm enrolled at a private college. They give individual tutoring. Not like here, where you are on your own."

"Must be expensive."

"I can afford it easily."

"This is a public college for everyone. They can't afford that."

"I cannot afford to fail for my future. I need to get those A-levels to get into Middlesex Medical School."

"The tutors are nice and helpful. I've gone to them after classes when I needed some help and they always helped me. You could do that." His insinuation of skin color for his failure offended my sensibilities and common sense. "English people here have been good to us and nice to us. No one has said anything racist. Please don't use your color as an excuse for your failure."

"I have to think about the future."

"You told me that as foreigners, we have to work ten times harder—do ten times better than an English kid to get the same thing because we are in their country. I followed your advice and it works. So please follow your own advice."

He kept looking around like a sleuth to ensure he wouldn't be spotted. It was clear nothing would dissuade him to return to college. I promised to help him with his studies and told him that all types of students came to me for help and that I was glad to help them because apart from helping fellow students, it made me a better student and consolidated my own knowledge of the subject matter.

I could do the same for him, give him priority, and he could stay with me in the library after college for a few hours. But that was too much for his ego to handle. Why would my mentor and my "spiritual knowledge guru" accept a subordinate role? He didn't want others to see him being taught by me, like a pop being taught by his kid. My entreaties to induce him to return were futile.

"I did not hear you mention 'black man' if anyone asks me why you left. Sounds really bad. Especially after your pro-British speech in class."

"Don't mention that. Tell them you don't know why I left or where I am." He left and I thought I would not see him again. The next day, I attended the last class of the day, our biology class.

The biology teacher was a medium-built man in his thirties with prominent cheeks and flat black hair combed to one side. He had a somewhat serious effect and rarely smiled. He always wore a black suit and a tie. The day after Norbert's apparition, I was completing some extra notes after class while the tutor was gathering his stuff at the front desk. After a while, he picked up his teaching material and stood near the exit door as if waiting for me, and it was obvious to me he wanted to talk to me. When I approached him, he asked me if I knew where Norbert was and why he was not back. This was the first time a tutor had asked me about this. I felt that since biology, as per Norbert's bravado, was his "best subject" and he was failed by this tutor, the tutor may have some concern that he was culpable in Norbert's disappearance. I had to lie to the tutor, per Norbert's request, that I didn't know where he was or why he left. From the conversation, I got a vague impression that the tutor was gathering information as there seemed to be disquiet among the teaching staff about why Norbert had bolted, a reflection of the deep positive impression Norbert had made on all, especially after his pro-British speech.

Norbert had endeared himself to everyone with his socializing; albeit, if he'd paid some attention to his studies, he would not be in this predicament. After we parted, I felt the tutor was also concerned that since we were the best of friends, he didn't want me to think he was responsible for Norbert's disappearance. Obviously, he was not the cause. He examined the exam papers fairly as he gave me the highest score in the class in the same exam. However, he carefully avoided alluding to the exam results, but I felt he suspected it as a cause. In any case, Norbert had also badly failed physics and chemistry exams, but his score in biology was abysmally low, the lowest of all in the class.

I didn't want to get distracted by this and soon forgot about Norbert, like, "Good to know you friend, and now goodbye and good riddance." One day, I was the last student preparing to leave our chemistry class, when I saw that the tutor, Mr. Hill, had also stayed behind. He was the first chemistry teacher, out of the three, who had started teaching us chemistry at the start of the first term. He looked like a recent university graduate who took teaching chemistry seriously, always drawing nice annotated diagrams on the board to explain the subject matter and equations. He was looking at me and called me to come over to the long desk in front next to the blackboard. I thought, *Oh no, not another grilling about Norbert.*

After I stood across the desk from him, he said that he was a graduate of Cambridge University. "I'm sure they would like to have you." He said if I was interested, he would write a recommendation letter to the master of his college, Trinity Hall, whom he knew. I was flattered—thrilled—but also nervous. It was an offer I could not refuse. However, I did not know anything about Cambridge, except that it was a famous university and our final high school graduating exams in Tanzania and many of Great Britain's ex-colonies were proctored by it. I felt my travails were starting to pay off.

Though, soon I would be facing a problem of serious distraction that would blow up and hit me hard like a typhoon, upendeding my concentration, the basis of my success so far. Its genesis was a speech given by a politician I had never heard of.

Chapter 10

The Invisible Hand of Enoch Powell

The honorable Enoch Powell was a British politician, a powerful orator, and a member of the British parliament who gained national, and perhaps international, prominence for his speech delivered on April 20, 1968, in which he blasted the immigration of non-white people from the new Commonwealth countries. His speech was dubbed "The Rivers of Blood" because he said, "As I look ahead, I am filled with foreboding. Like the Roman, I seem to see the River Tiber foaming with much blood." He referred to the violent riots in some cities of the United States in the 1960s and the assassination of Dr. Martin Luther King Jr. as harbingers of Britain's future before the end of the twentieth century. "The black man will hold a whip over the white man." Powell demanded resolute and immediate action to halt further immigration of non-white people into Great Britain and to voluntarily repatriate those with generous stipends. He had dropped a bombshell.

Powell used metaphors of the ancient Roman poets, who often used metaphors related to rivers, most likely stemming from his time as a top student in classics at Cambridge. Powell's boss, Mr. Edward Heath, the head of the Tory, or Conservative Party, in the British parliament, fired him as the shadow defense secretary with a phone call and told him he considered the speech "racialist in tone and liable to exacerbate racial tensions." However, Powell became a household name and got widespread support from the British public. Several polls showed his approval rating exceeding seventy percent, even though most of the British press lambasted him. His home in Wolverhampton received numerous bags full of mail daily, and over 80% of the letters were in support of him per his pronouncements. There were large demonstrations in London by the dock workers—traditionally the backbone of the ruling left-leaning Labor Party—supporting Powell, a conservative, right-wing politician, confirming the adage, "Politics makes strange bedfellows."

Powell infected most of the British public. He ensured the topic would not fade away with interview after interview, speech after speech, and a widely watched TV debate with a well-known and respected English journalist and TV host, David Frost. Frost argued that the dire prophecies used by politicians against Jews migrating to Great Britain in the early 1900s had not panned out, as current British Jews were a wealthy, prosperous group, holding leadership positions in politics, business, medicine, and science. Powell argued that assimilation had been a matter of the number admitted, as Jewish immigration had been restricted by law after the outcry when they had arrived. As Frost and Powell went back and forth, most viewers backed Powell, and those present during the exchange cheered him. One letter to a national paper called the contest, "David versus Goliath in reverse." Many expressed anger at their long-dead empire-building ancestors for their miserable failure to anticipate the consequences of their far-flung colonial endeavors.

Soon, I found out that I was not immune to Powell's invisible hand. As I walked past a bus stop one day to go to my Midland Bank branch to withdraw some money from my passbook account, a red bus full of young English school kids wearing their cute school uniforms, standing both on its lower and upper deck, stopped at the curb. The first time I realized I was being taunted was when I heard loud chants in unison.

"Immigrant. Immigrant. Immigrant...." When I stopped and turned my head to look at the bus, all the kids from both the decks were chanting together and waving, among the white faces was a black kid in the middle of the top deck, also fully participating with infected enthusiasm. I could understand his predicament, and it reminded me of the old saying, "If you want to live in the river, you must be friendly to the crocodile."

Confused and embarrassed, I increased my pace. It became apparent that the bus driver and the conductor were in cahoots with the kids and very likely had coached them. This was confirmed as the bus slowly followed me while the kids chanted. It seemed that they had done this to other victims because it was too well rehearsed to be impromptu. I made a U-turn and rapidly walked in the opposite direction.

To add insult to injury, as I walked past a store to go back to college, a very old English woman in a black outfit thumped her feet as I passed her and repeatedly shouted, "Get out of our country." I walked faster to get away from her. Some days later, I made another attempt to go to the bank. As I passed an office building containing several stories with balconies, someone poured water over my head. When I glanced up, there was no one. At least it had not been a hard object. Now I understood what Mr. Edward Heath, the Tory Party chief, meant when he told Powell that he considered the speech likely to exacerbate racial tensions—in one direction, like a one-way street, the British majority now viewed its minority as a threat because of their color and race, and the minority was cowering with fear. Powell admonished that in several decades, British cities would be engulfed in race riots, and the majority took that as prescience.

It was a distraction for me as I read the newspapers in the library to learn more about Powell and his past and try to analyze his motives. I was deeply worried and became self-conscious of what people thought of me as I watched these debates on TV that I'd avoided before as a form of distraction. Sham and I watched a Sunday TV program on a South Asian immigrant channel talking about this situation, urging South Asian immigrants to disperse in areas they had sizable populations, like the town of South Hall near the Heathrow airport, London's premier international airport. This had happened in the fifties and sixties, as immigrants from India came to work at the airport to do menial jobs unfilled by locals.

A day later, I was pushed off the sidewalk onto the street by a young English couple, walking arms locked, with the man telling the woman, "Push him to the street," and when I left for school one morning, there were two younger English women standing near Rafi's old black car at the curbside in front of the house. As I walked past them slowly, the younger woman looked at me, and with her eyes toward me like she wanted me to hear her, said to the other older one, "Now they have a car, a house, a job, and a suit and tie." I still wore my old suit and tie to college. I stopped and turned to them.

"I'm only a student renting out a room here. This is the same old jacket and tie I have worn every day for the last year that my dad bought me in Africa for college. He could barely afford it."

"You are?" the older one said, looking confused.

"You can have a car and a house," I said. "Do what my landlord does."

"What?" the younger woman said.

"Work two factory jobs starting at six in the morning. Come home at night. His brother lives here. Does the same. Rent out some rooms."

"Really?"

"You have all the opportunities. The factory hired him, but they will hire you first because you are English. He hardly speaks English."

"Sounds like hard labor."

"I worked at one to pay for college. Got nightmares of soda bottles crashing down a fast-moving conveyor belt as I could not remove them fast enough."

They looked amused. We parted on a friendly note when they realized I was nobody—just a student and a renter who was at the receiving end of their wrath triggered by forces Powell had unleashed. It made me think that frank communication helped to dispel erroneous notions. After walking around several streets, I walked down a long, straight sidewalk leading to the back of the college when I passed two older men wearing long black coats, talking to each other and looking at me when I approached. After I passed them and walked a considerable distance, I glanced back, and the two men were staring at me. Before Powell's speech, they would have ignored me.

Some days later, I'd heard Miss Betts tell a tutor about a nice entertaining movie she had seen, so I decided to cheer myself up and see it as I'd never been to a movie cinema in England. The seats were relatively inexpensive, and I was sitting toward the front as the movie seemed popular, with a lot of people in the rows behind mine. The lights were on, and the movie had not commenced yet. A piece of popcorn hit my head hard, and when I turned back, everyone was quiet, like it was a collective conspiracy, looking straight as if nothing happened. I left the theater, worried about my safety.

I was also worried about my physical safety after Sham came back from work one night with stitches. While riding a bus home, someone had rapidly made a cut on his head with a razor blade and had darted out of the bus before Sham had even known what happened. He had felt blood on his fingers when he had touched the top of his scalp and had had to go to a hospital to get stitches to stop the bleeding. I felt bad for him as it could have been me.

While I was apprehensive and distracted, I wondered what the English students and tutors at college thought of people like me now. Generally, the British students and tutors were a liberal lot; I had never heard anyone at the college say anything even close to being racist. However, I was certain they talked about this hot topic in private. Miss Betts was as friendly as before, but I had heard her tell a tutor she belonged to the British Liberal Party, the smallest of the three national political parties. The largest was the Labor Party, which was in power, and there was also the Conservative Party, or the Tories, who were in opposition. The Liberal Party's policies were "liberal," just like its name, and its leader, Jeremy Thorpe, lambasted Powell. My fears were confirmed when I walked down a hallway between classes. An older English lady, possibly in her fifties, with silvery-gray hair just touching her upper neck, was heading in the opposite direction and looked at me. When she approached me, she stopped and said, "Mr. Sharma?"

"Yes. Hello." I stopped.

"I'm Mrs. Nance."

"Good to meet you. You are a tutor here?"

"Yes, I teach vocational students. You are from Tanzania?"

"I am. Have you been there?"

"No. We lived in Malawi. My husband was a provincial commissioner."

Malawi was a small country bordering south of Tanzania and a previous British colony like Tanzania.

"You are our neighbor then!" I smiled.

"I miss the natural beauty of Africa."

"Africa's landscape is unmatched. In Tanzania, we have the tall savannah grasslands, the rift valley, the Ngoro Ngoro crater with a lake in its middle, and the Serengeti."

After a brief chat about Africa and its uniqueness, she came down to the real business.

"My vocational students have misconceptions about Asians coming from East Africa. Would you be willing to discuss that with the class?"

Actually, while the British press and the politicians called them East-African Asians, they were actually all South Asians, originally from the Indian subcontinent whose ancestors had migrated to Africa. This was a hot potato. I wanted to drop it, say no, and run, but how could I? This was an ex-provincial commissioner's wife. They were like gods in Africa, who would not even look at me there. Dare I refuse a goddess?

"Yes, of course. I will be glad to do so," I said, lying through my teeth. The meeting was set for a mutually compatible day a week later, which gave me time to study the problem and its historical background. Again, this was a distraction, as it took time away from my studies. Not to mention, it was an added challenge and stress, as I had never held a debate with a group of students in Africa, and I would have to do so with a weaker command of the English language.

However, I was certain Enoch Powell would crop up during the discussions, since he had started the whole façade, and I had to be prepared for that by learning about him and what motivated him. After reading newspaper articles in some major British newspapers like *The Times*, *The Telegraph*, and *News of the World*, I concluded that Mr. Powell wanted to trigger a national debate on strict immigration control of people from the new Commonwealth countries because of their different cultural background, race, and color, which he believed threatened the native British identity and culture of a country that was essentially white Anglo-Saxon. To do so, he used language that his party chief, Edward Heath, considered "racialist in tone" as the reason to fire him.

Ostensibly, the events culminating in Powell's speech commenced around February of 1968 when Kenya, the neighbor of my home country of Tanzania, started deporting its Indian-origin population who had British citizenship, originally bestowed to them by the British colonial government. Now I realized why there were so many Indians in the plane that brought me to London from Tanzania on July 7, 1967; they were British passport holders, like those in Kenya migrating to Great Britain from Tanzania.

When the British ruled East Africa, which comprised of three countries, Tanzania, Kenya and Uganda, each country was divided into large geographical areas called provinces. Each province had a de facto head called the provincial commissioner. So obviously Mrs. Nance's husband, as a provincial commissioner, was a powerful man in Malawi during the British rule. Each country had a representative of the British government sent from England, the governor, who was the most powerful person in the country and lived in a palatial mansion in the nation's capital. While the British, few in number, ruled the country, the country was run and developed by its Indian population, originally brought there by the British in large numbers as indentured laborers to build the railroads, especially in Kenya, at the turn of the twentieth century. The new railroad began at Mombasa on the Indian Ocean coast and went inland over six hundred miles across Kenya into Uganda. Several thousand died during the construction from tropical diseases and wild animals, and many returned to India with the money they had made, but most stayed and went into business using their money. While Indian traders had come to East Africa for centuries, their numbers increased with development promoted by the new railroads. In the remotest corners of East Africa, you would find an Indian shop, as observed by Sir Winston Churchill, who traveled there in his younger days at the end of the nineteenth century. Most Indians originally came to escape poverty in India, and many were barefooted when they arrived.

A person's present beliefs and pronouncements are often molded in their early years of life. Powell was a highly educated and intelligent person who was the top student at Trinity College, Cambridge, where he graduated in 1933 and became the professor of Greek at the University of Sidney in Australia at twenty-five. In those years, when Great Britain ruled a large swath of the world, he was a staunch imperialist. India was its largest and prized colony, called the "Jewel in the Crown" due to its vast resources, location, and size. It was also called the Indian subcontinent. The British governor-general of India, commonly referred to as the viceroy, like an assistant to the Roy or king in London, was one of the most powerful men on Earth, holding life and death over one-fifth of humanity.

As I carefully read the "Rivers of Blood" speech many times, I discerned a man seething internally with rage, especially at the part of the speech stating, "The black man will hold a whip over the white man."

Here was Great Britain, a country that ruled vast areas of Africa, Asia, and America at various times; its resolute people valiantly fought off the Nazis and the heavy bombing of London during WWII—this is what their future held? What I had experienced, and I was sure most, if not all South Asians were experiencing, was Powell's invisible hand at work.

On a deeper study of Powell to decipher the reason for his controlled rage, I found that he had cherished a burning ambition to become the viceroy of India and had left no stone unturned in his quest for that ultimate glory, including learning the common language spoken in North India, Urdu, an amalgam of Hindi, Farsi, and Arabic that evolved during the five-hundred-plus years of Mughal misrule in India before the gradual British conquest of large parts of India under Robert Clive's machinations in the seventeenth century. During WWII, Powell was with the British intelligence in India, avidly reading any book he could find about India and wrote to his parents, "I soaked up India like a sponge soaks up water." He stayed in India when rest of his colleagues were transferred to Ceylon, now called Sri Lanka, ostensibly to give him an edge when the new viceroy was picked.

After the war, Powell, a conservative, voted for the British Labor party, who won the election, because of his anger at the Conservatives for the Munich agreement that didn't prevent the war. However, the new Labor Prime Minister Clement Attlee, announced in February 1947 that India's independence was imminent. Deeply shocked by this impending collapse of the British Raj, as his dream crumbled, Powell walked the streets of London all night and later took a U-turn to become fiercely anti-imperialist and now believed the rest of the empire would follow India's lead. He wanted Britain to break from the ex-colonies, hence his contempt for the new Commonwealth that replaced the empire.

To keep the bond with the ex-colonies that they had ruled and nurtured for so long and to retain some influence with the newly independent nations, the European powers, mainly the British and French, formed loose voluntary unions. In fact, Sir Winston Churchill, who was in opposition in the British parliament and voraciously opposed India's independence, claimed, "It would relegate Great Britain to the status of a minor power," and reluctantly dropped his opposition when he was assured that India would stay in the British Commonwealth after independence. There were advantages for the newly independent countries in these unions, but one consequence that these colonial powers failed to predict and anticipate was that immigrants from the ex-colonies, like a reverse flow, would come to their shores in large unanticipated numbers within a decade as air travel became easier and cheaper.

But what had changed since Powell's viceregal dream collapsed in 1947 to trigger his angst? Ostensibly, he was leading a quieter life as the member of parliament for Wolverhampton, an industrial constituency of England, then as the health minister in the Tory government of the early sixties, which collapsed under the Profumo sex scandal, and also the defense minister in the party's shadow cabinet when they went into opposition. In the fifties, and accelerating in the sixties, the area he represented as the MP underwent a demographic shift as it was an industrial area that attracted immigrants from the new Commonwealth who flocked there attracted to the abundance of factory jobs.

My analysis was that the very people he wanted to rule over and would have had thousands of them as his servants in the grandiose Viceroy House in New Delhi with its 340 rooms spread over 320 acres, now were his equal neighbors in his own country and city. He could not accept or fathom that reality, and his angst boiled over publicly. If he were an MP of some other area with few immigrants, like most of the UK at the time, maybe he would have used milder language, if at all. There were some very right-wing conservative MPs to the right of Mr. Powell, like Sir Gerald Nabarro, who backed Powell's speech, but none of them gave such speeches themselves because they had few immigrants in the areas they represented.

While I felt I was prepared enough, I had little idea what I could be asked. I felt it would be good to discuss the matter frankly to dispel any preconceived notions and get a feel of what the English students really thought. At the same time, I wanted to keep the focus on the immigration crisis from East Africa, as I came from there and had a better understanding of it now.

On the day of our discussion, Mrs. Nance was waiting at the class-room door and waved me in as I approached her. On entering her class, I was surprised it was packed with English students, none of whom I'd seen before. They all stopped chatting when they saw me. Mrs. Nance asked me to take a seat at the front tutor's wooden table while she stood at the side of the table to my left. I was somewhat embarrassed and nervous; here was the wife of a once powerful person in Africa, yet she gave me her seat while she stood aside. It showed her humility and made me realize that our distant impressions of other people are not always accurate. Her students had no idea about how much power her husband wielded in Malawi, a country they hadn't even heard about. I sat with my elbows and forearms resting on the table, and my hands were folded in front. Mrs. Nance gave a brief introduction to the students.

"This is Mr. Sharma. He is a student from Tanzania, a country in East Africa. You have expressed worries about immigration from East Africa. He is here to discuss that with you."

She waved her hand to me to start.

"Thank you, Mrs. Nance, and thank you all for inviting me. Very kind of you. I feel honored, and a bit nervous." Some students smiled at that. "I watch TV like you, and I understand you have worries and fears about people who look like me and have different cultural back-grounds, races, and colors, that are coming here in larger numbers. At present, the immigration is from Kenya, the country north of my own country of Tanzania, but this problem affects all three countries of East Africa."

A student sitting in front asked, "We see plane-loads of people coming from Africa on the evening TV news. Why are they coming here?"

"Excellent question. It is a consequence of British colonial history." Mrs. Nance nodded her head in agreement. "First, how many of you know that Great Britain had an empire that extended to large parts of the world and Africa?" Hands went up but not as many as I expected. Most of the students were born after the sun set on the British Empire when the British gave India, its largest colony, independence in 1947, and later other colonies followed suit.

"Before Great Britain gave independence to Kenya in 1963, the Indians living there could get citizenship from the United Kingdom based on the British Nationality Act of 1948. The same for the Indians in Tanzania and Uganda."

Most students had expressions of surprise on their faces, like why would they pass such an absurd law? Great Britain consisted of England, Wales, and Scotland, and the United Kingdom consisted of Great Britain and Northern Ireland.

"The law was passed by the British parliament?" a student asked.

"Yes. When Great Britain had an empire, all the citizens of the colonies were considered British citizens under the classification of citizens of the United Kingdom and colonies. They could choose to come here and have the same rights you have under the law."

Again, there were sighs of surprise, and I looked at Mrs. Nance and said, "Mrs. Nance could possibly confirm that." I was aware that many Indians also lived in Malawi, and she would be familiar with this issue.

"That is a fact," she said.

I continued. "Actually, the British Nationality Act of 1948 was passed because after the Second World War, Great Britain badly needed workers to rebuild the country devastated by the war, and the only places where they could get them was from its ex-colonies, or colonies at the time. However, because of the difficulty of travel and its unaffordability, the number of people was not as large as needed, but they eventually started coming, like many came from the West Indies in the fifties to fill the shortage of bus drivers.

"Back to Africa. When the British ruled East Africa, they were fewer in numbers and so all the civil services, or the government machinery, including the railways, were run by the Indians. The economy was also built and controlled by the Indians. Obviously, they were worried about their future when the countries approached independence in the early sixties, and most of them took the British citizenship under the British Nationality Act of 1948. After independence, the new government of Kenya allowed the Indians to become Kenyan citizens within two years and renounce their British citizenship. Most of them did not do so within the time frame and now, the government wants those who failed to do so out. That is why you see plane-loads of them arriving at the airports here, as they are really facing deportation from Kenya, or they would be jailed there."

"Why did they not become Kenyan citizens when they were born there?"

"Good question. They procrastinated, thinking that the status quo would continue, and the vast majority failed to apply for the Kenyan citizenship. This resulted in the Kenyan government becoming suspicious of their allegiance to Kenya and decided to kick them out."

"We are worried these people will become a social burden to our country and a new underclass on permanent welfare," one student opined.

"Let me assure you that this will definitely not happen. You can drop an Indian with no money in any corner of the world where there is minimal economic freedom, except India, where it does not exist. You can follow that Indian for ten years, and I bet that he will soon find a job, any job that a local person does not want, to make his first pound, or whatever the local currency is, and then he will save that to double, triple, and so on, multiplying it, saving like crazy. He will buy a house so he does not have to pay rent, and rent out some rooms, and will have sponsored his family from his home country and educated his kids as a priority, no matter how many more sacrifices he must make. In ten years, he will be prosperous.

"Now the East-African Asians are already a step ahead and have already proven themselves. Their ancestors came around the turn of this century from India when East Africa was basically a jungle with a lot of dangerous wild animals and snakes. They braved that, and many died, eaten by lions. They built the railroads inland for the British. They built the present-day booming towns and cities in the jungles. They do not show on TV the capital of Kenya, Nairobi, for example, built by their ancestors and the present Asians there. They only show them as refugees getting off the planes at the airport here. If they could build towns and cities in the most difficult environment, they will prosper here. You don't have the wild animals and snakes here they braved in Africa." Everyone laughed at that.

"I never came across a poor Indian in Africa. Everyone was either employed or involved in a private business, be it a shop, jeweler, or shoemaker. When the British ruled these countries, the Indians ran all the civil service and transportation. Their kids study hard because they know they will have no future otherwise and their parents value education. It is their top priority. They will bring their business acumen here and prosper even more and contribute greatly to Great Britain's economy, creating jobs just like they did in Africa."

Then came the question I feared, but I was prepared for it after my extensive research.

"What do you think of Mr. Powell?" a student in the back of the class asked.

"He is a politician, but he is also a product of British imperial history. When he was young, he wanted to be the viceroy of India, but his dream collapsed when India was given independence in 1947. The area he represents has seen a significant increase in its immigrant population because it is an industrial area, so they go there for jobs. He is upset that people he would have ruled over are his neighbors. I may be wrong, but that may have contributed to his anger against immigrants from the new Commonwealth."

"Mr. Powell says he is not a racist. You think he is a racist?" one student asked.

"As a rough analogy, it reminds me of what my dad once told me. He said, 'If you are walking with your mother and someone asks you if that is your mother, you would not be offended and tell them yes. There is nothing impolite about that question. However, instead, if the person asks you if that is your father's wife, you would be offended and insulted.' Mr. Powell could have stated the same views without offending anyone. His language and tone is more in line with the second question in my father's analogy, like when he calls children of people of African ancestry piccaninnies."

The meeting ended on a very cordial note, and some students and Mrs. Nance thanked me and told me that they understood the problem better. I thanked them again for inviting me as it showed frank discourse between people could reduce misunderstanding.

One unintended consequence of Powell's apocalyptic-sounding anti-immigration campaign was that it scared many English people into leaving Great Britain for Australia that needed people and workers and had strict "whites" only immigration policy. The Australian government, seeing an opportunity in Britain's predicament, advertised at workplaces and the newspapers an Assisted Package Migration Scheme, where you paid only ten pounds sterling, and the rest of the transportation and other costs to Australia were borne by the Aussie government.

When Sham told me that he had applied, I was deeply worried, and even horrified, because if Sham left, I would be alone. Who would pay my rent? The money sent by my dad was barely adequate for food. However, my worries were laid to rest when Sham told me a month later that all the white applicants got accepted, including one from an East European communist country, and were departing for Australia on the assisted passage, while he never even got a negative response for his application from the Australian high commissioner. This was the first time I felt happy about someone being discriminated against, even though he was my brother, as it suited my purpose, which shows how a person's selfish interests can overshadow that of another's. This left Sham's employer scrambling for workers, and he beseeched that if Sham knew any immigrant friends who would like to work there, he was offering higher pay, but all the ones Sham knew were already over-employed. The worker shortages created by the "assisted passage" scheme gave further impetus for more to immigrate to the UK, including many illegal immigrants from the Indian subcontinent that Powell was hoping to stop with his dire warnings. So, for each English person who left scared by Powell's dire warnings, another immigrant came, and the percentage of the native-born population gradually decreased. Sham was even approached by a yelling English lady, asking him if he wanted to buy her home for a bargain basement price as she was soon leaving for Australia. He was not interested, and I'm sure she found some other immigrant taker.

My worries multiplied as I thought it would be harder to get admission to a medical school now. Since the polls showed the vast majority of the public supporting Powell, the deans might be less inclined to admit me. The passions aroused by Powell cooled somewhat in 1971, when the newly elected British government, led by Edward Heath, who had fired Powell, rammed a restrictive immigration bill through the parliament in a record three days to allay the public's fears that the immigration problem was out of control. The new immigration law restricted entry into Great Britain for settlement basically on the basis of color as only people from the old Commonwealth, like Australia, Canada, and South Africa, who had historical connections to the United Kingdom, could settle. The admission of East-African Asians was restricted to a quota of a thousand families per year, cooling local tempers. The irony was they formed a small percentage of the total immigration from the new Commonwealth, and many looked for other countries to migrate to as their British passports were worthless. Many were quietly allowed in by Canada who had a labor shortage. While the governments that expelled them, especially from Uganda by dictator Idi Amin, dispossessed them of their wealth and possessions, they could not do so to their business acumen, knowledge, and experience that they would use to excel in Great Britain. Many had already stashed money in British banks long before their expulsion for a rainy day. It was estimated by *The Times of London* that just the money from Nairobi's Asian residents in British banks totaled 400 million pounds, a staggering sum for those days.

However, Powell's invisible hand continued to play a role in national politics as the Labor Party lost the general election of 1971 to the Tories. It was postulated by political pundits that it was due to traditional Labor Party supporters, the so-called working-class people, like the dockworkers who had led massive demonstrations to support Powell after his speech, bolting to vote for the Tories to show their support for Powell. However, during the next 1974 general election, Powell, now a backbencher and the member of parliament from some Northern Ireland district with no major party backing him, switched sides and blasted the Tories for their shift to join the European Economic Union, leading to their defeat, per analysis of the political wonks. Powell told people to vote for the Labor Party, who opposed the European Union. That was also Powell's undoing and his star faded, especially because of the betrayal felt by many of his loyal and core Conservative Party supporters. He was finding out that he could only influence the game when he was in it; having left a major political party, he was just another independent member of parliament unable to influence any party's policies.

The irony was in all these immediate years after Powell delivered his speech and the numerous public discourses, discussions, and demonstrations for his support, no one really asked or discussed with the immigrants what they thought or felt about it. They were exhausted and tired of the hostility and were relieved about the new immigration bill so tempers against them could cool off. They had no control or input into the UK's immigration policy or laws and were bystanders at the receiving end of forces unleashed by Powell's invisible hand.

April 20, 2018, was the fiftieth anniversary of Powell's "Rivers of Blood" speech. Powell died in February of 1998 at eighty-five from Parkinson's disease. His legacy lives on in many YouTube videos with limited views and supportive commentators calling him "the prime minister we never had."

Chapter 11

The Biology Dividend

The animal dissections that I had started performing at home in January of 1968 paid off. In a few months, I was adept at dissections and drew dissected specimen views within the time limit of the exam. During Easter break when Sham was gone for work, I studied most of the day, starting at eight in the morning and ending when he returned at five in the evening. Most of the time, I concentrated on biology chapters that would be taught in the third term and in the second year because I had to be fully ready for the exam in early June of that year.

One thing I could not practice on my own was plant dissection because the plant specimens differed, but I had familiarized myself with the basics as much as I could. I had found that before taking the exam, I had to feel confident to get a grade A. If I didn't, then I'd not prepared adequately.

I took the A-level exam in biology and also an S-level, or special paper exam. The S-level originally stood for the scholarship level and was a hangover from past years when, according to Norbert, the British government gave you a scholarship if you passed it, but now it was just a feather in your hat. The S-level was a much shorter written exam with only two questions, but more difficult than the regular A-level exam. It had only two grades, 1 (Distinction) or 2 (Merit).

After I finished the written portion, I was certain I would get a high score because I could manipulate the subject matter to answer any question in the exam in full detail. The lab portion of the exam was held the following day. I got a dogfish for dissection to display all its cranial nerves on both sides. This would have been a difficult task if I had done only one dogfish dissection seven months ago. It was easier for me with all the Saturday dissection practices. The botany part was somewhat challenging as I hadn't seen such the plant specimen given before, and the question asked for a dissection of the trunk and to draw a piece of the transverse section to show the various bundles and layers of the plant's stem.

After I finished the sketching and labeling of diagrams of all the dissections before the exam time was over, I asked our biology tutor who was supervising the exam to certify them. He carefully compared them to my actual dissections and signed the papers with a brief smile. He took them to be sent to the examiners, with those of the other examinees, all from the second year.

About six weeks later, a large envelope came in the mail from the Associated Examining Board. Our landlord, Rafi, who left our mail in front of our room door, had left it leaning against the door. Initially, I was anxious and hesitant to open it as I feared the worst. *What if I am all wrong and got a low grade?* I left the envelope on the table in our room and looked out the window. I contemplated for a while and then mused, *What the hell? Even if I got a low grade, it was good practice for me to take an actual A-level examination.* I was already ahead of the game and could retake it again at the end of the second year when everyone else in the class would do so. It had to be opened, now or later, and might as well be now. With fidgety hands, I gingerly opened the envelope, pulling out the grade certificate at a snail's pace and peeked at it.

When Sham came home that evening from work, I shook his hand. He was surprised and asked, "What happened?" I was speechless and pointed to the certificate on the table and told him to read the middle part. He slowly read, "Advanced Level. In 1 subject(s). BIOLOGY A2."

He looked at me and asked, "What does that mean?"

"I got a grade A in biology and a 2, or merit, in the S-level examination. S stands for scholarship level."

"Congratulations, brother!"

I profusely thanked him for the help he had given me, the sacrifices he had made for me, the evenings he had cooked for both of us, and especially for vacating the room on Saturdays so I could concentrate on improving my animal dissections, without which a grade A would not have been achievable.

With the top grade in A-level biology at the end of my first year, I felt more confident that I had a potent weapon in my application arsenal for medical school admission because if I could get one A in one year, I could get them for sure in other subjects, like physics and chemistry, at the end of the second and final year.

The college had closed for the summer break. Things were back to normal at home. We cooked together, visited our cousin Naresh living in Shepherd's Bush on Saturdays, and chatted in the evening after we ate and cleaned up the dishes. There was no pressure because when Sham was gone to work, I studied physics, chemistry, and pure and applied math, which I planned to take as a backup subject in my second year. Things were tranquil in the house in the middle of my summer vacation. However, a potential domestic crisis was stealthily brewing up that would upend our lives.

Chapter 12

The Girls

During the summer of 1968, our landlords, the Rafis, rented a bedroom at the top floor of the house to two young Indians, a brother and a sister, who were from Tanzania like us but spoke a different language, Gujarati. As we found out later in our occasional conversations with them, their grandparents originally came to Africa from a small area called Kutch, located in India's western state called Gujarat. The sister was a pretty skinny girl with shoulder-length hair who wore short skirts, and Sham was soon enamored of her but had to tread cautiously because the brother, like a chaperone, was often around as the brother-sister team cooked together.

I faced a different problem that many young men might consider an opportunity, if not for my obsession with studies. In the day time when Sham was at work, I occasionally went out, mostly in the afternoons, to a local shop to buy a chocolate snack for my afternoon tea as I had no breakfast or lunch. I would leave through the hallway next to our room and pass through a short courtyard to the narrow stairs leading to the sidewalk. The door was usually ajar as England was a safe country in those days, and the door was locked only at night.

I often found a Pakistani girl, about the same age as me, who lived across the street, waiting at the door with her back against the doorjamb and arms folded in front, like she was guarding the hallway entry door. She wore the typical tight silk Punjabi dress from the old country. As I left the room and went through the narrow hallway, she would turn her head to look at me. No words were exchanged, but her pensive look bothered me as I passed her, and she barely budged to let me though. I had to pass through sideways to avoid physical contact. As I went up the steps to the sidewalk and down the street, I glanced back, and she was staring at me.

The first few times, I thought she was just waiting for someone. But who could that be? The Rafis, except *Bhabhiji*, worked late. I never saw the girl or her parents visit the Rafis. The two brother-sister tenants were at work, and they lived upstairs. The only persons in the basement were Sham and me, but Sham returned from work after five o'clock when she was long gone. Fleetingly, it crossed my mind that she could be waiting for me. But waiting all this time, hoping I would come out, and still waiting there when I returned? It didn't make any sense; no one in their right mind would do that. Then I thought of a novel idea. I made tea in the afternoon in the kitchen and usually, *Bhabhiji* was there or often waddled in when she heard any noise in the kitchen. She was there when I went up one afternoon.

"*Bhabhiji*, how is Alam doing?" I asked in our native Punjabi, the only language she spoke fluently. Alam was Rafi's younger single brother who lived in one of the rooms there and worked late hours, like Rafi, in a factory.

"Doing well."

"When will he get married?"

"We are looking for a girl for him in Pakistan."

"But *Bhabhiji*, why look that far when the girl is right here."

"Who?"

"That neighbor's daughter."

"She is too dark."

This surprised me because the girl was light-complexioned and Alam was a dark fellow. It exposed the color prejudice permeating the Pakistani and Indian societies.

"Will you go to Pakistan to look for his bride?"

"Our family there will find one. Alam can talk to her on the phone."

"He will marry her over the phone?" This was when I learned it was common for single Pakistani men in England to marry this way, like "phone brides.'"

"He will go Pakistan to marry her. Girl's family arranges that. He will bring her back."

"Who pays for the wedding?"

"Girl's family pays all."

"But *Bhabhiji*, if boys want to marry back home, then how will girls here find husbands?"

"I don't know. Too much TV." It seemed like she wanted to add to it but was hesitant. So, I persisted.

"But they live with their parents."

"Too much freedom. Spoiled."

My bright idea to dump the girl on Alam was stupid when I learned this eye-opening reality. Sham returned that evening, and during our post-dinner chat in the room, I asked him what *Bhabhiji* meant that the Pakistani girls here were spoiled. He said she meant they were not virgins anymore; the girls back home were supposedly virgins, and these boys wanted only virgins.

I didn't give it further thought as whatever the reason, I didn't want to be involved or be part of a new problem, another distraction. But the behavior of the girls at the college aroused my suspicion about this girl's motives and desires. With their new-found freedom and watching programs on TV, the repressed girls from the old country, often from the villages, where the only time they could be with a strange male was when they got married, arranged-style often to their cousins, were now tempted with other stranger boys in close proximity. Like a spring that was compressed tightly, when released, it decompressed fast in the opposite direction.

One afternoon, when I was leaving, she was again waiting. However, this time, her back was resting against the doorjamb, but her legs were bent forty-five degrees vertically so her feet rested against the bottom of the opposite doorjamb. For me to pass her, she would have to stand upright, or I would have to hop over her legs. Her whole posture looked provocative and ridiculous. As I approached her, I told her in Punjabi, "I want to go through here." This was the first time I'd spoken to her as she turned her head toward me, looking intently.

"What do you do here?"

"I'm a student."

She pulled her legs back and straightened up her body, allowing me to pass, but then partially pulled the door closed so there was only a narrow gap to the outside, like she did not want anyone from outside to look in. I stopped, wondering what the hell was going on as this was a very audacious act on the part of a girl.

With the door almost shut, she talked to me in Punjabi. It roughly translated into English as, "Let us kiss and adjust my *nala.*" *Nala* was the drawstring on the upper part of the *salwaar* or the pants part of the Punjabi dress that was tied into a knot in front to hold the *salwaar* in place so it would not drop down. This was a blatant sexual proposition as the *nala* was a very private part; in a case of reversed roles, it would be like a boy asking a girl to adjust his underwear.

Really surprised at such an unexpected proposal, I said, firmly, "No. Your mother will not like that."

"I will not tell her."

"Your father will kill me."

"He is in Pakistan."

"I don't know these things." I was worried someone would see us or *Bhabhiji* would hear us, though she spoke softly. I thought hard to get out this mess without offending the girl.

"We can learn together," she said.

Then an idea struck. "You must go. My brother will return from work soon." She got scared and opened the door ajar and bolted and never returned.

While this problem was solved, another had been brewing up. I had long suspected that *Bhabhiji* was attracted to Sham, but I was certain Sham was not attracted to her. She was an amiable person but not particularly physically attractive, and she was married. The situation that created this attraction scenario was evident. Here was the lady of the house, ostensibly from a village in Pakistan whose husband was absent most of the day. Her main conversation partner was Sham, who was a good conversationalist in Punjabi, the only language she could speak. No wonder she always found some excuse to come to the kitchen when he was there.

While Sham went to the kitchen when he heard the new tenant girl was there cooking, it also attracted *Bhabhiji* who did not cook in the evening as she had already done so in the afternoon when no one was home, except me who went up to make some tea. I rarely saw her two daughters and never knew if they went to school. With her woman's intuition, *Bhabhiji* suspected Sham was attracted to the girl; both were young, and she was pretty. I had noticed she was always cold to the girl, glaring and acting upset, sighing loudly and passing rude comments against her in Punjabi, a language the girl did not understand. While with Sham and me, we could do no wrong in her eyes, but she complained about any small mess or dishes left in the sink by the girl, who often came after eating in her room to clean up. With us, in similar situations, it was, "I'll take care of it. Don't worry." In a contest for creating messiness in a kitchen, no one could outdo us young guys.

As the one-sided tension and the temperature between *Bhabhiji* and the girl rose, it was a matter of time before it became too hot for the girl to stay in the kitchen. At this stage of my life, it had not occurred to me that if the kitchen was a jungle and a woman's domain, then there could only be one lion king of that jungle. Two women in a kitchen together could be a recipe for disaster. One afternoon,

I was going up the stairs to the kitchen when I saw the brother-sister team scooting hurriedly down the ground-floor hallway with their bags in tow and soon blasted out of the main door, slamming it shut behind them. I had anticipated this day from the way *Bhabhiji* had treated her.

When Sham returned home that evening, I told him about the hurried exit. He was surprised and disappointed. The following day was a Saturday, and Sham saw Rafi leaving for work from our room's window, and he rushed out to inquire about the eviction. I saw them talking for a while through our room window curtains. When Sham returned, he said Rafi was evasive about the reasons why the two left. However, Sham said he was surprised as Rafi kept insisting and apologizing that the reason for the eviction was not a Hindu-Muslim issue or problem.

We deduced Rafi had the wrong idea and ostensibly deeply worried that Sham thought they were asked to leave because they were Hindus like us. We never thought that way because if Rafi had any antagonism toward Hindus, he would not have rented to her or us in the first place. Sham assured him that we never thought it was a religious issue and that Rafi was the homeowner who could rent to anyone or ask them to leave for any reason. That was not our problem. Rafi did not want to tell Sham that this was really his wife's doing, nor did Sham want to tell him his inordinate concern was because he was attracted to the girl.

I knew the real reason. I had noticed that *Bhabhiji* had become overly sensitive to what Sham had said and at one time, had cried at some innocuous remark. Sham had had to apologize profusely to calm her. She had been hurt and upset at Sham's attraction to the girl and so she had taken her wrath on the girl and had gotten her husband to remove her from the premises. The husband had been a pawn in her game without being aware of what had really gone on.

I guessed *Bhabhiji* had fed negative stories about the girl to Rafi to end her tenancy as she dare not tell him the real reason. During our post-dinner conversation, we mused about moving out to rent somewhere else. However, we didn't want to hurt Rafi's feelings because he could construe this as we were moving out because it was to do with the removal of the girl and her brother. Unbeknownst to us, another game-changing event happened that gave us the believable excuse we needed to move out.

Early during that summer, my dad wrote to Sham and me that my younger brother, Raj, who was a year younger than me and two years younger than Sham, would join us as he had completed his high school in Tanzania and could enroll at my college. This made it imperative for me and Sham to look for another place with two adjoining rooms as we could not stay three of us in one bedroom and such rooms would be cheaper than two separate rooms.

There was a small eatery opened by an Indian who sold a myriad of Indian snacks and sweetmeats with Indian tea. The sweetmeats of different types were arranged attractively in square tin containers, enclosed in glass countertop cabinets like at jewelry stores. We occasionally went there to eat some Indian sweetmeats and drink tea. Most customers came to buy takeout sweetmeats or snacks and were Indians or Pakistanis. I never saw, at least when we were there, any English person; I guess Indian sweetmeats were not their cup of tea. We looked at some handwritten advertisements on pieces of paper on a small bulletin board hung on a wall. One ad was for a two-bedroom rental that seemed perfect for us as it wasn't too far from my college and Sham's work. We went there on a Saturday.

To our surprise, it was a shop. As Indian immigrants arrived, many were buying the small cute English shops that the owners were selling as they were aging or were offered a price they could not refuse, in accordance with the adage that everything was for sale if the price was right. However, the new Indians shopkeepers kept them open till late at night, like nine or ten o'clock, which was unheard of for the English-owned shops that usually closed at five in the evening in those days. How they bought the shops became evident from what the Indian owner told us.

He had worked in a factory, like most immigrants, doing as much overtime he could get and had saved every penny he could over a few years. He had made an offer to buy the shop from its aging

English owner. Once he had bought it, he had quit his factory job and had tended the shop for long hours, adding products for Indians, like Indian groceries. Above the shop was his four-bedroom home, which came with the shop, and he was renting two of the rooms. Our conversation gravitated to the room rentals.

"Your ad said you are renting two rooms?" Sham asked.

"Yes. But you cannot bring girls here." That condition surprised us. So, Sham responded, "We don't know any girls. Why?"

"No girlfriends here."

I interjected. "We are good guys. We don't have girlfriends. No girls want to go with us."

"No dating here." He repeated firmly.

That condition was a deal breaker, and we were offended by his precondition before even showing us the product. On parting, in his typical humorous way, Sham told the guy, "If you know any girls who want to date us, please give them our address." The man fumed and turned away. We were astounded at this puritanism.

Sham had another advertisement from a local paper about a rental, so we went there. It was even further than this place, but we were exploring. We knocked on the typical brick house door. A Jamaican opened it. Jamaicans started coming to Britain in the fifties when there was a shortage of bus drivers, many working as bus drivers and conductors.

"We are here for rooms to rent. Are you the owner?" Sham asked.

"Yes," he said with a broad smile. "Two rooms. Upstairs." He pointed up with a finger, moving it up and down.

"How much is the rent?"

"Five pounds per week." While that was a hefty sum, it was cheaper than the six pounds the Indian shop keeper wanted. We followed the man upstairs and saw the rooms. They were adjoining and acceptable. There was a bed in each room with a chair and a small table. We wanted to clarify that there were no inordinate preconditions.

"Any conditions?"

"Yes," he said and suddenly looked serious. We got anxious and thought, *Oh no, not the same condition as the last landlord.*

"Pay your rent!" We looked at each other for a second, and all burst out laughing, starting with him. After the laugh, Sham cautiously broached the subject of girls. "Any restriction on bringing girls?"

"Girls? Hell no!"

"Actually, we don't have girlfriends. The last landlord we met didn't want any girl visitors."

"Man! Bring them. The last tenant banged one so hard on the bed it creaked downstairs. Cracked a ceiling. It was all loud groans and moans."

Sham and I looked at each other really surprised. We had gone from a puritan to a free spirit as we listened to his elaborations on the sexual freedom allowed in his place in gory details. We were two virgin boys, and his sexual innuendos worried us so we left after excusing ourselves that we would be back with our third brother.

Some days later, Sham found another place that was about the same distance to my college as our existing abode at the Rafis. We decided not to ask about possible female visitors unless the landlord mentioned it. We went to a house on Brewery Road in Plumstead in the evening. It was dark outside, and we could see through the partially opaque door window the silhouette of a person approaching. A beefy man with thick hair opened the door.

"We've come to meet Harbans Singh," Sham told the man in Punjabi, our common native language.

"I'm Harbans," the man said. We were somewhat surprised as he did not wear a turban or have a beard like most Sikhs. However, many Sikhs in England were discarding the key tenets of their religion—shaving, trimming their hair, and discarding turbans—for various reasons, such as to reduce discrimination, to easily maintain short hair, and to attract girls, as even Sikh girls preferred their boyfriends clean-shaven.

"You have two rooms to rent?"

"Yes, yes. Right here." He showed us two rooms to the left of the entry hallway where he was standing. The front room had a large window facing the street, and it was a little larger than the back room. Each of the rooms had a door that opened into the hallway and also a double door in the wall, separating the two rooms. It was like a one-bedroom apartment, with the front being a living room and the back being the bedroom. Sham made a deal with the man that we would move in in a week based on a handshake, a common practice of conducting business in the third world. We were glad that there was no mention of any preconditions and told Rafi of our planned move. He was very disappointed and said he thought of us as family. We told him we felt the same, but he understood our need for two adjoining rooms as our third brother would soon be arriving from Tanzania to live with us.

At the beginning of my second year in England, in July of 1968, with a beautiful summer blooming with long days, we settled into our new two-bedroom rental at the house owned by Harbans Singh on Brewery Road in Plumstead that was about a fifteen-minute walk from Woolwich College.

Chapter 13

The Elephant in the Room

Long before Norbert disappeared from the college after his rout in the college exams, I had researched the steps required in the medical school application process and how to navigate them successfully. I had gathered from Norbert that an invitation for an interview at a medical school was the key first step in the admission process, but it was difficult to get as the number of qualified applicants overwhelmed the number of admission spots.

The applicants had just finished their first year of college and had not taken their A-level exams, which they took at the end of their second, or final, college year. Since there were no standardized preliminary screening exams for medical school admissions in those days, the student's performance in the three college term exams in the first year acted as a proxy.

I was certain the headmaster gave his opinion about the suitability of the students, and this was not a problem for Norbert, as the dean of Middlesex Medical School had promised him a place if he passed his A-levels. However, he had underestimated the difficulties in passing his A-levels. He was good in human anatomy as he claimed, but that had no relevance to what the medical school admission requirements were.

I'd figured out the critical role of recommendations when I had taken my application to Mr. Cooper, the acting headmaster and the head of the math and science department, whom I had visited in the hospital after his heart attack. He observed that my communication skills were lacking and that it was difficult for me to answer a general question easily, like I needed some time to answer. It was also that, suddenly, I became nervous. However, he told me at the end of the interview, "I'll give you a strong recommendation." I felt better. I assumed his statement was based on my strong academic performance throughout the year and in all three exams.

I was aware of my disability of slow thinking in answering questions not related to science. What Norbert had told me would guide my preparation for the medical school interview, if I got one. He said they always asked why you wanted to go into medicine and what your plans were after graduation from the medical school. "Never tell them," he advised, "you want to make a lot of money or that you want to stay in England after graduation. You must say you will return back to your country because then you will have a better chance, as they know you will be prescribing medications and ordering other medical equipment from England."

I'd told him I did not want to stay here as the weather was too cold for me, and I could live like a king in Tanzania as a doctor, with a large property and ranch with servants and a new American car—the very reason that I wanted to be a doctor since fifth grade. He said, "You have to give answers they want to hear."

The coveted interview invitations were mailed when the students were on their summer break after the end of their first year of college. With the added tailwind from a strong recommendation letter by my chemistry tutor, Mr. Hill, to the senior tutor at Trinity Hall College, or commonly called Trinity Hall, one of the twenty-five Cambridge University colleges where he'd graduated from, I received an interview letter from the director of medical studies there. I was excited and anxious, but happy I'd disproved Norbert's claim of not getting into a British medical school as I had now achieved the important and difficult initial step of getting an interview. But an interview did not guarantee anything, as the medical schools could cherry pick. All his negativity had actually made me try harder and taught me a life-long lesson to avoid people with negative attitudes who want you to fail. I was glad he was gone and hoped I'd seen the last of him. For the interview, I rehearsed hard, just like for an exam, acting the dean's role as the interviewer and then reversing the role as the interviewee.

My interview at Cambridge was scheduled for early afternoon. Not knowing how long it would take to reach Trinity Hall, I left early in the morning and took several trains from Woolwich and reached King's Cross station in London from where trains left for Cambridge hourly. I bought a cheaper day return ticket. The train sped at fifty miles per hour, and the ride lasted an hour as I looked out to see rows of red-brick homes and apartments passing by. The train was low on passengers, and I was alone in the compartment, so I kept practicing for the interview using rote memorization due to my communication problem.

On disembarking at the Cambridge train station, I asked around for directions and grabbed a map of the city from a ticket booth. A bus that took passengers to Cambridge city center arrived at the bus stop in front of the station after going halfway around a large roundabout. I boarded the bus and went to the upper deck front seat to see the city. From the station, the bus went down a main thoroughfare with shops and restaurants on either side. I disembarked at the city center, the Cambridge Market, where there were numerous market stalls selling vegetables and fruits in a large rectangular area surrounded by shops. From the market, I went through some narrow alleys using my map and occasionally asking a local resident to reach Trinity Hall, which was surprisingly close to the market.

I was early and entered the porter's lodge at the entrance of the college where the porter pointed through a window toward the interview room across a large square lawn. From the lodge, I took a right through the entry archway that led to the square courtyard with neatly trimmed grass and wandered around the college and went to its rear where it was bordered by the River Cam. I was admiring the college's beauty and its 800-year-old architecture, as Cambridge was one of the oldest universities in the UK.

I decided to go back to the city center to find a cheap place to eat as I had a few hours to kill. As I looked at the prices of food items from café to café to find the cheapest one, an Indian approached me. He asked me if I could lend him some money to reach another town further north of Cambridge where his friends lived as he had exhausted what he had to reach Cambridge from London. He was a recent, fresh off the boat arrival. At first, I politely refused, telling him that I was only a student with barely enough money for lunch. He apologized and thanked me and moved on, but then I remembered what Sham had told me when he first arrived from India at Gatwick airport. He had no money and was wandering around when some Pakistanis approached him as they saw him looking around aimlessly and bought him lunch at the airport restaurant and invited him to come and stay with them in Leeds, a city in northern England, also offering to help him find a job at a factory where they worked. They had just picked up a friend who had arrived from Pakistan. Sham declined the offer and told them he wanted to stay in London and had a friend he could stay with. So, the men bought him a train ticket for his destination.

I felt bad and called the man back and gave him my lunch money. He profusely thanked me and asked me if I could write down my address so he could refund my money when he found a job. I told him it was no problem, and that I was glad to help a fellow countryman. I was not that hungry anyhow and went around to see some other places like the famous King's College chapel that was near Trinity Hall.

Afterward, I arrived at the room where I was to meet the director of medical studies for my afternoon appointment. I knocked at the door and was invited in by Dr. H.F. (Bill) Grundy, a slim man with a longish nose and thinning hair on top of his head, wearing a black jacket and a tie. He had high cheeks and a prominent smile and asked me to take a seat across from him. He did not have any paperwork or folder in front of him. I assumed he had reviewed all my information beforehand. After the introductions and niceties, he came to the main pointed questions.

"Why do you want to study medicine?"

If I were truthful, I would have said, "Because I wanted to have my own private medical office and make a lot of money and have a big house with a huge yard and several servants to do different chores like gardening, cooking, and housekeeping. I also want to buy a new luxurious American car, called the Rambler, that the only doctor in my town owned. It would be a win-win situation as I would alleviate my patient's suffering and diseases and also make a lot of money."

However, the real answer I gave Dr. Grundy was, "I want to help and alleviate the pain and suffering of my fellow human beings caused by diseases. I know that firsthand because I suffered from malaria as a child, and it was awful, with high fever, shivering, and pain. The only doctor in my town came to our house. He was very kind to me, held my hand, and told me, 'You will get well.' He gave me medicine and cured me. In fifth grade, I passed by his office and wanted to be just like him. I want to learn about the anatomy of my body, how it functions, how it is affected by diseases, and how to treat them. It is truly a noble profession, and I will always act in the best interest of my patients and always treat them with kindness and respect, just like I would like someone else to treat me."

"What will you do after you complete medical school?"

"I will go back to my home country of Tanzania. There is a tremendous need for medical doctors there. I would like to have my own private practice like most doctors there so I can be my own boss and support my future family. I would also like to help poor people who cannot afford medical care by volunteering in free medical clinics, or even allocate certain hours or days at my own private clinic or volunteer part time at the government hospital for the poor where the lines are very long."

Dr. Grundy asked me some more questions about that and about the available medical care in Tanzania that I was able to answer easily. Like an actor, I had rehearsed all these answers many times, so they flowed naturally and did not sound like they were learned by rote like a parrot.

Then he asked me a question that caught me by surprise as I hadn't thought about it. "What will you do if you do not get into a medical school?"

I became stiff and thought hard and took a few seconds to respond. Then a thought occurred. My thoughts went back to Mr. Hill, my chemistry tutor; I admired him, and he was the reason I was here or even knew about this place. "I will study chemistry and become a chemistry tutor. We are short of chemistry tutors in Tanzania."

Dr. Grundy smiled a little and said chemistry was one of his favorite subjects as he did research in pharmacology on how drugs affected the body. I was pleased I had hit the right note. After the interview, I thanked him for inviting me, but he gave no indication or a hint as to what his final decision would be, except that I would be hearing from the admissions office.

I had applied to four other medical schools, some not well known, as my backup plan. The modus operandi of those days was whenever I went to any medical school interview, only the dean of the medical school interviewed me. There were no medical school admission committees; the dean was the judge, jury, and executioner for admissions. At all these interviews, I conjectured the very reason I was invited in the first place was the elephant in the room—the grade A that I got in A-level biology. Not only that, but metaphorically speaking, the accompanying baby elephant was I got this grade at the end of my first year and that I also passed the scholarship level exam, an extra feather in my hat. These interview letters came after I sent proof of my biology grades to the deans. I'd proven myself and had a definite edge over my competitors who had only strong college headmaster recommendations but might not be able to get the A-level grades the deans would ask for. During the interviews, the deans never mentioned or discussed this elephant in the room.

My last back up was the medical school at the University of Leeds. Here, the dean was seated at a desk in a large sprawling clinic, where there were many men in white coats among throngs of patients. I assumed they were doctors in training. Every dean asked just about the same questions, with some variations, and I was good at the answers from the interviews with four previous deans.

Acceptance letters from the four medical schools, except Cambridge, arrived in the mail soon after my interviews. Most wanted only a grade C in one of the remaining A-level subjects, like physics or chemistry, an indicator of how much the grade A I already got weighed in. But it was dead silence from Trinity Hall.

Finally, at the end of September 1968, I received an acceptance letter from Trinity Hall. Surprisingly, it was an unassuming standard pre-printed letter, in which the essential details were typed in darker ink. It was dated September 28, 1968, and started, "Dear Sharma," with Sharma typed in. The first paragraph read, "I am glad to be able to tell you that we intend to offer you a place in October 1968 to read medicine. You will in due course receive a formal notification from the UCCA Central Office." "Medicine" and "8" were typed in the blank spaces. I guessed UCCA stood for University of Cambridge Council on Admissions. The second paragraph was crossed out with two hand-drawn lines with a pen. I assumed it did not apply to me and read, "We expect you to take the Joint Examination this autumn and hope that you may win an award. The completed application for this exam-ination must be in our hands by October at the latest." I didn't know anything about this Joint Examination and that it led to some award. I regretted it later for not pursuing this matter to find out more and take the exam if it applied to me to win an award.

The last paragraph read, "Please let me know as soon as possible whether you intend to accept this offer." The next line stated, "Yours sincerely, Senior Tutor." Senior was typed in. The letter was signed by E.K. Frankl. Below that was a typed message: "P.S. This offer is conditional on your obtaining one further grade A at A-level."

I saw that the offer was for October 1968, only a few days from the date on the letter and it was already October! Then, how would I get another A in a few days? It seemed like a typo as I assumed the offer was for October 1969 and confirmed later it was a mistake.

Our second year at college had started at the beginning of September 1968. I felt content and happy that I had achieved the difficult and important task of securing a conditional offer at several medical schools. This was a far cry from when I started college with the discouragements and negativity from Norbert. Thinking out of the box had worked.

But now my conundrum was which one to accept. While Cambridge wanted another grade A, the others would accept a grade C, which would be easy for me. I could only accept one, and the clock was ticking. Again, I decided to think outside the box.

At this stage, I thought all the medical schools in England were equivalent, and the London medical schools who had accepted me were a better choice as I was living in one of its suburbs. But if I did that, I imagined it would disappoint Mr. Hill, our Cambridge graduate chemistry tutor who had recommended that I go to Cambridge and had written a recommendation for me. I decided that I could not, in clear conscience, accept a London medical school offer, without first passing this by Mr. Hill.

At the end of the next chemistry class, after all the students had left, I took out my acceptance letter from Trinity Hall and walked to Mr. Hill who was at his desk in the front of the lab preparing to leave.

"Mr. Hill, could I talk to you for a minute?"

"Yes, of course."

"Thank you. I have an acceptance letter from Trinity Hall," I said excitedly as I handed him the letter.

Before even reading the letter, he congratulated me. I did not want to mention my acceptance at other medical schools unless it was absolutely necessary. He read the letter.

"They want me to get another grade A," I said as he neared the end of the letter.

He looked at me in the eyes and replied as if that was not a problem. "You can get that."

His confidence in me was why he had placed his reputation on the line with the senior tutor at Trinity Hall for me.

"So, I should accept the offer?"

"Yes, of course. They only want the best."

I was flattered and that solved my conundrum again by thinking outside the box. Getting another A would not be a problem as I had spent most of the summer studying chemistry and physics for the second year and the backup pure and applied math. College chemistry was a difficult subject because part of it was organic chemistry, or chemistry of the carbon, a subject in itself with its benzene rings. I had become good at it as I got an organic chemistry backup textbook to familiarize myself with the subject.

At college, it was apparent no other student got an interview as they were a social bunch and liked telling each other personal stuff. No student knew about my progress, interviews, or that I got an A in biology as I kept my cards close to my chest. It was clear that the difficult part was to get an interview with so many good applicants. Most of my colleagues' failure in first-term exams and their later mediocre performance weighed heavily on their prospects as it was obvious Mr. Cooper gave recommendations based on this performance.

Chapter 14

A Tale of Two Sikhs

As the beautiful summer of 1968 progressed, we were well settled in our adjoining two bedrooms at the house on Brewery Road in Plumstead owned by Harbans Singh when a taxi arrived from the Gatwick International Airport and dropped off our two remaining brothers, the oldest Ram and the youngest Raj. Ram, older than me by three years, was an adventurous guy who had worked as a traveling salesman for Cadbury, a well-known British chocolate company, in Tanzania, carrying Cadbury chocolates to the smallest towns to sell to shops. He had saved enough money to pay his airfare to California where he had secured admission at National Technical College in Los Angeles.

Some days later, I accompanied Raj to my college and helped him register for his first-year classes in math and science starting in September of 1968, just like I had done the previous year for myself. Raj and I lived in the smaller of the two rooms at the rear while Sham and Ram lived in the larger front room with a large window facing the road. It doubled up as our living room as we had a small TV on a wooden stand close to the window, and there was a tiny couch and a low table in the middle and a small bed. Our two rooms were separated by double doors as a partition, but we kept them open for easy movement between the rooms as there were no privacy issues being four single guys. Ram stayed with us for a month and then left for Los Angeles.

As the summer cooled, my second and final year of college started in September of 1968. I stopped studying late in an empty classroom as I'd done in the first year when the library closed. It was redundant now as I had studied well during the summer break to make up for any extra study, and I did not have to study for biology anymore, but I continued studying at home after leaving college at five o'clock because there was nothing else to do.

Our landlord, Harbans Singh, was an Indian Sikh, but unlike most Sikhs, he was clean-shaven. Sikhs, an energetic group of people and physically strong, were Indians whose sine qua non was their articles of faith, a turban, covering unshorn hair folded into a bun on top of the head, an unshorn beard, a steel bangle on the right wrist, a comb inside the turban, and underwear and a small knife. They mostly resided in India's northern state called Punjab from where my father had originally migrated to East Africa in the 1920s.

When Indians went overseas, they faced discrimination for a myriad of reasons, like accent, color, food, and because of India's low international standing from years of dogmatic economic malfeasance. On a scale of one to ten, where one was minimal or subtle discrimination and ten was the worst, an Indian faced a discrimination of seven in a Western country, but a Sikh faced an eight because he had the additional baggage of his articles of faith. If an Indian had to wake up at six o'clock in the morning to prepare for work or school, then a Sikh Indian would have to wake up at five o'clock in the morning as he needed additional time to tend to his long hair that would badly entangle if not fully groomed.

The epitome of this was as described by Dr. Manmohan Singh, who was originally a refugee from the newly created country of Pakistan during the 1947 partition of the Indian subcontinent and became the prime minister of India in 2004. When he was at St. John's College at Cambridge University and graduated from there with a first in economics in 1957, he would get up early at four o'clock in the morning to go to shower, take care of his hair and beard, and make his turban—long before anyone else got up, so no one would see him doing all this. Like the tale of two cities, my life would soon be intertwined and affected by two Sikhs.

One day, I was sitting at a library table reviewing what I'd just studied when a Sikh student, Gajinder Singh, or GS, who sat quietly in a back corner of the pure and applied math class I attended, took a seat next to me. He wore a large blue turban that was firmly enveloped around the top of his forehead and covered half of his earlobes, fanning upwards and outwards, like straight slanting sides of a large bowl, to the crown of the head, where it was flat on the top like a helicopter landing pad. Ostensibly, he was fresh off the boat as his turban style was definitely old country. His facial hairs were sprouting into a partial beard as his testosterone levels rose, propelling him into adulthood. He asked for my help with math. I closed my book and tried to explain to him in simple math language the difficulty he was having. After a while, I felt his comprehension of the subject matter was poor, and he simply didn't get it. I tried various methods for a while, including explaining some parts quietly in Punjabi, even though I'd sworn not to speak in any Indian language at college as it could cause a misunderstanding with the British students. It was getting closer to my next class when an English classmate named Griffiths, with curly blond hair, took a seat across from us at the table and looked at GS and asked him a pointed question. "Why do you wear a turban?"

"My father wants me to wear it. He will be very upset if I remove it," GS replied, looking exasperated at the question. My time was up, and I excused myself. When I met Griffiths again alone, I told him that the real reason GS wore a turban was because it was a religious requirement and gave him a brief background of its genesis. The tenth Sikh guru, or their spiritual leader, Guru Gobind Singh Ji (Ji was added for respect in Punjabi), had ordained his followers over three hundred years ago to keep their hair unshorn and wear some other articles of faith to give them a unique identity so that they would stand out in a crowd, never deny their faith, and be willing to die for it. It had nothing to do with his father. Griffiths appreciated my explanation and said GS could have explained that instead of blaming his father. GS came back in the library one day to learn some more math, and I confronted him, demanding to know why he lied to Griffiths about his turban. He said he felt embarrassed. So, I asked him if he would keep blaming his father when other English people asked him the same question. Why not tell them the truth and be proud of his faith and state? Just like other religions had certain unique beliefs and articles of faith, Sikhs had their own too. He agreed.

GS now came around often when I was studying, which diverted my concentration from physics and chemistry. His background in math from his schooling in India was rudimentary, and he would have difficulty comprehending basic concepts despite my best efforts, so I decided to dump him on Raj, as math was his main subject. At first, Raj was accommodating but soon ran into the same roadblock I had and found GS was not suited for high-level math. However, unbeknownst to me, as the year progressed, this would lead to tensions between us at home as Raj realized this problem was dumped on him by me.

Meanwhile, another Sikh student, Bhamra, or Bham for brevity, rented a room on the second floor of the house we were living in. He was also in his first year of college, like Raj, but taking different subjects. He was six-two with a sturdy athletic frame and wore a tightly fitting compact red turban and had a smooth short black beard that was rapidly increasing in density and length by the week, too fast for his comfort. We occasionally bumped into him when he was in the kitchen, and Sham indulged in casual chit-chat and gossip in Punjabi with him. Soon, we detected a regression in his external physical features as gradually the beard got trimmer. Not long after that, the full transformation took place, as Bham shorn his long hair, discarded his turban, and shaved his remaining beard.

He detailed his evolutionary tale to us: He attended the Sikh temple, called a *gurudwara*, every Sunday morning like most Sikhs where they also served lunch cooked by volunteers after the prayers, devotional songs, and readings from their holy book called the *Guru Granth Sahib*. Everyone sat on the floor, and while he was there, the Sikh elders waved him over to sit next to them. They respected his observation of their faith as they worried about their co-religionists shaving their hair and abandoning the key tenets of their religion in their new adopted country. However, as they saw his gradual transformation, like the thinning and trimming of his beard, they looked at him suspiciously and cooled off toward him. Soon, when his transformation from a Sikh to a regular clean-shaven Indian was complete, they totally ignored him, and embarrassed, he stopped going to the *gurudwara*.

The new Bham cut a reasonably handsome figure, with nicely cut thick hair, clean-shaven full cheeks, and a square jaw. The motives for his drastic step eventually surfaced. Bham was enamored of a pretty Pakistani Muslim Punjabi girl named Naaz in his class at Woolwich College, whose brother was also a classmate. She wore sexy, tight silk Punjabi outfits. However, in his former self, girls, including Sikh girls, were not interested in him. Now it was a different story. I often saw the trio, Bham, Naaz, and her brother, wandering the college halls and eating lunch together. In normal circumstances, any such tango between a Sikh boy and a Muslim girl would be taboo, like tasting the forbidden fruit, and would infuriate parents on both sides of the religious divide. However, love had transcended religion because love was a separate unique religion in itself. Since immemorial times, love did not allow manmade religion to encroach on its turf, and when it did, the results were often catastrophic. Here, the youth had abandoned the key tenets of his present religion for the religion of love.

The new, metamorphosed Bham was popular with girls. The skinny Sikh girl who had tried to befriend me unsuccessfully and was later insulted by Norbert's faux pas asked Bham if he would come to her house. When he asked why, she said, "I want to make tea for you." He walked away without responding. She had rejected him before, and now she wanted to make tea for him! No dice. Eventually, her search for a suitable boyfriend came to fruition when she started dating a shorter and chubbier clean-shaven Sikh boy a year behind her in class.

However, things were not moving fast enough for Bham. He wanted some real action with Naaz, but she was always under the watchful eyes of a chaperone, her elder brother. Bham thought he had done everything right. The three of them were often canvassing the students and campaigning for Naaz's brother to become the president of the college's student body. Bham made extra efforts to lobby me at home, cajoling me to use my influence over my classmates to vote for the brother, even though I was not interested in student politics. Then they visited me during lunchtime, and the sister asked me to help her brother. I agreed but was not sure what I could do. The brother was eventually elected, partly from lack of another contender. At our rental house, the situation was evolving. Bham usually returned later at night as he went to Naaz's house after school with her brother. While this was none of our business, we would soon be affected indirectly.

Things at our house were getting chaotic, to put it mildly. To start with, our landlord, whose wife was in India, got greedy and rented one room above us to two other Sikhs, but these guys were traditional Sikhs in their early thirties who observed their faith strictly. They had long, freely flowing lush black beards and turbans covering the long hair on their heads. They were village boys from Punjab belonging to the Sikh farmers' caste called the *Jats*, who were sturdy fellows and worked hard in the farms. The other room upstairs was rented to Bham, and the last room was where Harbans lived. The two new Sikhs who worked in some factory doing the night shift soon left for India and returned with two young brides—a common practice among the Sikh men in England who were from Punjab in India because they got the added benefit of fleecing a hefty dowry from the girl's struggling parents back home who had to mortgage their land possessions just to send a daughter overseas for better prospects. So, in one room, there were now four people and nine people in the entire house. However, at any time, because of people at work or college, the actual number was less, like when the two newlyweds left for work at night. But problems arose.

Our two adjoining rooms opened into the common hallway of the house on the first floor and spanned to the common kitchen. Behind the kitchen was the common bathroom with a bathtub. Harbans was a good cook but didn't like cooking often, so he cooked a large pot of dry vegetable curry that lasted a week. We hardly cooked at that time, so I used to get tempted and occasionally went to the kitchen on my return from college to scoop some of the curry using a steel ladle and stir the rest in the pot to hide any surface appearance of theft, covering the pot with its lid. I had to be cautious to take just enough, or none at all, if the pot was running low to avoid suspicion of pilfering.

In our room, Raj and I would study after college early in the evening, when we would occasionally hear disturbing creaking and thumping sounds coming from the ceiling. It reminded me of what that Jamaican landlord had described when we had been searching for rentals. The newlyweds, all four of them holed in one room, could only have communal sex. This became apparent one day when Sham arrived home from work, and we went to the kitchen to cook some Indian food for the three of us brothers while Raj, who did not cook, stayed in the room studying. While we were chopping vegetables, the two village girls wearing their tight Punjabi outfits came down the stairs and entered the kitchen giggling at each other, becoming somewhat quiet when their gazes met ours. After they scurried behind us, they started giggling again and entered the bathroom, slamming the door, like they were annoyed we were in the kitchen even though we were there before them, minding our own business. After that, we heard a lot of splashing water in the bathtub. The brides reemerged from the bathroom after a while and went back past us into the hallway and up the stairs quietly.

Then Sham explained to me in lower tones what had transpired. He told me that women washed their private parts after having sex and that explained why they had gone to the bathroom and we had heard all that splashing water. While Sham was a virgin like me, he knew more about such stuff having lived in India where there was a serious population explosion. I opined why the guys did not do the same, wash their dirty organs after sex, and perhaps they should also do so before sex. After that, we started talking loosely about the noise from the creaking ceiling and further indulged in cheap talk about the two *Jats'* penises to have some fun and laugh. The situation was getting out of hand when Sham said a *Jat* told him that they don't get any sex as single guys, but once they marry, their wives give them a lot, and we laughed louder. However, I used a derogatory term in Punjabi for a large dirty penis, *ganda laan,* and our voices had been getting louder unconsciously. Sham looked past me and put his finger on his mouth, and I turned my head to look at the hallway just as someone cleared his throat loudly. At the bottom of the staircase, one of the two *Jats* was glaring at me. His thick black hair was unfolded and flowing freely over his shoulders and back as he was not wearing a turban, like most Sikh men at home. With his long freely flowing black beard, he looked like a young muscular version of Rip Van Winkle—somewhat scary with a hairy chest separated from hairy legs with a white towel. He eyed us meanly without a word, but he meant, "Juniors, watch your dirty, wagging tongues." One positive outcome was that we did not hear the loud, disturbing thumping anymore as the newlyweds presumably toned down their hyperactive procreative acts.

In the aftermath of this unspoken confrontation, our living situation rapidly deteriorated. Bham's metamorphosis made him attractive to the two village brides and aroused their husbands' suspicion and ire. Bham confided to Sham that when he went to his room at night after the two husbands had left for work, one of the brides would open her door partially to furtively peek at him and even winked at him once, insinuating, "Come to our parlor; the lions have left the den for the night," which was an audacious act for a Punjabi village girl. When Sham jested that he should take her up on her offer, Bham emphatically rejected the idea as he was scared shitless the two husbands would kill him. In fact, now one of them stood outside the house entry door like a guard. I could see his silhouette in the hallway light through the front door's opaque glass as he stayed up for as late as he could, waiting for Bham to return and intimidate him just by waiting there.

By now, Bham had given up on Naaz, who had confided in him she desired to move to the highest level of relationships but would not due to the fear of her brother. A British Jewish girl in Bham's class, who had previously ignored Bham when he wore a turban, now saw him as an opportunity and was soon dating and visiting Bham in his room. That suited Bham because now the hostile husbands on his heels cooled off when they saw he had a prettier girlfriend than their village wives and who satisfied his urges.

It was raucous in the house with all this action. To add to the chaos and our woes, another event transpired. Sham had occasionally complained of a painless small bump on one side of his nose since his younger days in Africa. The local doctor had no idea what it was and had placed a stethoscope on that side of his nose to listen, an ostensibly a dumb act. But with good medical care in England, he went to see his doctor who referred him to a surgical specialist at a local hospital where they removed the benign mass. At the hospital, Sham made a fast recovery with the help of an Indian nurse from Mauritius, a beautiful island off the coast of East Africa. She became a close friend and started visiting him daily during the evenings after Sham returned from work. For their privacy, the double doors separating our two rooms were closed. Raj and I were now confined to one small room, but Sham paid the rent, and he had the right to his larger room and privacy.

As Sham's relationship with the nurse blossomed, the disturbance from their talking, laughing, and watching television disturbed us and made it harder to concentrate on our studies. One day, I lost my cool, resulting in a loud verbal altercation with him. I yelled at him to stop bringing the girl home. With Raj and I stuck in one room, our relationship was deteriorating, as Raj figured out I had dumped Gajinder Singh on him for math tutoring. He also had resentment toward me because he thought I was a poor role model. He wanted more guidance as to what studies he should pursue after college. It led to an argument evolving into a shouting match and ultimately, a physical fight. I was at my wits' end and reflexively grabbed his neck and started squeezing like a man possessed. When I suddenly realized I was doing something horrible, I immediately stopped, and we went to our own corners of the small room without another word. I realized Raj's allegations were true—I was a poor role model who was self-centered. I had to change.

When I went to the kitchen a day later, I bumped into Harbans Singh, our landlord, who confided in me that he had been liberal with us only because of me and Raj, and he disapproved of Sham's activities. It was then I realized he was fishing in troubled waters, trying to divide the brothers as he had heard my shouting match with Sham. It occurred to me how the others in the house were gleeful of the discord among us, and it was a warning to us to circle the wagons. I was getting despondent as we were heading toward a disaster with all the internal tensions and strife among us brothers. At that point in time, we were staying together only for mutual survival and convenience.

Chapter 15

The Bonhomie

It was during this hopeless dark period when I felt depressed and hopeless, like the roof was caving in on me with no relief in sight, that Sham opened the door between the rooms one Saturday morning. He looked distraught and said his female friend had gone back to her home country. We all made up, reminding each other we were brothers after all and needed to move on. So, we all huddled into his room to watch the morning TV. We had finished watching an hour-long discussion panel about South Asian immigrant problems on an Indian-Pakistani immigrant channel when a four-door sleek black car arrived and parked in front of our house.

We three brothers peeked curiously through the transparent curtains of the front window, wondering if the driver had made a mistake, as there wasn't any important individual living at our abode, only some factory workers and broke students. Sham, in his usual joking fashion, commented, "They think the British prime minister lives here? Even the Indian prime minister wouldn't visit us."

For a minute, nothing moved inside the car, its tinted windows making it difficult to look inside. With our curiosity mounting, we huddled closer, our heads together, and Sham pulled one part of the curtain a little to get a clearer view. The front door of the car opened and out came a beefy, balding African man, wearing a black suit with a waistcoat and tie. He straightened himself, looked around, and then stared down at a piece of paper in his hand and gazed up at our house.

Sham again jested, "Seems like our *mwanainchi*." *Mwanainchi* is a Swahili word for a countryman.

"Maybe he is the president of Tanzania visiting us," Raj said.

As Sham and Raj laughed, I carefully observed the man as it was déjà vu for me—the face rang a bell. Laughing out loud, I said, "That is Norbert Eliumelu!"

"Who the hell is *Aloomaloo*? Does not sound like a Tanzanian name." Sham and Raj looked at me curiously. *Aloo* was the Punjabi word for potato.

"He is from Biafra," I said. "He was my friend at Woolwich College. He left before the year was over."

"Isn't that part of Nigeria trying to break away?" Sham said.

"Yes, yes."

"Maybe he will be the next president of Biafra," Raj said. We chuckled.

"Invite him in," Sham said.

I left the room and opened the front door and called out loudly, "Norbert!" as he looked again at the paper. Our gazes met, and he came forward with a big smile and open arms, and we hugged in front of the door.

"Sharma. Good to see you," he said.

"Really happy to see you. Come in. Meet my two brothers."

We all were seated in the living room, and I introduced Norbert to my brothers, telling them how close of friends we had been at the college and about his background of having lived in England since 1953.

"What do you do these days?" I asked.

"I'm at the private college I told you about."

"Studies going well?"

"Yes. I get private instructions."

"That's why they call it private college," Sham interjected, and we all laughed.

"I got accepted at Cambridge medical school. They want another A."

Norbert looked stunned or surprised; I couldn't decipher which one. Here was a man who had done everything to dissuade me, saying it was impossible for me to get a place in a British medical school being a foreign student, and I proved him wrong. Like someone in a boxing ring who just recovered from a stunning punch by his opponent, he asked, "How'd that happen?"

"Remember my idea about getting a grade A in biology?"

I didn't want to remind him of the highly negative response he had given to the idea that it was impossible and his attempts to dissuade me from even trying.

"You took the A-level biology exam?" He shook his head.

"Got an A. Also passed the scholarship level exam."

It was a second blow. Norbert tried to change the topic, like it was unimportant. I told him that I got accepted to all the other four medical schools I had applied to, conditional on just one more A-level grade C. However, I did not want to rub it in. He was our guest, and we believed in treating our guests with the utmost respect and humility, like a member of our family. In Tanzania, my mom would offer him tea and sweetmeats; here we only had tap water.

The rest of our conversation was exciting for my brothers, who asked him about the situation in Nigeria and Biafra's problems. We also talked about Tanzania, but we were curious about the luxury car, and Sham asked him if it was rented. Norbert said he owned it. When it was time to leave, I went out with him and looked inside the car when he got in. It was truly a luxurious car, nothing like anything I'd seen before. Most of the cars in England were small, like the iconic Morris minor. Most people took public transport as owning a car was really a privilege.

Norbert offered to take me for a ride. I was excited and really wanted my brothers to come along, but he was the car owner, and I didn't want to overreach. I sat in the passenger's seat in front, and he took off. The car rode smoothly. Norbert drove me to a ferry terminal near the Thames River where ferries went across to a town called East Ham. It was a beautiful day with clear skies, and the river flowed quietly. He parked the car, and we took a ferry across the river and back as we talked about old times. He dropped me home and wanted to return the following Saturday to take me to his house.

When I saw my brothers, they asked me excitedly about my car experience. I felt guilty having enjoyed the car ride without their participation and underplayed it. "Just a boring car ride," I said.

The following Saturday, Norbert returned with his car. This time, I was surprised he brought along a blond-haired lady with a blond-haired boy. He told me that she was Irish, and they had been living together for six years but were not married. We all drove to his house, which he said he owned, quite a distance from Woolwich. It was a cute four-bedroom house attached to neighboring typical London homes. After an inside tour of the house, he took us all to lunch at a restaurant.

He was familiar, from our college days together, with my being a vegetarian and helped me order some boiled vegetables. While I enjoyed talking to his lady, I was in the dark about their relationship and avoided asking personal questions except how they met. He said he had met her at the Middlesex Medical School when he had worked there as the chief anatomy technician for eight years. I peeked at the lunch bill that looked pricy; Norbert didn't seem to be concerned and paid it. After the fine dining, Norbert dropped his live-in lady and her son back home and drove me back to my house. At first, that surprised me because I thought it would make sense for all of us to drop me off first. However, his motive became clear.

On the way to my house, he asked me a loaded question that was beyond my knowledge or expertise. He claimed his girlfriend insisted the boy was his son because she was living with him when he was conceived. They had lived together for six years and the kid was five years old, so the timeframe made sense. He asked me pointedly if the boy was really his son or sired by another "bull." The boy had short cut hair, like a bowl-cut, blond like the mother, and I did not see an iota of African features that would suggest Norbert was the dad— not even close. The lady was nice and soft-spoken, and I did not want to say anything that would jeopardize their relationship. I was taken off guard because know-it-all Norbert asked me a question whose answer could have repercussions. Of course, I told him confidently that it was entirely possible for the boy to be his son because rarely, only the mother's genes dominate totally, as was the case here. Thank God Norbert bought my contrived implausible explanation and thanked me for restoring his full trust in her and his blond "son."

Chapter 16

Quid Pro Quo

My Saturdays were now exciting as Norbert regularly arrived later in the morning and took me out in his car to different places, like a wonderful alternate world limited to Saturdays. Afterward, I returned to reality when he dropped me back home late in the afternoon. One Saturday, he came in a sports outfit with white shorts and a nice t-shirt. He took me out to a tennis court to teach me tennis. I was in my regular long pants as he taught me the basics of the game, and eventually, we played some games, but I was a starter, and he played like a pro, at least to me. It was a lot of fun. After that, he took me to lunch. He never brought his live-in partner and her kid after the first time nor did he invite me back to his home. We were like two guys on a date.

Another Saturday, he took me to the British Museum in Russel Square, far from Woolwich. It was fascinating, especially when I saw the real Rosetta stone that had helped decipher the lost ancient Egyptian language of hieroglyphics because one part of the stone had Greek writing carved on its face and the other was in hiero-glyphics. The black rock was over 2,000 years old and had been discovered by Napoleon's soldiers in 1799, who found it sticking out of the ground when they were reconstructing an old Ottoman Fort in the town of el-Rashid (Rosetta) in Egypt. The British got its possession, as spoils of war, after defeating the French in North Africa. I first learned about the Rosetta stone from our eighth-grade history teacher in Tanzania. He was a tall American with a neat, long beard who worked with the Peace Corps sent by President John Kennedy. He gave us a summary of his lectures in legal-sized typed pages stapled together like a booklet. Seeing the real stone was the ultimate treat. After the museum tour, which included seeing a room full of ancient Egyptian mummies, we had lunch at the sprawling museum cafeteria where there were many tourists.

While at Woolwich College, just like in the first year, my scores in term exams in physics, chemistry, and pure and applied math were in the high nineties. I felt I was almost guaranteed to get a grade A in these subjects in the final A-level exams.

Norbert's visits were exhilarating, and like most excitements, there had to be a climax, but at what price for me? I felt like a virgin being wined and dined, even though I did not drink, for I had no idea what the sacrifice would be, or when the ax would fall. At that point, I thought Norbert's guiding motive was a sense of deep friendship, but I also wondered why a guy twice my age, living with a nice lady and a kid, would want to cohort with a young, broke student; *especially on Saturdays, should he not be enjoying the weekend with his family?* There was all this display of wealth—the car, the house, the outings, and the dinners. All this should have been a red flag if I were street smart, but I was not, and I let it pass to enjoy the Saturdays.

One sunny Saturday with white clouds in the sky, Norbert came in a black suit, waistcoat and tie, like he was going to a formal place. He asked me to wear my tie and jacket, but the only reason he gave was we were going to Veeraswamy. I scratched my head and inquired if he'd gotten into religion and if we were visiting a *swamy*, which meant a Hindu religious teacher in my native Punjabi and also Hindi, called *veera*. He laughed and told me it was a surprise and adamantly refused to divulge anything about this mysterious person. We drove for almost an hour.

I thought Veeraswamy must be a Hindu guru, and at least I could get his blessings. That could be the surprise Norbert did not want to divulge. So, I put on my tie and black jacket as it made sense to dress properly in front of a *swamy*, even though *swamis* wore cheap, simple clothes.

We drove to central London, and Norbert parked his car in a public parking lot under a large multistory building. From there, we walked down Regent Street, a well-known street with fancy designer shops near central London, popular with tourists. It was bustling with people, and as we headed toward an arch on the side of the building, I saw a reddish-purple flag fluttering from a flagpole attached to a second-floor balcony on top of a shop with a sign that read, *Veeraswamy,* and below it in smaller letters, *1926*. At first, it didn't quite register in my brain, as I was thinking of a person. Then we turned right into an elegant arch of the long building, and I saw another long vertical rectangular sign, reading, *Veeraswamy 1926.* An Indian man in a traditional Indian outfit and turban was standing at the entrance just past the sign.

"Is this a shop or what?" I asked curiously as a real *swamy* would not be living in such a pricy fancy place.

"You will see," Norbert said with a smile as the man greeted us and guided us toward an elevator that we rode to the second floor. We were warmly greeted and welcomed at the entrance of an elegant Indian restaurant by an Indian lady dressed in an elegant red Indian sari with a gold border. She guided us and seated us at a table and chairs fit for a maharaja. The décor of the place was stupendous—like an Indian maharaja's palace during the British Raj, with antique chandeliers, chairs, and tables. I felt I had been transplanted to an opulent palace of the past. The tables had a beautiful silk tablecloth, and the restaurant had big windows looking out to the street. There were pictures of the glorious British Raj and some of the restaurant's famous diners.

In those days, Indian restaurants were a rarity in the UK. The only few were operated mainly by Pakistanis, Sikhs, or Bangladeshis, and most were struggling as the clientele were mostly their countrymen who rarely ate out to save money. Amazingly, English people did not know much about Indian food, even though they had ruled India for over two hundred years.

I read about the brief history of the restaurant on the last page of the menu. Veeraswamy was the oldest surviving high-end Indian restaurant in the UK, opened in 1926 by Edward Palmer, a retired Indian army officer who was very conversant with Indian food and was the grandson of an English general married to an Indian princess, whose family surname was Veeraswamy. In its early days, most of the clientele were British ex-India civil servants, military officers, and others who had lived in India; famous subsequent diners included Sir Winston Churchill, European kings, and the late Indian prime minister, Jawaharlal Nehru.

I was in awe as I admired this opulence and quietly asked Norbert if he was sure we should eat here, as I saw the menu was proportionally priced with the rich ambiance. I didn't have any money. Norbert reassured me it was his treat, and that I could order whatever I liked. I hadn't eaten tasty Indian food cooked by my mom since I had left Tanzania. The waiters were all Indians, and one came to ask us if we wanted any drinks. Norbert ordered an alcoholic drink, and I settled for a coke. The waiter gave us some menu recommendations, and I ordered some *kachoris* as appetizers. They were small and round, like large golf balls, made of spicy lentil stuffing covered by a thin layer of dough and fried. We ate them with mint and lime chutney. Norbert loved them and ordered some more. The service was stupendous as the waiters checked on us frequently as if they thought Norbert the president of some African country. All the other diners were English or European, dressed in suits and ties, while their wives were in elegant dresses. Norbert ordered lamb curry, and I ordered *daal* or lentils and mixed vegetables with saffron rice and *naan*, north Indian bread cooked in a clay oven. The food was delicious, and I felt like I was in a palace. While savoring the delicious food, I was not concentrating well on what Norbert was saying, and my answers were always to agree with him as he did most of the talking. How could I disagree with one paying for this expensive lunch? That would be sacrilegious. Unbeknownst to me, he started asking me some loaded questions.

"You believe friends should help each other?"

"Of course," I replied as I put another spoonful of rice soaked in the rich *daal* in my mouth.

"A friend who doesn't help his friend is not a friend, but an enemy." I laughed and looked around, but Norbert was serious, looking directly at me.

"Who do you consider your best friend?" The question surprised me as I'd no other friends.

"He is sitting in front of me."

Norbert smiled. "So, you would help your best friend?"

"Of course," I said. However, I was concerned with this line of questioning. What help could I offer? I was broke. I tried to change the topic to the ambiance.

"It is a beautiful restaurant."

"Yes, yes," he said, impatiently looking around.

Luckily, the waiter interrupted and asked if we wanted any dessert and gave his recommendations as we had finished the main portion of the lunch. I ordered some *gulab jaman*, which were small brownish red balls made of fried milk powder soaked in thick, warm sugary syrup. They came as three pieces in a small bowl with the sugar syrup covering them. We also ordered some Indian tea, which was made of tea leaves boiled with spices like cardamom, cloves, fennel seed, cinnamon, and milk. Norbert loved these *gulab jaman* so we had to order another batch. It had been many years since I had last eaten this delicious dessert.

Then Norbert probed me again. "How are you going to finance your medical school?"

He had a knack for knowing my weaknesses. From our conversations, he knew I'd applied for a grant with the Inner London Education Authority who had rejected the application. That had been my main worry, but I thought that was my dad's problem and replied, "My dad will pay for it. It's his duty."

"But your people are told to leave Africa. It's on TV."

"That is Kenya. My parents live in Tanzania."

"You don't think it will happen in Tanzania?"

"My dad has not mentioned that."

"Tanzania is restricting money sent out." Norbert was simply reiterating what I had told him casually before. Then he got to the point.

"Will you help your best friend with physics and chemistry A-levels?" He looked at me in the eyes.

"Yes, I offered that before. You refused. You are getting personal instructions at some private college."

It seemed we were talking across each other.

"I need two A-level subjects, grade C in physics and chemistry or biology."

"You should have no problem with the private tuition you got."

"I can't get the grades."

"What have you been doing these last two years?"

He came to the real point. "Will you please take A-level exams for me?"

"You must be joking." I was incredulous at this preposterous proposition.

"No. Please help me, your best friend."

I realized why he started this talk about best friends. "I can't do that." I was firm. "They will catch me. Do I look like Norbert Eliumelu? I look like Ashok Sharma."

"There are many exam centers. You take the University of London A-level exams." Our college offered exams given by the Associated Examining Board, an association of several British universities that offered A-level examinations, so if I took exams given by the University of London, it would be at a different place where no one would know me.

"Look, I can help you with the studies. I can't lie and cheat to take the exams for you."

When we drove back, he continued threatening me that medical schools were expensive and that I could not go, or should not, without a firm financing plan for the six years. He warned me that medical schools needed proof of financing from foreign students before admission that I didn't have and impressed on me how there was no way a third-world country like Tanzania would allow the amount of foreign exchange needed to be sent to me, just one person, when they had to think about the masses, even if my dad was not told to leave the country. When we reached my home, I thanked him for lunch to end the conversation going nowhere, but he kept on haranguing me.

"Norbert, you have money and you had a great job at the medical school. Why bother with these A-levels?"

"I taught anatomy to medical students in white coats. I want to be like them and become a physician." Here he went on again, lecturing like a politician.

"You said the medical school dean was your friend. He can take you in without the A-levels if he wants because I found only the dean decides who to accept. He has all the power."

"No. The medical school has basic A-level admission requirements. He must comply with that. He wants me to pass A-levels and will take me with passes to fill the requirement."

"Then you should have basic knowledge to pass physics and chemistry." To change the subject and test his knowledge to convince him that he could do it, I asked a basic question that a high school physics student could answer. "What are Newton's three laws of motion? Give an example of each." It drew a blank on his face as he just looked at me.

"Well, then just tell me the third law of motion and forget the example." Again, a blank. "Ok, let's test your chemistry. How many electrons are in the first electron shell of an atom?" No response.

"I don't know any fucking shells. Fuck the shells and its atom, especially the nucleus." He was irate at my line of testing.

"My God! What have you been doing for the last two years of college?" Again, he looked at me like a dunce.

"I'll make the best physician. I know more human anatomy than physicians. These requirements—chemistry, physics, biology—are stupid, stupid, stupid. They have nothing to do with medicine," he said sarcastically, stressing each word.

It was a wasted effort to convince him his idea was asinine and dangerous and could be disastrous for both of us. Then he came to the point. "We help each other. Let's make a fair exchange. I will pay for your medical school. You take my A-level exams. We both go to medical school." This quid pro quo proposal was dead on arrival for me.

My response was an emphatic no, but it was directed at the man who would not take no as an answer. Eventually, he beseeched me, as his best friend, to at least seriously consider this quid pro quo proposal and to do so fast, as time was running out for him. To get rid of him, I told him I would think about it but told him not to come the following Saturday because my brothers and I were going to pick up my mom who was visiting us from Tanzania for two weeks. Our dad had written to us about her desire to visit us a month before. Norbert latched onto that idea and insisted he could take me to the airport to pick her up.

"No! Definitely not. My oldest brother is planning that. We will take the trains."

Eventually, he left after I told him, at his insistence, when we three brothers planned to leave for the airport. I smelled a rat and deliberately gave him a later time, off by two hours, in case he showed up. Honestly, I did not want to see this man anymore. I had lost all my respect for him. It reminded me of an adage, "With this type of friend, you don't need an enemy."

Chapter 17

Seduction and Temptation

The following Saturday, we three brothers were ready to leave early in the morning as planned because we had to change several trains and did not want to be late to the airport as our mom did not speak any English. Lo and behold, the silhouette of a black car parked at the curb of our house appeared through the glazed glass of the front door as we were about to exit. It was Norbert. He'd figured out my game plan and had out-flanked me. He was standing outside the car with his arms folded in front of his chest, looking at our house.

Sham left out of the door first as I followed him.

"Your friend is here!"

I couldn't tell my brothers why I did not want this noxious "friend" here, and it was not my idea for him to show up.

"I'm here to take you to the airport to fetch your mother!" Norbert said with a broad smile.

"We are taking trains. Too many people for a car," I said.

"Easy. Three in the back. One in front."

However, I was undercut by my brothers, who had no clue why I acted unfriendly to Norbert or why I was resistant to his great offer. They were thrilled to experience a free ride in a fancy car and not bother with all the trains we would have to take, not to mention the fare money saved by Sham on a tight budget. I sat in the back with Raj and insisted Sham sit in front as I had already ridden in front several times. I wanted to minimize chatting with Norbert as I saw this was a further attempt to keep up the pressure on me to take his exams. However, I did not want my brothers to suspect anything was amiss. Sham asked Norbert about the car's performance and the functions of the dashboard dials, and Raj asked more questions about its maximum speed and if he had driven at that speed. It took two hours to reach the airport.

As we got closer to the airport, Norbert asked me, "What do you call your mother?"

"*Mama.* That's mother in Swahili, the native language of Tanzania. Also, the first word a baby learns to speak."

"You call your dad *dada* and a baby learns this with mama?"

"No," Sham interrupted. "*Pita Ji.*"

"Swahili for father?"

"No, it's the Punjabi word for father. The actual word is *pita* but *ji* is added for respect."

"We speak Punjabi at home, which is spoken in the north Indian state of Punjab where my dad came from," I told Norbert.

"Why call your mother with a Swahili word but not your father?"

"Because *dada* in Swahili means a sister." We all laughed. "Dad wouldn't like that!"

"What is the Swahili word for father?" Norbert asked.

"*Baba*, like in Ali Baba," I said. "Swahili has many Arabic words."

He did not ask nor did I volunteer that that was a legacy of the two-thousand-year history of brutal slave trade conducted by Arabs in East Africa, with their heart-wrenching sprawling public slave-markets on the offshore island of Zanzibar—now a European tourist hotspot located twenty miles from the Tanzanian coast—stopped forcibly by the British navy in the Indian Ocean in the eighteenth century. History of slavery, subjugation, and abject discrimination had left a deep gash in the African psyche.

At the Gatwick airport, Norbert parked at the curb and stayed in his car as it was only for passenger drop-off and pick-up. The rest of us left for the arrival terminal. Since we were delayed as driving took longer than the trains, we saw far ahead that *Mama* had just cleared immigration and was placing her passport into her purse. As she looked around, confused about where to go, we approached her. Sham, in his usual humorous way, shouted to draw her attention.

"Mama, *jambo!*" *Jambo* was the Swahili greeting that meant hello. Mama smiled, and we all rushed and stooped to touch her feet with both hands, a sign of deep respect among Hindus for their parents. One of us grabbed her suitcase and the other her purse.

Mama was a sweet, short lady at four-eleven, and wore a traditional Indian sari and a red dot on her forehead, signifying she was married. We deeply loved our mama as she had fed and nurtured us as we had grown up in Tanzania. She had really sacrificed her life for our welfare, including braving painful poisonous stings of yellow scorpions hiding in firewood when she fetched wood in the dark to cook for the family at night, as there was no electricity in our house when we were kids. She would cry for hours from the severe pain as the poison took hold until the only doctor in town arrived and gave her a shot. As we headed to the curb, I told her our friend from Africa was waiting in his car.

When we reached the car, Norbert was standing outside and greeted Mama with folded hands in front of his chest, bowed, and said, "*Namaste, Mama.*" Mama was surprised and flattered and replied, "*Jambo!*" We laughed. I forgot to tell Mama Norbert was not from Tanzania and did not speak Swahili. Norbert looked confused, but I explained to him the misunderstanding. He laughed.

On our way back, Mama commented to me that the well-fed Norbert looked like a heavier version of Joshia, our native servant in Tanzania when we were kids. In those days, many Indians in East Africa had native servants who did the daily chores like washing dishes, cleaning the house, helping with the kids, and occasionally cooking. I did not translate that to Norbert and simply said that he looked like someone she knew back home. Mama told us how much she missed cooking for us, and that it was quiet and lonely back home since we'd all left.

Returning to our house, we invited Norbert in at Mama's insistence to thank him for his help, which he eagerly accepted as if he couldn't wait to be asked. Earlier in the week, we had gotten Indian groceries to cook a nice meal for Mama after her long flight. We were rotten intermittent cooks when that rare event of cooking did transpire, like a lunar eclipse, but for our beloved Mama we were determined to show off and put forth our best efforts like our lives depended on it. Sham had been watching our landlord Harbans Singh cook to improve his own skills.

After we sat in the living room, Sham stood up and told Mama we were heading to the kitchen to cook and that she should rest and talk with Norbert with Raj translating. We were in for a shock as Mama jumped up, rushed to the door, and insisted she wanted to cook for us because she really missed it and that was why she came to visit us. We were dumbfounded. Anyone would be thrilled if they did not have to cook for anyone else anymore. Not our mama, who had traveled thousands of miles just for that! After a lot of back-and-forth tug-of-war, haggling and pleading that she rest after a long flight and that it was highly unfair and inappropriate to impose cooking on her, we agreed to let her cook if we could show her where the stuff was in the kitchen and help her.

To us, Mama was the best cook in the world. It was from years of experience and dedication. I was certain everyone else thought that of their moms too. Mama cooked us a delicious mouth-watering Indian dinner of yellow *moong dal* made of small yellow split mung beans, *aloo gobi* cooked with potatoes, cauliflower, and curry, rice, and *parathas*, literally cooked dough, a thick wheat flatbread fried on a pan with ghee. We all enjoyed the food and cleaned off our plates. When Norbert told Mama her food was more delicious and tastier than the food at Veeraswamy, I put a finger on my mouth, and he realized he was not supposed to tell my brothers we had been there. My brothers did not know what Veeraswamy was and ignored his comment, unsuspicious as to why I hushed him up. When it was time for Norbert to leave, I thought I could use the excuse that we wanted to show Mama around the following Saturday, but she already inadvertently invited Norbert, with Raj still translating, to come, as she planned to make an Indian sweetmeat called *mohanthal*, and he could have some with tea. Like a leech, Norbert latched onto the offer and thanked her profusely, saying it would be an honor for him. Then he asked Mama if he could also call her Mama, as he thought of me as his brother. Mama, who had no idea what his game plan was, was flattered and opined she would like that.

When I went out to see Norbert off, he implored me again, begging with crocodile tears in his eyes that his future lay in my hands, and that we must help each other for mutual survival. Without admission into a medical school, he would be destroyed as he had resigned from his well-paying job as the chief anatomy lab technician to prepare for A-levels. It flummoxed me that this was the same man who had repeatedly urged me, when our friendship was blooming at Woolwich College, to go to India to study medicine because it was impossible for me to get in. He was now stooping low to get my help so he could get admittance to Middlesex Medical School illegally. I felt like telling him, "Just think if I were in India because of your advice. I wouldn't be able to help you." I told him this was unlawful, unethical, and immoral, and I could get caught and deported as I was on a student visa that had to be renewed annually after certification by my college. He cried some more, begging and admonishing me that time was running out for him. He was correct on that point because the end of May was approaching and the exams were during the first two weeks of June. Our college took them earlier with the Associated Examining Board (AEB). He tried to hand me his examination admission confirmations letter for the University of London, whose exams were a week or so after the AEB exams. My attitude had softened with all he had done for me, ostensibly with his nefarious plan in mind. However, he was dangling a carrot in front of me that I needed desperately—to pay for my medical education. Yet I held hope that my dad would come through with a plan to finance my schooling. I refused to commit to anything but knew Norbert would return the following Saturday to double down. I planned to hold my ground.

The three brothers huddled in the front room at night to sleep as we reserved the back room for Mama for privacy. However, she insisted one of us sleep in the empty bed as there were two beds in the room, and it was unconscionable that three of us sleep in the front room with only one bed and a couch. So, Raj, being the youngest, got the short end of the stick and was outvoted, reluctantly agreeing to sleep in the back room. Our first week with Mama passed fast, as she loved cooking for us, and we were getting three meals a day—a luxury we only had back home. She was not interested in our proposals to take her out sightseeing and only went with us to the open market and an Indian-owned shop that sold Indian groceries to get raw materials for cooking and for the sweetmeats she had planned to make.

We discussed with Mama more about the situation in Kenya surrounding the expulsion of Indians who were British citizens and if this could spread to Tanzania. I found out that she had a British passport, and she said Dad had one also. Raj and I had Tanzanian passports as we were born in Tanzania, but Sham, despite his birth in Tanzania, had a British passport. Mama's passport had a two-week visa from the British High Commission in Dar es Salaam to allow her to come to the UK only as a temporary visitor to see us because of the new immigration law that severely restricted entry of East-African Indians with British passports. This was the most byzantine state of affairs I could imagine in immigration. The British passports my parents held were worthless, and if Tanzania kicked them out, they would be stateless and not admissible to the UK.

I asked her why Dad had not mentioned any problems. He had queried in a recent letter, when I mentioned the high cost of medical education at six hundred pounds per year at Cambridge, if it could be paid in installments. Mama divulged he wanted us to concentrate on our studies and not worry about this. Dad was well paid by Tanzanian standards, working as an accountant for a foreign company. But he had many to support: Raj and I in college here, his aging parents in India, and my sister, the oldest of the five siblings, studying in a college in India, himself and Mama, and costly rent for their apartment in Dar es Salaam, Tanzania's capital city where they lived. He would have no money to pay for the medical school. The fear Norbert had instilled in me and the unsavory proposal was reverberating in my mind— loosening my protective armor against this nefarious plan. The wild card was what would happen if the Kenya virus spread to Tanzania. Disastrous for us. Mama said Dad did not see a future for us in Africa. With that ominous warning and prophesy, my dread of Norbert's visit the following Saturday did not seem so foreboding anymore.

I was soon reminded of what our English phonetics teacher, an older English gentleman who had traveled extensively in Europe, had told us in my first-year class: "In France, even a girl who was not pretty, easily got married if she knew how to cook well." In contrast, he was contemptuous of the poor cooking skills of English girls, as he claimed. Hence, if the dictum that the path to a man's heart was through his stomach, then not to be left out was it was also indirectly through his mother—charm and cajole her to the threshold where she did her son's bidding because sons had a special soft spot and unbending respect for their mom's commands and opinions. Norbert had already figured that out in my case, and the fireworks were yet to come.

That would be Norbert's next modus operandi when he arrived the following Saturday to savor the Indian sweetmeat *mohanthal* that Mama had made to thank him for transporting her from the airport. *Mohanthal* was made with gram flour cooked in ghee with spices like cardamom and crushed pistachios and sugar syrup added. To make it the right consistency and softness required skill and experience, and Mama had mastered it. Norbert came, and while we were eating another delicious lunch that Mama had cooked, Norbert continued flattering Mama about how delicious the food was and how outstanding her cooking was, the best he had ever tasted. He continued showering her praise about me too—how a truly a great friend I was who always helped him. It was astounding how he could impart his feeling to Mama despite the language barrier between them. There was also his body language, the smiles, and the mannerisms that conveyed his intended meaning. He then broached a topic I found confounding. He would become the president of Biafra one day, he emphatically boasted, and he would make me the country's minister of health! This seemed like a pipe dream with the war going badly for the Biafran insurgents, and why would they pick him as their president, basking in the comforts of a foreign country with his suits and ties, when the real warlords and their barefoot starving boys were fighting in the trenches? But the climax was yet to come.

After we finished lunch, Mama went to the kitchen to make Indian tea, made by boiling chai masala and tea leaves in water, adding milk, boiling it all again, and allowing it to cool somewhat before sugar was added. She wanted it served with the *mohanthal*. Sham and I brought the cups full of the freshly made hot tea from the kitchen, followed by Mama with a plateful of *mohanthal*. Each golden-yellow *mohanthal* piece was shaped like a one-inch square brick, with ground pistachios and cardamoms sprinkled on top. They looked like small golden nuggets filling the plate. We ate one piece each, breaking a small piece off at a time, and savoring it with a sip of the hot tea. By the time the whole piece was eaten, the teacup was empty. The *mohanthal* melted in my mouth like connoisseur chocolate. However, Norbert kept eating, consuming each piece whole as he continued his flattery. Before we knew it, he had cleaned out the whole plate. We were happy for him as he was our guest, and we were flattered that he enjoyed Mama's food so much.

Then he stood up in front of the couch with each of my brothers sitting on his side and Mama and I seated on chairs across from the coffee table in the middle. He started giving an impassioned impromptu speech, looking at each person in the eyes like a real politician. He shook his finger in the air as he spoke rhetorically about his deep friendship with me, and the climax came when he waggled his right hand and index finger together, looking in turn at each of the brothers momentarily and then at Mama, and pronounced my first name for the first time. "I'll give Ashok a full scholarship. He deserves to study medicine. I'll pay for all his fees, books, and room and board. He will never have to worry about money for his medical school."

If I were a powerful politician and Norbert my minion, this would be the ultimate sycophancy. I was taken aback, mesmerized, flattered, and convinced he was the solution to my medical school financial problem. When I translated for her, she told me to tell him that I would do everything to help him also. The problem was I could not tell her what he wanted in return because she would have disapproved of me taking his exams. She was a moral and religious person; I had heard her read the Hindu religious epics like the Bhagwat Gita, the Mahabharata, and the Ramayana in Hindi to my dad. I was afraid to tell her because if she disapproved of what Norbert wanted me to do, then I would definitely not do it. My brothers nodded their approval but were also in the dark about what Norbert wanted in return for his largess.

When I went out to see Norbert off, my resistance to taking his exams had diminished, realizing the problems I faced, like no money to fund my medical education. He used the same pitch again, and he handed me an envelope that had his admission slips with addresses of the venues to take the physics and chemistry exams at the University of London centers. I hesitantly accepted it after he again warned me that the six hundred pounds in annual fees at Cambridge did not include the numerous medical textbooks and other equipment that I would need. These were expensive, he warned. He would pay for them also, he insisted. He again assuaged my serious concern about being caught by emphatically claiming that the English proctors monitoring the exams did not know about differences in names between various other races and were used to all kinds of international names. As a backup plan to explain my new Nigerian name, he made up a concocted story I could tell about being adopted by Nigerian parents.

The die was cast when I accepted the envelope with a firm caveat that I would return it to him next Saturday if I could not do it as I was still somewhat skeptical about his ability to give me a scholarship. However, he owned a house and a fancy car, and the way he had lavishly spent money on Saturdays convinced me otherwise. I was like a starving person who had ripe fruit dangling in front of him, except I needed money to buy it. During the week, I felt guilty that I had not been forthright to Mama about what his demand was and planned to accept Norbert's proposal. At the middle of the following week, Mama left for Tanzania as her visa on her British passport was expiring. Sham had a Muslim Bangladeshi acquaintance at work take her to the airport in his car so she would not have to take all those trains.

We were heart-broken to see Mama leave, and we cried hard and told her how much we loved her and would miss her, and she cried profusely and told us how much she loved us and missed us. Out of the door, we bowed low to touch her feet and cried again as she stood facing the house. She also cried and placed her hands on our heads to bless us and said, "May God protect you all." And we cried more. With teary eyes, she boarded the car with the back door held open by the Bangladeshi.

Chapter 18

Adieu Woolwich College

The following Saturday was June 1, 1969. Our A-level exams, given by the AEB, were held in the first week of June at our college, and I had applied to take physics, chemistry, and pure and applied math. The equivalent University of London exams that Norbert wanted me to take for him in physics and chemistry were scheduled in the second week of June, so the dates would not conflict with my exams. The master politician that Norbert was had noticed my hesitation in accepting the envelope containing his examinations admission slips and my caveat that I would return it next Saturday. On that fateful Saturday, I saw through the front window curtains Norbert's car arrive outside in the morning and waited for him to knock on the door instead of going out to meet him. He came toward the door and then disappeared from my view as he approached the front door. There was no knocking on the door, and then I saw him go back to his car and suddenly leave. *Why would he drive all the way from his home and then just leave?*

Confounded by this odd behavior, I went outside. In front of the door was a brown rectangular package that felt heavy. I took it inside and opened it. Inside was a hardcover book called *Gray's Anatomy, 34th Edition*. It had 1669 pages and an electron micrograph picture of part of a cell, its nucleus and organelles, on its cover. When I opened the book in awe, inside the hardcover was a paid invoice for the book for six pounds, made out to Norbert. Like the straw that broke the camel's back, it was the ultimate bribery to clinch the deal. Without saying another word, Norbert had presented me the book with the invoice to convince me how expensive medical school textbooks were, and as a good-faith down payment of what he could do financially to pay for my medical school. If he could afford a book costing six pounds as a throwaway gift, the amount that Sham earned from a week's hard labor, he could comfortably afford to pay for my medical school. At that moment, I became a corrupt bureaucrat. Like in the third world, I was bought—the temptation was too great, and the alternative was no medical school. I grabbed a blue ink pen and followed my Pavlovian routine of writing my full name on the first title page of the book: *Ashok Kumar Sharma.* Under that I wrote, *6/1/69,* the date I got the book. I'd officially accepted Norbert's ultimate bribe and was willing to accept the risk of taking his exams so he could get into Middlesex Medical School and pay for my medical school. That way, as he kept insisting, both of us would go to medical school, instead of none.

When the college had shut down for two weeks toward the end of May 1969 to give the second-year students time to study for their crucial A-level exams, everyone was preoccupied with preparing. However, I had studied so hard—with total focus on the exams to get A's—that even though Mama was visiting us, I had been ready way before she came. She was actually a boost and a great help because we didn't have to worry about scrounging for food, and she did not bother us. She was predominately there to feed us and was happy doing just that.

Younger brother Raj, who studied hard like me, was a brainy kid and so good in math that he was ready for his first-year college exams before the break and never asked me for help as he was better than me in math and it was his favorite subject. I was taking pure and applied math as extra icing on the cake, as my focus was on physics and chemistry. The math replaced the biology that I was done with.

The written exams in physics, chemistry, and math usually had three categories of questions. There were a few easier questions, or easier sub-sections of a question, like asking a definition of something in physics and chemistry; then there were questions of intermediate difficulty that formed the bulk, and lastly, there were some difficult analytical ones that screened out the top students. To get a grade A, a student would have to do well in all the categories, including the difficult ones. I had to prepare and focus to score well on the difficult questions because the rest would be easy. Those who had prepared reasonably well would be able to answer the easy questions, and with some correct answers on the intermediate questions, would be able to get a C or a D. A grade B would require doing well on some of the difficult ones.

I could now manipulate the extensive knowledge I'd acquired in such a way to virtually guarantee to get a grade A in physics and chemistry by thinking like an examiner—how I could ask the most difficult questions on any topic to trick the most astute examinee.

Like an exam addict, I looked forward to the battle, the final exams given by the AEB. The one more grade A Cambridge wanted to admit me was a joke because I planned to give them three more. This was a far cry from when I had started two years ago when I could not understand what the tutors were saying.

The A-level exams I took during the first week of June were held in the large gymnasium hall with double entry doors adjoining a long hallway on the second floor of our college. There were rows of desks and chairs set up on either side of an aisle running down the middle of the hall, like in a movie theater. I intentionally sat at the first desk in the aisle row closest to the left entry door so when the exam was over, my answer papers would be picked up first by the proctor, and I could simply bolt out without talking to anyone. The college was closed two weeks prior to the exams, and once the students took their exams, no one saw each other anymore to my knowledge. They went to the next stage of their lives and hopefully got into a university to study their chosen subject.

During my last exam, I sat in the same spot and glanced ahead at the students in front and saw one turned around and stared at me. It was Farida, seated at a desk diagonally across from me. When our gazes met, she gave me a genuine smile, but I hid behind a façade, with no hint of my feelings. I promptly looked down at my desk and checked I had the pencils and pens ready for the exam, but I could see from the corner of my right eye that she was still staring, waiting for a response. Soon the exam papers were handed out by the tutor close to the start time, and he told us to turn them to open them and start answering.

For the last exam, the new proctor changed the modus operandi. He collected exam papers from students in the front of the gym first and then moved backward. Students bolted after their papers were collected, like they could not wait to scoot. Farida passed by and exited while I checked my papers to avoid any eye contact. My papers were last to be collected, but I took my sweet time to leave to ensure all had left the college, except for the tutor who was stacking and preparing the papers to be shipped to the examining board. I picked up the cheap black leather briefcase that had served me well for two years resting against the back wall and placed all my pencils and pen in it, listening for any noise outside, but it was quiet. All the exams were over and like my beginning at college, it was an inauspicious end. I was positive I would get an A in physics and chemistry, and it was likely I would in pure and applied math as well.

I peeked at both sides of the hallway like a rat watching out for a cat. It was deserted and I took a left turn and walked slowly. As I turned right at the corner into a second hallway, there was Farida, waiting at the same spot she had been in December of 1967. I wanted to turn back and run, but that would be too obvious and rude. When I saw a paper in her hand, I thought, *Oh no! Not another invitation to a party,* which had caused so much friction, antagonism, and furor with her the last time because I didn't attend. But then why would she have a party when we were marching on to our separate paths? We were done with the college.

The A-level exams were hard for the average student, but I did not see any reason to rejoice with a party. I strolled timidly toward her.

She looked at me with a slight smile and was obviously waiting for me as there was no one else around to rescue me. As I approached her hesitantly, she greeted me with a broad smile and I greeted her back with a smirk, stopping two feet in front of her. She moved close to me and stood sideways so we formed an L-shape with our bodies and talked about how the two years had gone by fast but avoided saying anything about the exams or asking if I had received a place in a medical school. Being a horrible conversationalist, I just nodded to whatever she said. Apparently, she had not gained admission to any medical school or gotten an interview nor had anyone else in our class except me. They all talked and socialized, but I was a lone ranger and reticent. I felt uncomfortable and frozen in place as she slowly edged closer to me. She talked to me as I looked with my head twisted to my right so I could see her directly. This was a weird way for two people talking until her game plan became evident—she wanted close physical contact. She inched closer so her left breast was now firmly implanted against my right upper arm. Her breast felt firm, almost hard, with a stiff pointed nipple pushing into my arm like the cap of a pen. At that stage of my life, I thought a breast was supposed to be soft like dough. I stayed, still thinking it would be rude to move away as she pushed harder, like her body would soon push me from where I stood. She handed me the piece of paper in her hand—ostensibly a preplanned move—and told me it was her contact information and address and that she would love it if I contacted her. I took the paper, nodded, and placed it in the side pouch of my briefcase, just as I had done almost a year and a half ago when she had given me one for the party at her house.

On my face there was no smile or emotion, a mask, but the mask reflected the real face and feelings of the person behind it. For the first time, I guess when she realized I would be gone, she dropped her mask and divulged her true feelings toward me because what I saw on her face was genuine and sincere desire. As a last-ditch attempt, she was trying to entice me to form a relationship or a close friendship. I dreaded this, as I didn't see any future in a relationship, nor did I want any future relationship with her for the same reasons—religious differences and its complications—as when she had given me her address in December of 1967 for the party.

In my two years of college, I'd learned that the girls were much more mature than the boys. I was an immature twenty-year-old virgin boy who would not know what to say or do if we met alone. She would have to do all the talking and would eventually find out I was not worth it unless she had an ulterior motive. I left after the encounter as she looked at me, wondering why I never offered my contact information or mentioned my future plans. I went down the stairs and increased my pace at the bottom as I wanted to be out of there. When I reached home, I discarded the paper she had given me into a trash can so there would be no temptation, just like I had done with her contact information before. I was not ready to deal with the consequences or the fallout from any further involvement with her. This was the easiest, least painful, and cheapest exit for me—the least expensive divorce is one that takes place before marriage.

Chapter 19

The Faux Examinee

After my exams were over in the first week in June, in the second week of June my attention was now focused on acting as the fake substitute examinee for Norbert—a task I hated except for the part of actually taking the exam. Like a drug addict needing another quick fix, my fix was the exam—that was how much I looked forward to them.

I'd entered the physics exam hall after being checked in by a young Englishman at the front desk who ticked off my name on a list after I handed him my official exam authorization slip from the examining body, the University of London. He didn't blink an eye at my new name. I guess to him, Ashok Sharma wasn't much different from Norbert Eliumelu. Similar scenarios played out at the chemistry exam and its lab. Now it was easy sailing with only the physics lab portion left to take; why would there be any trouble? Norbert was right, so far, that they would not suspect my faux name was really a Nigerian name or that I was a real imposter. Only the lab portion of physics was left and then I would be home free.

The lab part for physics was scheduled a few days later at a university campus. I left early in the morning, took a train to central London from Woolwich, and then a few underground trains to the town where the exam venue was located. I had to ask someone on the way the location of the property. Luckily, most local people in any town knew the streets and locations and were always helpful. I reached an impressive solid gray brick building with broad stone steps leading up to a large heavy double-door entrance. For some unexpected reasons, like an epiphany, I had bad vibes about this last lab part of the physics exam.

Again, like what had happened at the previous exams I took for Norbert before I reached the venue, I felt deep angst. Could I go to jail and or be deported? Then I conjectured it was okay as I had no problem taking the other exams, including the chemistry lab portion, so why should I worry about the physics practical exam? But the game was not over yet, and this was the last lab portion for which I had to be checked in. When I entered the open doors into the foyer of the building, I looked at the young student seated at a table with a stack of papers in front of the lab entrance and another student standing across the table talking to him. There was a check-in sign in the foyer, pointing to the table.

In the remote case someone asked me at exam check-in, why, for an Indian, I had an ostensibly non-Indian name, I was to confidently respond that I had been adopted by Nigerian parents as a kid after my parents had been killed in Nigeria in a road accident. But Norbert had reassured me English people wouldn't ask or care about the name as Indians also had names that sounded weird to English ears.

He also assured me they dare not ask me why my name was Norbert Eliumelu as it may sound "prejudicial." That was the default plan A: a kind of "please don't ask why my name is Norbert Eliumelu (because you don't look Nigerian)," and plan B was the concocted Nigerian tragedy. He had repeatedly reassured me confidently that this would not be a problem, and he had been right so far because the English proctors at the previous exams had let me in after checking my exam confirmation slip against their official examinee list. Sometimes well-laid plans go awry when neither plan A nor B works because the conditions they were designed for do not pan out. There could be a slip between the cup and the lip, and the concocted Nigerian tragedy could turn into a real Greek tragedy. There was no plan C in case of such a scenario.

My face went pale, like blood had drained out of it, when I saw the young man checking the examinees in. My heart sank and raced as I took a deep breath in, afraid to breathe out. I stopped in my tracks and looked away, afraid to look at the guy at the desk. I fumbled and pretended to look around like I wasn't sure where I was going. Our gazes met as the student in front of me finished checking in. He saw I was acting lost and waved me over with a hand. I somewhat regained my composure as I had to check in, even though I wanted to run, but that was not an option now as I had taken the written exam, which would be invalidated if the practical exam was not taken.

This was England in the late 1960s, and the physics practical exam was being held at the University of London, a premier British university. So common sense dictated that the proctors would be English, or maybe Scottish, Irish, or Welch. The reason for my angst was something I had not anticipated, even in my worst nightmare—the guy checking in the examinees was an Indian! While an Indian might not question my first name, as some Indians were Christians and Norbert was a Christian name, he had to be a real imbecile to believe my last name was Indian. Maybe that's why they had him there—to nab imposters like me. However, I headed toward him, like going into a lion's den, as my mind raced faster. I decided no matter what he asked me, I would stick to my Nigerian story as he couldn't disprove it. In those days, we carried no photo IDs, as not many had them. Even a driver's license had no photo, so you could drive a car with someone else's license. The only photo ID I had was on my Tanzanian passport, which was at home.

The Indian looked me in the eyes for a few seconds that seemed like an eternity as I handed him my official exam admission slip. When he read my name, his eyes widened. He looked at me again, and then again at the slip, and then again at me as I waited for his questions and possible interrogation. He read the admission slip intently, like the name and the character standing in front of him didn't match. Apparently trying to mumble, he held the admission slip in his left hand and tapped it with his right index finger several times and then pointed the finger at me, again tapping it in the air, like asking, "Is this really you? You think I'm stupid?" I stayed frozen. However, he shook his head and returned my slip and finally and hesitantly ticked off my fake name on his examinee roster without saying a word. I was free to enter the lab entrance door behind him. I breathed a quiet sigh of relief when I entered the lab and glanced back as he shook his head again like he was saying, "I thought I'd seen everything, but this?" The Indian was onto me, and though he had let me in, I was now worried that he would pursue me. I had to be extra careful.

I went to my designated lab spot at one of the many long wooden lab tables near a corner of the table. From the materials provided, I guessed what the exam experiment was. Close to the exam start time, the Indian guy closed the entry doors and distributed the exam questions and told us to start after the last person had gotten his paper. I opened the exam question paper.

The materials provided on the table included a small roll of string, a pair of scissors to cut various lengths of the string, a ruler to measure the lengths of the cut strings, a retort stand, a small metal ball with a round hook to attach the string to it, a stop clock, and calipers. The exam question asked us to find experimentally how the period, or T, of a pendulum was related to L, its length, and use the results to calculate g, or the acceleration due to Earth's gravity, and to show all the results obtained in a tabular form and graph them. It also asked for the percentage error in experimental g as compared to the real known g in physics textbooks. The premise being the smaller the error, the more accurate the student's experimental results and higher the score as it was a gauge of his experimental expertise.

When I pulled the pendulum—that I would have to construct—to one side and let it go, it would swing back and forth in an arc, like a child on a swing set. T, or its period, was the time it took for the pendulum to reach its highest point from one side to the other and back to its starting point. The formula connecting T to L and g was not given as the student was supposed to know that.

In a physics practical exam, you wrote all your findings and calculations, including the rough calculations you did to show the examiner that you were not fudging your results. I was adept at physics experiments because during my college lab sessions, I paid close attention to the details of how to do the experiments and sought the tutor's help to improve and get more accurate results. For this experiment, I drew my columns on the answer paper and labeled them on a horizontal column at the top of the page as T (period, seconds), T^2 (square of T) and L (length, meters).

I constructed a pendulum by tying one end of a string to the small round metal hook of the metal ball and using my ruler, I cut the string at an appropriate length that would be easy to graph and hung the ball from the top end of the retort stand. I pulled the ball to one side and let it swing, using the stop clock to measure time in seconds for twenty back-and-forth swings and divided the result by twenty to get the average T and repeated the procedure with five different lengths of the pendulum to give me five points to plot on the graph.

In those days, to do the calculations, we used slide rules or math-table booklets, now relegated to math museums or vintage items for sale. We were allowed to bring those to the exams because some of the calculations would take too long to perform manually. I had a small math-table book that I had brought to the exam with me. It had a blue cover and had various tables for multiplication, division, squares, square roots, and calculations for trigonometric functions like sine, cosine, and tangent.

The equation that connected T to L, stated that T was equal to . If I did my experiment correctly, I should get a straight-line graph when the five T values obtained experimentally were squared and the resulting values were plotted against their corresponding L measurements.

It was much easier and time saving to do these calculations with the math-table book. I had placed my book on my right as I did the experiments. My hand moved to grab it, but it had disappeared. I looked around cautiously as you could not look at another person without being accused of cheating. The book was nowhere, and everyone was busy doing their experiments.

I scratched my head because I was certain I had brought it to the lab and had carefully placed it on the table to my right. I thought maybe it had fallen to the side of the table, so I stooped down to look around the table's corner, but nothing was on the floor. I heard a thud on the table to my right. I felt someone was standing close to me, and as I straightened up and turned around, the Indian was standing right there, glaring at me with a finger tapping quietly on the book. He had slammed my math-table booklet on the table after appearing from nowhere like a phantom. He stared at me for a few moments more and then removed his hand as I was in a controlled panic waiting for him to accuse me, but what would he say? I would insist that I was adopted by Nigerian parents and it was none of his business what name I had and or why it did not fit my face. However, he didn't say a word and left, but his grim silence spoke plenty. Then it occurred to me, and I cursed myself. When I opened the first page, I saw written in blue ink, "Ashok Kumar Sharma." That was my trademark, and I always did that to all my books as a proof of ownership.

Somehow, the Indian, who had not given up on me, had stealthily snatched my booklet when I was concentrating on the experiment. Obviously, he looked for some positive incriminating evidence that I was not the Norbert Eliumelu that I claimed to be. He saw it in the booklet, but maybe that would not hold if I said I just borrowed it from a friend called Ashok Kumar Sharma. The Indian did not bother me again and went about his business proctoring the examination. For whatever reason I would never know, he had let me off the hook without even questioning me. While I was using the book now to do my calculations, all sorts of fears went through my mind.

What if the Indian has another plan up his sleeve to really nail me down? I was worried about the consequences. *Will I be deported from the country, jailed, or disqualified from further exams?*

I finished my calculations, sketched my graph, and did all the calculations asked in the exam question. My results were solid as all my experimentally obtained points were on a straight line and my calculated experimental g was close to the real one. I was certain "Norbert" would get a grade A. After the exam papers were picked up by the Indian, I scooted from there as if I'd dodged a bullet, but only because the shooter deliberately didn't want to shoot me. I didn't look back, still paranoid that the Indian would follow me until I boarded the train at the tube station.

Chapter 20

The Subterfuge and the Patsy

After six weeks, the A-level exam results were out with the certificates arriving in the mail. As expected, I got a grade A in both physics and chemistry, and a grade B in pure and applied math, which was my backup subject. I was certain that Norbert, for whom I had been the surrogate examinee, also got grade A in physics and chemistry, assuring him a place at Middlesex Medical School. The results would have gone to his house or designated address. I even conjectured that the dean there, whom Norbert worked for, would have been thrilled that he placed his faith in this man who had served him well for eight years and it paid off big. The fact was Norbert wouldn't have even gotten an interview at any medical school otherwise.

However, Norbert had become incommunicado after he had dumped the expensive textbook, *Gray's Anatomy*, outside my front door as the last desperate attempt to make sure I would take his exams. There were no more Saturday visits, dining out, or going to museums. At first, I did not expect him to come for a few weeks in early June because of the exams, but exams were over by the second week, and still, he was a no-show.

I sensed something was wrong. I was so mesmerized by his rhetoric that he would finance my medical school that I had no plan B, except the hope my dad would take care of it in spite of severe restrictions placed by Tanzania on sending foreign exchange out of the country and the fact that Dad was now paying for two of us, Raj and I, not to mention he was overstretched and broke financially back home. My main worry was what would happen when Tanzania decided to expel him because he was a British citizen but could not come here because of the new immigration law. At first, I reassured myself there must be a reason or some explanation. I had to find out, so I went to the address where he lived, using his address on the paid invoice he had sent with the *Gray's Anatomy* book. I had been to his house once, so I had an idea of its general appearance and rough location.

After changing several buses, I finally arrived at his house on a Saturday morning, hoping to catch him. The window curtains were shut so I could not see a thing or attempt to peek inside as no one answered the door after several periodic knocks. The fancy car was absent from the front of the curb. After waiting there for a while, I left a note on the door for him to come to my home as we had no phones. I returned toward the middle of the following week as my fears intensified. The same scenario repeated. When I returned home, I mailed him a letter to please contact me or write to me, but he never answered. Again, I went back for the third time on Saturday, and it was as if he had disappeared. That was the last time I went there as I wanted to preserve my meager savings that I was spending on bus fares to visit his house.

The reality dawned on me that Norbert had deliberately absconded and was carefully avoiding me. There was no scholarship he had promised, just an elaborate ruse to induce me to take his exams. I was afraid to tell my brothers, my closest confidants, but I needed to get it off my chest that I was in deep trouble. Norbert had really shafted me with his fake promises because now I had lost the opportunity to at least work in a factory—like the Pepsi Cola factory where I worked when I first came to England—after my exams were over in the first week of June to earn some money to pay an initial down payment to the Trinity Hall bursar at Cambridge.

What good was admission to a medical school if there was no money to pay for it? It was already early August, and the medical school would commence in September of 1969.

Reluctantly, I went back to the admissions office at the now deserted Woolwich College and inquired about any sources of financial assistance for their students matriculating at a university. They advised me to apply to the Inner London Education Authority with my acceptance letter from the university I planned to attend and gave me their address. The next day, I went to the Inner London Education Authority's office that was far from Woolwich and filled out an application for a grant and handed it in to a lady at the reception who told me that I would get a written response as to the next step. My hopes were raised. A week later, I received a letter asking me to come for an interview and to bring my admissions letter from Cambridge and my A-level exam result certificates, which further raised my hopes. In those days, I had not seen any photocopy machines, so original documents had to be provided for verification, and the receiver returned them later.

I went to the office of the Inner London Education Authority and was interviewed by a Jamaican. My hopes now soared as I thought he would be considerate of someone from Africa. He asked me what I intended to do after completing medical school, and I gave him the same answer that I gave during my medical school interviews—return home to Tanzania to practice there. A week later, a letter came from the education author denying the grant that was usually based on parental income that I had no proof of. No reason was given.

I had previously written to my dad how this dear Nigerian friend from Biafra was going to give me a scholarship, and Mama had also told him on her return to Tanzania. Dad had been thrilled, and now I wrote to him that he had disappeared, and I could not find him because he had no intention of fulfilling his pledge. To show I was making other efforts, I sent him the rejection letter from the education authority. Now the burden was on him to pay for my medical education.

Dad had become lax after I'd written to him about Norbert's offer and had spent some of the funds he would have mailed me in summer on other urgent expenses. Now he was in a panic and sent me thirty pounds sterling, the limit allowed per month by Tanzania's new strict foreign exchange regulations as the country's foreign exchange reserves dwindled as a result of policies heavy on public spending.

I deposited that and kept ten pounds for our food expenses for the month and thought of another outside of the box plan, like a preemptive strike. Instead of worrying about the whole annual cost, I would pay what I had as a down payment and get into Cambridge. Then hopefully my dad would come up with a solution instead of me worrying about how to pay for the whole year and beyond. I mailed most of the money I had saved, totaling about sixty pounds, or equal to about ten percent of their total bill for the first year of medical school, to the bursar at Trinity Hall College, Cambridge with a letter that I could make monthly payments as my dad would send me more money. They were very accommodating and did not raise any objections. Dad also wrote to me that he would follow up by writing to the Inner London Education Authority to review and reopen the case about my grant rejection.

I deeply regretted the day I first met Norbert, waiting in front of me at the line for lunch at Woolwich College and wished I had ignored him. It was my curiosity that got me talking to him and then finding out that he worked for a dean of a medical school raised my hopes of having found someone who could guide me to gain medial school admission. His negativity toward my plans and discouragements should have been enough to keep me away from him, but I was impressionable and paying the price now.

This experience taught me a bitter life-long lesson not to commit a crime at the behest of a friend because such friends are worse than enemies. In this elaborately contrived and well-executed game of subterfuge perpetrated by Norbert, who turned out to be just a low-lying basic crook and con man, I was the patsy who denied another worthy applicant to medical school a place because his or her spot was taken by this smooth-talking thug harboring delusions of grandeur about making the best physician because of his self-claimed knowledge of anatomy. As to his advanced delusions of grandeur about becoming the future president of Biafra, its rebels seeking the breakaway province's independence were in full retreat, routed by the Nigerian army. Those who surrendered were often shot point blank in front of video-trotting foreign journalists to send a message of deterrence to other Nigerians who contemplated secession.

DEPARTING FROM THE THIRD WORLD FOR THE FIRST WORLD WITH THE AMBITION TO BECOME A MEDICAL DOCTOR. JULY, 1967

On July 7th, 1967, at the age of 18, I departed from the international airport at Dar-es-Salaam, the capital of my home country, Tanzania, East Africa, for England. I wore a new suit and tie because I thought all men there wore suits and ties. To my right is my only sister, Chandra, five years my senior and the oldest of my four siblings.

Telegrams: ....
Telephone:......2152...............
In reply please quote:

Ref. No. ...3/5/V/246....

KARIMJEE........... SECONDARY SCHOOL,

P.O. BOX .....330......,
Tanga
...................................,
TANGANYIKA.

30th August,1966

ASHOK KUMAR SHARMA

A   Ashok Kumar Sharma has been studying in this School
since January,1965.   He will sit the C.O.S.C. Exam.
Nov/Dec.1966.

Ashok Kumar is very brilliant academically. He
is always first in the school examinations. He got
distinctions in almost all the subjects in the recent
Regional form IV Examination of 1966. He is a very
hardworking, reliable obedient and well behaved pupil.
He is really an asset to the school. He is fit for
any Science course. He is a sure grade I pupil.

I wish him all success in his career.

DAP/AAM .   Ag.HEADMASTER

A STRONG REFERENCE LETTER FROM MY HIGH SCHOOL'S
INDIAN ASSISTANT HEADMASTER. AUGUST 1966

My reference letter from the assistant headmaster at the high
school I graduated from, with typo errors in the letter corrected by
him with a pen. The headmaster was an Englishman, and I doubt he
checked the letter. The school was still using old stationery from the
days the British ruled the country when it was called Tanganyika. After
independence in 1962, it was renamed Tanzania in 1964 after a merger
with the neighboring archipelago of Zanzibar.

UNIVERSITY OF CAMBRIDGE

LOCAL EXAMINATIONS SYNDICATE

This is to certify that the candidate named below sat for a Joint Examination for the School Certificate and General Certificate of Education and qualified for the award of a

SCHOOL CERTIFICATE

IN DIVISION ONE

incorporating a GENERAL CERTIFICATE OF EDUCATION. The candidate reached at least Grade 8 in the subjects named and attained the standard of the G.C.E. Ordinary Level pass where this is indicated.

ASHOK B SHARMA   H213   66

KARIMJEE SECONDARY SCHOOL TANGA

	Grade	G.C.E. Standard
ENGLISH LANGUAGE	6	ORDINARY
GEOGRAPHY	1	ORDINARY
MATHEMATICS	1	ORDINARY
ADDITIONAL MATHS	2	ORDINARY
PHYSICS	1	ORDINARY
CHEMISTRY	2	ORDINARY
BIOLOGY	3	ORDINARY

SUBJECTS RECORDED   SEVEN   G.C.E. PASSES   SEVEN

EXAMINATION OF NOVEMBER/DECEMBER 1966

A. L. Armitage

(See overleaf)   Vice-Chancellor

OUR HIGH SCHOOL GOLD STANDARD: THE C.O.S.C. EXAM OF NOV/DEC. 1966

The C.O.S.C. exam, stated in the assistant headmaster's letter, was an acronym for the Cambridge Overseas School Certificate examination that all the high school students in East Africa, and many other ex-British colonies, took to graduate. It made it easier for the British universities to gauge their qualification for college entry in Great Britain. Note my English language grade was the lowest of all due to my difficulty in the language. Interpretation of the grades: 1 & 2, Very Good; 3,4,5,6, Pass-with-Credit; 7&8, S.C. Pass.

ENOCH POWELL, THE MEMBER OF PARLIAMENT FOR
WOLVERHAMPTON, DELIVERING HIS FAMOUS SPEECH
DUBBED THE "RIVERS OF BLOOD" ON APRIL 20th, 1968

Enoch Powell delivering his apocalyptic-sounding speech, dubbed
the "Rivers of Blood," to a Conservative Association meeting in
Birmingham, England. "As I look ahead, I am filled with foreboding,"
Powell said, and "like the Roman, I seem to see the River Tiber foaming
with much blood"—a classical allusion to the Sybil's prophecy of civil
war in the Aeneid. Powell used it as a metaphor for race riots that he
predicted would engulf Great Britain in a few decades.

The nativist part of the speech, quote: "We must be mad, literally
mad, as a nation to be permitting the annual inflow of some 50,000
dependents, who are for the most part the material of the future growth
of the immigrant-descended population. It is like watching a nation
busily engaged in heaping up its own funeral pyre." Powell's burning
ambition to be the viceroy of India in his heyday—included inordinate
efforts, like he learned Urdu, the commonly spoken language of North
India—ended in a fiery crash with India's independence in 1947. As
the viceroy, he would have had thousands of Indian servants to serve
him in the palatial 340-room Viceroy's House, the world's fifth largest
palace located in New Delhi, and life and death power over a fifth of
humanity. Two decades later, like poetic justice, the burgeoning immigrant population from India in his constituency of Wolverhampton
triggered his wrath. The very people who would have been his subjects

were now his equal neighbors in his own town and country. The match that lit the powder keg for the speech was the massive demonstration by Indian Sikhs in Wolverhampton in March 1968, demanding to be allowed to wear turbans—mandated by their religion—as bus drivers. Headgear of any type for the bus drivers was proscribed by the city's transportation committee. The committee caved in to rescind the rule for Sikhs after one of them threatened self-immolation. Less kosher was Powell's description of his Caribbean immigrant constituents' children as "wide-grinning piccaninnis."

AT WOOLWICH COLLEGE, LONDON. HELPING AN AUSTRALIAN CLASSMATE IN THE CHEMISTRY LAB. MAY 10, 1968

Here I'm helping an Australian classmate with chemistry in the chemistry lab. Note how thick the chemistry textbook is. I always wore a tie at the college, even when doing chemistry experiments, when I had to take my jacket off.

THE ELEPHANT IN THE ROOM. MAY/JUNE 1968

When I went to the interviews with the deans of medical schools during the summer of 1968, the elephant in the room was this Grade A in A-level biology that I got at the end of my first year of college, instead of at the end of the second or the final year. S after the A stands for the more difficult scholarship level that I also passed, like icing on the cake. In fact, I believed the reason I was even invited for the interviews was because of this Grade A, which took a gargantuan effort to achieve.

TRINITY HALL
CAMBRIDGE

28   September 1968

Dear Sharma,

I am glad to be able to tell you that
we intend to offer you a place in October 1968 to
read **Medicine**   . You will in due course
receive a formal notification of this offer from the
UCCA Central Office.

We expect you to take the Joint Examination this
autumn, and hope that you may win an award. The completed application form for this examination must be
in our hands by   October at the latest.

Please let me know as soon as possible whether
you intend to accept this offer.

Yours sincerely,

[signature]

Senior Tutor

P.S.   This offer is conditional on your obtaining one
further grade A at A level.

THE CONDITIONAL ACCEPTANCE LETTER FROM TRINITY HALL, CAMBRIDGE

This conditional letter, accepting me to the Cambridge Medical School, the world's premier medical school, was an unassuming standard pre-printed letter with the essential details typed in. The offer was actually for October 1969, a typo error, as it was only October 1968 when I received the letter. The offer was conditional on my obtaining another grade A at A level that I would have to get at the end of my second year. UCCA was the acronym for University Central Council on Admissions.

GENERAL CERTIFICATE OF EDUCATION

This is to certify that   ASHOK KUMAR SHARMA

born   5 MAY 1949

sat for the General Certificate of Education at

WOOLWICH COLLEGE FOR FURTHER EDUCATION

and reached pass standard in the following subject(s) in

JUNE 1969

ADVANCED LEVEL

IN 3 SUBJECT(S)

CHEMISTRY	– A1 –
PURE AND APPLIED MATHEMATICS	– B –
PHYSICS	– A2 –

Signed on behalf of the Associated Examining Board

H.O. Childs

Secretary to the Board

THE DEPARTMENT OF EDUCATION AND SCIENCE ACCEPTS THE EXAMINATION
AS REACHING THE APPROVED STANDARD

Signed on behalf of the Department of Education and Science

CERTIFICATE No. 101154

CENTRE No./CANDIDATE No.   32/129   0337   *Geoffrey Cockerill*

Under-Secretary

JUNE 1969. TWO GRADE As AND ONE GRADE B, INSTEAD OF ONE GRADE A

Instead of one further Grade A at A level that Trinity Hall wanted in the conditional offer for admission to the medical school, I got them two more Grade As, in physics and chemistry, plus distinction, or 1, in the scholarship level exam in chemistry and merit, or 2, in physics. As icing on the cake, I also got a Grade B in pure and applied mathematics

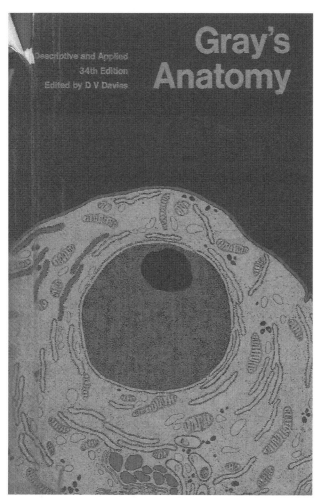

NORBERT'S ULTIMATE BRIBE TO INDUCE ME TO TAKE HIS A LEVEL EXAMS. JUNE 1st, 1969

Cover of Gray's Anatomy, 34th Edition, that Norbert dropped at my doorstep on 06/01/69 as the ultimate bribe to take his A level exams. I placed a protective red plastic cover over it decades later. The latest edition of the book, the 41st, was published in 2016.

GRAY'S ANATOMY

INSIDE PAGE OF GRAY'S ANATOMY.

As I did to all my textbooks, I wrote my name with pen and added the date Norbert left it outside my door.

BOOK TWO

Chapter 1

Cambridge

On September 9, 1969, I matriculated at Trinity Hall College, commonly called Trinity Hall to distinguish it from its first namesake college that adjoined it, Trinity College, the largest of all the Cambridge colleges first made famous by Sir Isaac Newton, who studied and made his scientific discoveries there in the sixteenth century. All the new undergraduate students gathered for a traditional formal group photo on an expansive lush green lawn on one side of a long dining hall that split the college into two halves with a connecting arched walkway. The lawn faced River Cam, which flowed through Cambridge. All of us wore the formal college attire: black gowns and a tie. A copy of the large photo pasted on a hard brown rectangular cardboard with our names at the bottom was given to each student for posterity after a few weeks.

Cambridge was a collegiate university made of twenty-five colleges. Students lived there or in dorms, ate meals there, and had study tutorials there, but the studies one pursued were administered at the university level by various faculties, like the Faculty of Medicine for those studying medicine. Each college had its own rules and regulations and picked its own students but was subject to certain university regulations and had officials sit on its various administrative bodies.

The medical school had 125 new first-year medical students from the twenty-five colleges starting in September of 1969. Six were from Trinity Hall, and five were women from the Girton College, the only women's college. The colleges were segregated by gender: women at Girton College and men in the other twenty-four colleges.

Our first introduction to medicine was the human anatomy dissection class, and it was like being thrown into the thickest of a battle without any preparation. I'd never even seen a cadaver before. We all waited with anticipation in an expansive foyer in front of the two large double wooden doors of the anatomy dissection hall. I was more excited and very curious about what lay beyond, as I'd wanted to be a medical doctor since I was in the fifth grade and still couldn't believe that it was becoming a reality after ten years. The space was crowded, with a lot of din from students chatting. I didn't know anyone. At exactly nine in the morning, the two doors opened from the inside, exposing a tall, beefy man with flat black wavy hair who was standing with a lady of similar height, wearing a red skirt. Suddenly, there was pin-drop silence as all eyes were fixated on him.

"Welcome to your first anatomy dissection class. Always be respectful of your cadaver. You will find your last names on the tables as you make your way in to my right. We are here to help," he said and waved to the right with a hand and then moved to one side with the lady. He was the professor of anatomy, and the lady was the anatomy lab technician. It reminded me of Norbert and what he did at Middlesex Medical School in London, the professor's right-hand man.

The students entered trepidly in an orderly fashion and entered the expansive dissection hall with rows of broad metal tables, each with a naked cadaver on it. The room was well lit from the overhead fluorescent lights. To the right stood several men who were anatomy instructors, wearing white coats with name tags. In front of each table, a complete human skeleton hung from a mobile made of a tall, thin vertical metal rod with a horizontal arm at the top of a heavy metal support base. Next to the skeleton, there was a deep bucket to discard dissected body parts.

I reached my table that was in the middle of the front row of tables. Since the body is externally symmetrical, with some exceptions, like the left male testis hangs lower than the right, two students were assigned to one cadaver to dissect each side. My partner, Mark Drayton, was a fellow medical student from Trinity Hall. Our cadaver was a sixty-two-year-old woman with short gray hair. All sorts of thoughts went through my mind as to who she was and what she did when she was alive and how she died. I felt grateful she had donated her body so we could learn human anatomy and eventually help others. It must have been a courageous, heartrending decision for her, and maybe she thought that even in death she could contribute to humanity.

Soon, the physician instructors who had chosen a career in teaching came around and told us to start dissecting. For dissection instructions, we had a thick brown book by Zuckerman with wide pages that had photos of a real cadaver dissected in various sequential stages with clear detailed instructions starting with the arms. The book lay near the head above the shoulder for easy access, and each student got a surgical scalpel, thick forceps to pull out dissected tissues, surgical scissors, and a steel probe. We were instructed to carefully identify the labeled parts in the guide, like the muscles, tendons, nerves, arteries, and veins on our own cadaver before removing any tissue and to ask the instructors if we could not find any structure as human anatomy could vary a little from person to person. The complete hanging skeletons were so we could identify where the various muscles or ligaments we dissected were attached to on the bones. It was harder to do that on the cadaver, as the bones and joints were surrounded by muscles, ligaments, and connective tissues. The instructors came around frequently and were very helpful. The body was turned over as we started the dissection from the upper back, exposing the muscles and nerves, and later turned it over as we dissected the arms.

A few days later, to watch a postmortem in a side room, we gathered around a young man found dead at a bench in a park one night. He was semi-reclined on a table so all could see, and the instructor made a vertical cut in the middle of his chest from below the neck to his abdomen as blood spurted out. The sternum was cut with a saw to expose the heart and lungs. He dissected the organs, like the heart, lungs, and stomach and explained his findings. We occasionally went to the mortuary where most of the postmortems were performed. There was a prominent sign that read, "Do not give me two diseases, one manmade and one doctor-made. Napoleon Bonaparte." At this stage, we didn't know anything about doctor-made diseases.

Anatomy lectures were given in a large spacious hall with semicircular rows of seating, like an amphitheater, and the professor stood at the podium in front with a screen for slides and a table for specimens of body parts whose anatomy was being taught on a white metal tray, like the liver, stomach, spleen, pancreas, and small and large bowel. For organs that were too small to dissect in humans, like the eyes, we were provided the large eyes of oxen in the side room to dissect with scissors and forceps.

Skeletons were not easy to procure. The skeletons were smaller in size as they were imported from Calcutta in India, where there was an abundance of unidentified bodies that were dissolved in various chemicals to remove the soft tissues and the skeletons then shipped to England for sale. For over one hundred years, India's skeleton trade followed from its villages to world's distinguished medical schools and was known for its pristine quality. Rumors of people there bludgeoned to death to profit from their skeletons by unscrupulous crooks in this trade persisted. We were required to buy our own private dismantled skeleton, without the skull, to study the anatomy and parts of the numerous bones of the human skeleton. This was required in the first year only as we did anatomy of the body below the neck. Second-year medical students sold their skeletons to the first-year ones. For that, I followed directions in an ad, leaving Trinity Hall and passing through various narrow streets and alleys to Queens College, where I met the seller at his room and paid him five pounds. He gave me a long rectangular brown cardboard box, like a mini-casket, with the skeletal bones inside.

For an hour every evening, except Fridays, we had tutorials—a common modus operandi at Cambridge colleges as a teaching medium—in physiology and anatomy. The physiology tutorials were given by Dr. Bill Grundy, who was also the director of medical studies at Trinity Hall and had interviewed me. Dr. Grundy sat at one end of a round table in his office, facing the six medical students. As he taught and explained the subject matter, he wrote and drew relevant diagrams on a pad upside down so that we could read and take notes at the same time, without him having to turn the pad. The tutorial was a two-way street, where he asked us questions and taught the subject matter relating to what we were studying. One of the weekly anatomy tutorials were given by Professor Roy Calne, now Professor Sir Roy Calne, who was the professor of surgery at the Addenbrooke's Hospital in Cambridge and a fellow of Trinity Hall. He would later do the world's first liver transplant. In his office, each person sat on small sofas with armrests as he faced us on his own sofa. The tutorials were useful for the students to understand the subject matter and also be able to discuss any problem with a topic they had. Later, I realized the tutorials were also a way for each college to help their students to get higher grades at the year-end examinations that were like an intercollegiate competition.

Mark Drayton, my anatomy dissection partner, was of similar built as me, about five-eight and wore plastic-rimmed glasses. The anatomy dissection class was on Friday afternoons, and after the class, we would have tea and biscuits and chat, alternating Fridays between my room and his room. I learned interesting things from him as he was in the British army's home guards and spent some weekends there for training. He told me about how flares worked in the dark to track enemy positions and that you froze in place if a flare went up into the sky at night to prevent detection by the enemy. We went to the public swimming pool in Cambridge where he taught me how to swim, dog-paddle style, as I was afraid to put my head under the water. I will always be indebted to him for that as I lost my fear of drowning.

At Trinity Hall, the three meals of the day were served at the spacious dining hall, with long, black wooden tables and benches on either side of the entry doors. The kitchen staff was kind to make modified semi-vegetarian meals, especially with eggs, for me. Later, I threw in the towel as I got tired of eating eggs for breakfast, lunch, and dinner and became a non-vegetarian but never really got used to eating meat either as the English food was too bland for me. Dinners were formal, and we had to wear our black college gowns. The tutors, who also wore black gowns, had a separate table at the far end of the hall from the entry doors, and they only came for dinner.

Each first-year student had their own room, and each floor had a butler, or caretaker, for the students living there. The butlers wore white suits with bowties and addressed each student as "sir." They were humble, very respectful of us, provided excellent care, and took pride in their work. I never quite got used to being called "sir" as they were much older than us and I thought we should be calling them that. They also served us breakfast, lunch, and dinner in the dining hall like waiters. My floor, labeled F in the Trinity Hall map, was served by an older gentleman and his wife, who were very kind and wonderful. They picked up my clothes for washing and delivered them weekly, clean and meticulously ironed. One day, when I went down the stairs, I found the wife crying. She said her husband died from a heart attack the day before, yet she still came to work. I cried with her. Here was a man I saw and talked with daily, and the next day, he was gone. That inspired me to do the research we were required to do in our third year on the role of diet in the genesis of atherosclerosis, the cause of most heart attacks and strokes.

Norbert had faded from my mind like a bad dream, but the memory of his deception and angst he had caused me left a mental scar. Here was a crook, who did not know any physics, chemistry, or biology yet had a grade A in both the subjects because of me. I assumed he was now a first-year medical student at the Middlesex Medical School in London. One of the three subjects we had to study in the first year of medical school was biochemistry. It required some knowledge of A-level biology but especially organic chemistry, a vital component of A-level chemistry—no wonder these subjects were a prerequisite for medical school admission. This dawned on me one day when we had to spend a whole afternoon in biochemistry lab doing experiments using and mixing chemicals found in mammalian cells. We had to write up certain reactions that occur in our cells and the calculations from the results we obtained that required knowledge of A-level chemistry.

I wondered how Norbert was faring in all this. Maybe the curriculum at London medical schools was different, and he didn't have to possess the same knowledge base—or maybe he found another sucker. But it was medical school, and having someone do experiments and calculations for you didn't fly. I came up with the hypothesis that while he had gotten into medical school and got away in anatomy and physiology, he would get caught in biochemistry because he would not be able to do the calculations, even if he did the experiments somehow by copying or asking gullible students. The system would weed him out, sooner or later, I theorized. I decided to discard the notion as pure conjecturing because I had nothing more to do with him.

Not long after that when I went to check my mailbox at the porter's lodge, there were two letters, one from my dad in Tanzania with an airmail stamp on it and another white envelope that had my name and address written in nice handwriting in blue pen that looked somewhat familiar but there was no return name or address on the left upper corner, like the sender wanted to stay anonymous. The envelope's thickness suggested it contained several pages. I went back to my room and opened my dad's letter and read it. He had sent me my monthly official bank check worth twenty pounds that I usually took straight to the bursar's office as payment for my medical education. My account was always in arrears as my payments were inadequate, but that was the maximum Dad could send me as he was sending the remaining ten pounds allowed under Tanzania's restricted foreign exchange allowance to my brother Raj in London.

Then I opened the white envelope. The papers had details of a biochemistry experiment above a plea for me to do the calculations and send it to an address given at the end of the letter. I could smell the rat—it was from Norbert. My hypothesis was proven. I could not believe this dastardly act after what he had done. What nerve! He thought I would just do the calculations so he could submit it to his biochemistry professor? I went to the bursar's office to pay, and on the way dumped the letter in a trash bin at the porter's lodge. Years later, I wished I had kept it for posterity to show how evil some individuals could be.

Having proven my hypothesis, my next follow-up hypothesis was he would be kicked out of the medical school because he would flunk the exams held at the end of the first year, especially in biochemistry. That was not my concern anymore nor did I care. The medical school would do itself a favor by expelling him earlier than later.

However, I wasn't gloating over Norbert's present predicament or my hypothesis that the system would catch up to him and eject him from the medical school because next day I received a threat that could derail my career but for a different reason. I was in serious arrear of my bill from the bursar's office, and I had no money to pay. I'd gotten into Cambridge with strong academics but weak financials—the very reason I took all the risk for Norbert. The billing was done on a term basis, and I had promised them regular payments after a small down payment. It reminded me of what Mahatma Gandhi had once said: "A postdated check issued by a crashing bank," in response to a British envoy sent at the height of WWII to negotiate with a promise of India's independence once Britain won the war with India's help. Here, I was the crashing bank. As matters stood in the second quarter, I had been able to pay about eighty pounds of the first term's bill of 200 pounds, and only fifty pounds of the second term of a term bill of 200 pounds, leaving a hefty total balance of 270 pounds, including a balance of 120 pounds for the first term. I was close to presenting my plight to the senior tutor of Trinity Hall, Mr. Frankyl, who was originally a refugee

from Germany fleeing Nazi persecution before WWII and was impris-
oned in England during the war as were all people of German ancestry
living in England, irrespective of their background or reason for
being in England. I felt he would sympathize with me. However, I felt
embarrassed as I had pride, and it would be construed as I made a false
promise to pay knowing I could not do so while my account was on life
support.

Chapter 2

A Far-Fetched Rescue Plan

The end of our second semester in April of 1970 approached fast, and our college would close for six weeks for the Easter break. During this time, all the students had to vacate their college rooms, which would be locked. All the English students went home to their families. I was postponing my fateful visit to Mr. Frankyl, counting days till the college closed, like waiting for some miracle to rescue me. My options were bleak because if my appeal to Mr. Frankly failed, I was out luck and options—and then what?

Again, I thought of a novel outside of the box solution, like the one that had gotten me into the medical school in the first place. What if I created conditions that would make it harder to eject me, or make Trinity Hall administration seriously consider why I should be allowed to stay, despite my impending default? However, I realized that first, I would have to see my tutor about this because each student was assigned a tutor, who was like his supervisor or mentor and dealt with any problems he had. It would be inappropriate and rude of me to approach Mr. Frankyl first as his secretary probably would ask me to see my tutor first.

But I had another conundrum. When the college closed for six weeks, I had nowhere to go. My two brothers were renting one room to save money with me gone. The two rooms we had rented at Harbans Singh's house were too pricy as the money Dad sent was insufficient. We came full circle as they were now renting the same room in the basement Sham had at Rafi's when I had arrived in England. If I moved back with them and slept on the floor, the room would be too crowded and cause resentment and fights, and I would be unable to study. That was the default plan if nothing worked, so I went to see my tutor, Dr. David Cove, a PhD with a handsome reddish beard and brown plastic-rimmed spectacles. We had a designated time per week when he was available in his office and all six medical students from Trinity Hall were under his supervision. I told him I had nowhere to go for the holidays and asked if I could stay in my room at the college. He told me the college would be closed, and I could not stay there, but he would allow me to stay in one of the rooms in the college dormitory for second-year students as it was located next to his house on the outskirts of Cambridge. "Also, I can keep an eye on you," he quipped. All the first-year students stayed on the college campus but had to move out in the second year. I made no mention of my other serious problem because with his acceding to my request, it would help me implement my out of the box plan.

My plan was far-fetched and based on the premise that if I wanted the college to help me with the defaulting problem, then like a quid pro quo, what would I offer in return? Why would they take the long-term risk? What did the college covet?

My first year, 125 first-year medical school students at the Cambridge University Faculty of Medicine were the cream of the crop from around the world. I questioned myself about how I could shine among this distinguished crowd? What if I got a grade 1, the top grade, in the first-year final examinations? Would they then hesitate to kick me out and perhaps give me more time, more breathing space, so Dad could come up with something and I could work in a factory with higher pay in summer to pay off the arrears? I had no idea how many of the students could get a grade 1.

The medical school exam at the end of the first year, called the Tripos, was given in the three major subjects we studied: anatomy, biochemistry, and physiology. Anatomy also had an oral exam in addition to a written one. Each subject was graded by four categories as 1, 2(1), 2(2) and 3 in that order. To get an overall 1, we had to get 1 in two of the subjects and a minimum 2(1) in the third—a tall order. My plan was to receive a 1 by getting a 1 in all three subjects. That would make my 1 stand out on the assumption that most of the 1s would be made of two 1s and one 2(1). It was like a pyramid, and I would be the top rock of that pyramid.

Since I started medical school, I had continued with my study habits and techniques from my college days, especially with a focus on the final exams, helped by the quiet privacy of my room and also studying in the Trinity Hall library. At the library, I carefully documented in a notebook questions that were asked in each of the subjects in the previous five years to discern a pattern. Some questions were repeated at random, but most were new questions. I concluded that my primary focus would be on topics that had not been asked in the previous five years, and less on the ones asked. Some questions were analytical and of somewhat difficult nature like, "Discuss how ontogeny recapitulates phylogeny," based on the premise that when an organism develops (ontogeny), starting with its embryonic stage, it expresses the intermediate stages of its ancestors throughout evolution (phylogeny).

All the Cambridge colleges closed for the Easter break of April 1970, and the city was suddenly empty of twenty-five percent of its population. I was now staying at a four-story rectangular brick building next to a wide, neatly trimmed lush grass lawn. Each dorm room facing the lawn had a small balcony. Dr. Cove allowed me to stay in a room on the third floor facing the lawn and his small, cute house. The dorm room had a wooden desk with compartments for papers, books, pens, and pencils. I settled into the room with my books and bought several small cans of baked beans, bread, and tea bags at a local store to cook in the common kitchen, which was present on each floor.

The dormitory was like a ghost building. I had it all to myself, except when the cleaning ladies came weekly to check on and maintain the deserted building.

My daily routine was the same. After waking up at seven o'clock in the morning, I showered and then boiled some water in a kettle on a stove in the kitchen, poured it into a cup with a teabag, and sipped it slowly in my room as I planned my day. I studied from eight o'clock in the morning to ten o'clock at night, almost fourteen hours daily, except for two short breaks at the kitchen for lunch and an early dinner consisting of a small can of baked beans heated in a saucepan and spread on a toast. I took occasional quick breaks to go to the balcony to look out, take some deep breaths, and review what I had studied in my brain as I admired the beauty of the lawn.

One afternoon, it was nice and sunny with a clear sky when I went to the balcony and saw Dr. Cove working on his garden at the edge of the lawn to my left. I always admired the dedication of English people to their tiny, well-tended gardens in the front and back of their homes, and Dr. Cove was following that tradition. You could always tell if a house that had a small garden in front belonged to an immigrant or an English person because the immigrant's was untended and had weeds, while the English person's was manicured, had no weeds, and was a beautiful sight to behold. Dr. Cove had a hoe in his hands and looked up, sensing my presence. Our gazes met for a few seconds as the sun hit his face. I could see beads of sweat dripping down his forehead, and then I went back into the room to study more.

In my six weeks at the dorm, I prepared for the exams. The anatomy portion had separate branches like histology, or the microscopic anatomy of tissues. For the oral anatomy exam, we could be handed an individual bone from the skeleton and asked to describe its structure and any unique features, what muscles and tendons were attached to it, and the nerves and blood vessels in its vicinity. I impersonated the examiner, asking a question, then reversed the roles as the examinee and answered the question.

I always looked for the atypical bone or features, like the atypical first rib, which was more likely to be asked. Examiners didn't ask the expected as that wouldn't be challenging.

My modus operandi was changed to fit the unique local medical school conditions, unlike the university-based A-level final exams where we didn't know the examiners. Here, I knew the examiners were the professors, and I got a feel of what made them tick, gauged from what they taught during their lectures. I took good rough notes during the lectures and then wrote detailed notes in nice writing from the rough notes on the same day while my memory of the lecture was fresh, just like I did in college.

At the end of the six weeks, when I returned to my room at Trinity Hall, I had studied almost six hundred hours, or the equivalent to about twenty-five days round the clock. I was ready for the exam and looked forward to it.

As I expected, the exams were difficult, but that is what I'd prepared for. During the oral anatomy exam, the examiner handed me the first rib, which was atypical, from the many on a table in our anatomy hall just as I had predicted. Then he took me to a cadaver with muscles around one shoulder dissected and displayed, and he asked me to identify them by name, demonstrate what shoulder movements they performed, and their attachments and nerve supplies. After the exams, no one talked about them as if nothing had happened, like a taboo topic, for the same reason students did not do so in our junior college days.

We were required to report to Dr. Cove at regular intervals, especially after the exams, as he wanted to discuss any problems we were facing and inform us about updates to our residency and studies at Trinity Hall. After the exams, when I went to see him, it became obvious that most of the other five medical students from Trinity Hall had already seen him as one was just leaving when I entered his room. He was quiet and didn't look very happy.

When I entered Dr. Cove's office after knocking, I immediately thanked him for his generosity in allowing me to stay at the dorm during the break. "Didn't see much of you," he remarked. Then he asked, "How did you do in the Tripos?"

"I did well," I responded casually as that was the truth. He looked surprised and grinned and did not say anything more. It was obvious that the other students had not done well. I could gauge from his face, which read, *How could this dude have done well when the others did not and all were cream of the crop?* It was like he didn't believe me or didn't like the casualness in my response as if I were not serious. He seemed perturbed that I would say that after all, he did for me. It was an unusually short meeting, and I left somewhat worried that I had given the wrong response while trying to be honest. I wanted his help with my financial meltdown, and I wondered if I should have feigned how difficult the exam was. Then he would be comforting and empathize with me. I never gave him the chance to be my mentor. Deeply worried I had destroyed the opportunity to ask for his help with my poor finances, I left without broaching the topic.

Medical school exam results came out much earlier than at the junior colleges, and they were prominently displayed on typed papers in a large glass wall cabinet at one of the medical school's buildings. Only five medical students got a grade 1, several got 2(1), many more got 2(2), and most of the rest got 3. As there were twenty-five colleges, it meant no one from at least twenty colleges got a grade 1. Out of the five students who got a 1, I was the only one from Trinity Hall to get a 1, and out of these five who got 1, I was the only one to get a 1 in all the three subjects of anatomy, biochemistry, and physiology; the other four had a 1 in two of these subjects and a 2(1) in the third subject. This meant that I was the first out of all the 125 students, and thus shining among the cream of the crop.

The college closed down for the summer toward the end of May 1970, except I would have to stay for another six weeks in my room for a mandatory summer course in introductory pharmacology, or the study and uses of drugs, their structure, classification, and effects on living animals, that all medical school students after completing the first year were required to take in preparation for their second year. I was happy about this extended stay because while I was planning to go and stay with my brothers, it would mean less time to cause congestion in the room. My plan after the course was to work in a factory as they paid higher for the summer to pay off my college arrears.

I went to pick up my mail from my college mailbox at the porter's office and dreaded another letter from the bursar about my overdue account balance. I saw two letters sticking out, recognizing one as an airmail letter from Dad. I grabbed them and was about to leave when the porter at the front desk said I had forgotten my postcard in the mailbox. I apologized as it was a small white card and lay deep inside the box, so unless I really looked in, it would be easily missed. It was a small, blank three-inch white square. I wondered if this was a prank as there was no name or address or stamp. I took the card and pocketed it, embarrassed to tell the porter it was a blank card. I planned to trash it when I returned to my room, but it fell out of my pocket onto the floor when I pulled my room key out of my pocket. I picked it up and dumped it in a small trash bin next to my desk without further thought.

Of the two envelopes, I opened my dad's first, expecting some money that I could pay to cool the bursar's heels. There was a bank check for twenty pounds, and I started reading Dad's letter. Dad always wrote long letters to me in response to my brief ones that mostly stated my studies were progressing well without dwelling into any details. In his letter, he told me for the first time that he had never stopped pursuing the grant rejection matter with the Inner London Education Authority after I had sent him their grant rejection letter the previous year in summer after Norbert had disappeared. Dad had communications with the education authority and impressed on them that he was a British citizen and he was willing to come to the United Kingdom and work there to pay for my education, but he could not enter the country because of the new severe immigration restrictions, which required him to get an immigration voucher from the British High Commission in Tanzania. He was so far down the line that it would be years before he was even considered. He was making progress, albeit slowly, partly due to the time it took the mail to reach from one country to another so far apart. They had reopened the case and had asked for his proof of income. This heartened me somewhat even though I was skeptical anything would materialize to help me.

When I looked at the second letter, I was surprised, as the return address stated it was from the Inner London Education Authority. I opened the letter with trepidation, expecting a rejection. The letter dated May 28, 1970, was not a rejection letter but informed me of an award to fund my education for the six years! The letter stated that ILEA would pay for my academic fees plus a grant for college lodging equaling 395 pounds of which my parents would have to pay 160—an amount I had just paid from what Dad had sent me per month. The ILEA was truly my savior, and I had to thank my dad for his perseverance to help me as otherwise, I would be out of medical school. I was truly ecstatic as my defaulted academic fees and the lodging fees for the first year would be paid directly to the college.

Chapter 3

The Visitor from Caius College

When I threw the piece of unwanted paper into the trash bin next to my desk, I hadn't realized the card had a hand-written note on it. The postcard had writing on only one side and was blank on the other, and that was the only side I had seen. I picked up the card and started reading. At the top of the card was a printed line that read: *From DR. D. J. COVE, TRINITY HALL, CAMBRIDGE, CB2 1TJ TEL. 51401.* Under that was a solid black line to separate it from the blank part below for the handwritten note. The note read: *Congratulations, you got a first—a truly magnificent result! I confess I was a little cynical when you told me you had done well—please forgive me!* It was signed DJ Cove. I was thrilled, and here I was going to throw away the card. Elated, I mailed the card to my dad in Tanzania as I felt proud for Trinity Hall and for myself. Later, Dad returned the card as it really belonged to me, but added at the top of the note, *Dear Ashok.* Dad was proud of me and added this to leave no doubt that the note was written to me.

Our summer school started, and except for the six medical students, all the other students, many reading law, went home. They were replaced by many American students doing a summer stint at Cambridge. They were a jovial lot, friendly, and easy going—not formal like the typical

Cambridge student when I met them during the meal times in the college dining hall. Sometimes, some of them gathered in the lush green lawn that covered the middle of the square building where my room was located and played frisbee, a sport that I'd never seen before.

One morning, I was at my desk studying pharmacology in front of the open window facing the lawn when a face appeared in front of it. He was a slender, tall English student with a longish nose from Caius College, who I saw during the lectures but had not spoken with him before. We looked at each other, and he raised one arm and asked me a question that no student had ever asked me during all my years of schooling, "How do you get a first?" I waved at him to climb the stairs and come to my room.

When he opened the door and peeked in, I invited him to take a seat and said, "To get a first, you study for it right from day one of your college like I'm doing now. It will be the most important priority of your life that must be done first every day. You study at a desk and a chair with a pencil in hand and a pad for hours and hours, except for eating, going to the bathroom, and sleeping for eight hours. No studying on the bed, in an armchair, or where there are any distractions or comfort. Studying is an active process. Study in the library or a quiet room.

"You think like an examiner whenever you study any topic and ask yourself how you can ask the student the most difficult trick question on this topic. Take good rough notes during lectures, especially the labeled diagrams drawn on the board to explain subject matter, and write detailed notes in nice writing on the same day while the material is fresh in your brain. Imagine the lecturer speaking. Just remembering and cramming a lot of facts will do no good if you don't learn how to use them in an exam. Facts learned are only the different pieces of the jigsaw puzzle. You need to learn how to manipulate and fit them together to complete the puzzle that is the answer to your exam question. That takes a lot of practice.

"Go and review in the library all the exam questions asked in the last five years to get an idea what the examiners think and spend most, like seventy percent, of your time on topics that were not asked." He seemed mesmerized, like listening to a preacher.

"No late-night studying after ten o'clock or burning the midnight oil—the most wasteful and damaging habit. Don't drink tea or coffee to stay awake at night." I offered him tea, but he politely declined as he wanted me to continue. "Say you are a military commander with one thousand soldiers, but your enemy commander has ten thousand soldiers. Who will win the battle?"

He looked confused and replied, "My enemy."

"But what if you changed strategy and trained your army specifically for the battle, day in and day out till the day of the battle, in the trenches preparing for any eventuality, thinking like your enemy commander and ready for a battle any day—unlike your enemy, whose army does long maneuvers and spends more time in comfy barracks than training. Who will win now?"

"I think my army will win."

"You got it. The battle is a metaphor for the exam. I was that small army training in the trenches, while you were the big army, as were most of the other students. When you were gone home for your six-week Easter break, I was here studying long hours daily, thinking like the examiner. That's why I got a first. Now you do the same as I did, and you will get a first next year."

Then I explained to him in detail my other basic study strategies at the desk that I had used successfully in college and high school to consolidate information in my long-term memory.

"Also take your own timed mock exams, full exams, like a full mock battle. It will give you an edge over others. You can use the previous exam questions and see how you can answer all the questions in the allocated time. Use simple, labeled diagrams to explain clearly and save time instead of writing long descriptions that the diagram can explain simply. Answer the question in simple language to convince the examiner of your full understanding. Do not waste time on anything irrelevant to the question. If you can answer the same question in one page concisely with a labeled diagram that another student takes two pages to describe, you have saved time to complete the exam in time. If you cannot explain in simple terms what the question asks, then you do not fully understand the subject matter and the examiner will mark you down."

After I was done and he was leaving, I said, "And here is one for the road. When you are not studying, like walking back to your college or eating, still think about that difficult problem or fact you just studied and consolidate it in your mind further and ask yourself what the trickiest question you can ask on that topic is. Make full use of that six-week break they give us before the final exams. What I told you takes time to do!"

The student left, followed my advice, and got a first at the next year-end exam.

After completing the six weeks of pharmacology, I went to London to stay with my two brothers, renting the same room at Rafi's house in Woolwich where Sham had lived when I arrived from Tanzania in July of 1967. It was a tight fit for the three of us at night, so Sham rented an attic in the home of a Sikh family he knew for me to sleep in at night for one pound per week. I would climb up to the attic via a ladder, and there was not enough room to stand up, except in the middle where the two slanting roofs on either side met. I would leave early in the morning back to my brothers. Sham had already left for work, and I would stay with Raj. With the summer break greatly shortened by the six-week pharmacology course, I was back to Cambridge after six weeks of staying with my brothers and glad to be done with sleeping in the attic like a rat.

Chapter 4

The *Karjamai*

When our second year at Cambridge started in September of 1970, the financial pressure and the stress of expulsion from the medical school for failure to pay their fees was off my brain thanks to the largesse of ILEA who now paid my academic fees and a large part of my lodging expenses directly to Trinity Hall. I had been struggling to stay afloat with a big rock around my neck, and now I was free of the rock just as I had been about to sink.

The biochemistry we studied in the first year was replaced by pathology, or the causes and effects of disease on the body, and microbiology, or study of disease-causing microorganisms like bacteria, viruses, and fungi. As we had completed the anatomy of the body below the neck, we concentrated on anatomy above the neck, the skull and anatomy of the central nervous system, the spinal cord, and the evolution of humans through millions of years. The physiology of the first year was replaced by neurophysiology, and we learned about the brain and the spinal cord function and how they controlled the various functions of the body and the consequences of damage to its parts.

We attended the sprawling neuroanatomy lab with rows of long wooden laboratory tables and sinks spaced apart. When we entered the lab for our first class, on the front table of the lab there was a freshly removed brain from the postmortem of a deceased person lying on a white tray. The neuroanatomy professor told us that the brain, especially from someone who had died recently, was like a sponge or "thick porridge," and we would not be able to dissect it to learn. The brain, with its convolutions, was somewhat flattened and sagging from its own weight on the tray, with fresh blood around it. The convolutions consisted of groves called the sulci and raised ridges called gyri between them. The brain was delicate and soft and a vital part of the body, which was why it was protected inside a bony skull. The spinal cord was its lower extension that was protected inside the bony canal, the spinal canal, located inside the vertebral column. We were each given a white bucket with a grayish-white brain that was preserved with formalin and hardened over time, like it was baked, so we could dissect it using a scalpel and forceps.

Hand-in-glove with the study of the brain was the study of the skull that encased and protected it and some anthropology, mainly concentrating on how the skull evolved from the early ancestors of humans to the present-day humans, or *Homo sapiens*. One day we had all these old human skulls from archeological expeditions in Africa lined up chronologically, dating back to hundreds of thousands of years to the present. It was fascinating to see the early bulky skulls with prominent eyebrows and a bony ridge in the middle of the cranium of the skull where the strong muscles connected to the heavy lower jaws originated. The early skulls had a smaller volume, indicating smaller brains, which later evolved into larger volume skulls with lighter lower jaws, disappearing prominent heavy eyebrows and the median ridge on top of the skull and increasing brain volume as the early man evolved and became smarter. There were skulls from 200,000 years ago when it was theorized humans migrated out of Africa.

Neuroanatomy lectures were often given by neurosurgeons from the Addenbrooke's Hospital as they also taught the functional applied neuroanatomy and explained what happened when various parts of the brain were damaged by trauma or disease with photo slides. For our neuroanatomy and neurophysiology tutorials, the students from Trinity Hall went to Claire College as the relevant professors were fellows there. The human skull had many holes to allow for the entry and egress of the various cranial nerves, arteries, and veins, and the neuroanatomy tutor always brought a skull during the evening tutorials to demonstrate these using a thin metal pointer and questioned us.

We were also taught introductory human reproductive biology, and one day, we got a shock treatment when we were invited to an evening show in a large auditorium with tiers of seats climbing high, like in an amphitheater. It was an hour-long documentary shown on a large screen using a front projector, showing a series of different couples having sex—white couples, a black and white couple, among others, with the projector man commenting that some couples like the color contrast during sex, which included other combinations of races. After it was over, we were shell-shocked as most of us were virgins who did not really know the mechanics of human sexuality, but we needed to learn them. Then the announcer pronounced that if you were a male, then you should find a girlfriend and if you were a female, then find a boyfriend; many laughed because only five of the 125 medical students were female, and they already had boyfriends in their hometowns. Medicine was a male-dominated field in that era— definitely not by choice.

In my third year of medical school, commencing in September of 1971, there were no year-end exams as the year was devoted to research, and we had to submit a final thesis. Each student was assigned a professor, or a medical researcher, to work with for a medical research topic of our preference and to get an understanding of how research was done and to discover new knowledge and facts. My research topic was the role of diet in the etiology of atherosclerosis, or plaque forma-tion in the arteries, which was the cause of most heart attacks and strokes. Like I mentioned previously, I had decided to do that after my butler who took care of me in my first year died of a heart attack.

While I had to spend a lot of time at various Cambridge libraries searching for numerous papers on this topic published by different researchers, fully reviewing them, and discussing my findings with my professor, my weekends were now free. A small city like Cambridge was boring, so I went to visit my brothers in London, always a very lively city. When I reached Sham's rental room at the Rafis in Woolwich that first weekend, he was alone and said our youngest brother Raj had left.

Raj had moved out from Woolwich as he had finished his two years at Woolwich College and was now enrolled at a University of London campus to get a bachelor's degree in science and was renting a room at an Indian widow's home closer to his campus as Woolwich was too far. The lady had a good-looking teenage daughter, and the rent was well below the market rent. As a bonus, he got an Indian dinner in the evening cooked by the widow.

We decided to visit him and then planned to take him to eat at a small, cheap Indian restaurant, almost a café, called Diwana located on Drummond Street in the town of Euston only a few tube stations away from where Raj lived. We knocked at the door of the house, and a thin Indian lady wearing a gray sari opened the door and looked at us suspiciously before we told her we were his older brothers. The daughter was sitting on a couch with folded arms in the living room watching TV. We passed her and climbed the nearby stairs as she glanced at us without saying anything. We were happy to see Raj, and he was happy to see us but declined our offer to eat out as he had already eaten dinner cooked by the landlady; however, he accompanied us to Diwana and once there, joined us in eating some appetizers called *pakoras* that were made of potatoes, peas, onions, and some other vegetables, soaked in gram flour batter, and deep fried. We dipped each one in mint chutney before eating. Raj said he was happy at his new place but was somewhat evasive about the full situation there.

On his occasional weekend visits to Raj, Sham was suspicious that this was a deal too good to be true and conjectured that the widow was eying Raj as a potential future groom for her daughter, but Raj was a student who was broke and not ready for prime time. The widow did not care as she owned the house and apparently had a comfortable income from her job. Sham's suspicion was aroused further when finding out Raj had not paid his rent for months, partly from lack of affordability but mainly from disincentive to pay as the widow never asked for it. Sham was a street-smart guy as he had lived in India where you were forced to become street smart to survive or perish, so I believed his theory. He quietly urged Raj to bail out of there before he got deeply entangled into a well-laid trap, leading to betrothal by this widow from India. Raj was furious at any such insinuations so on our future weekend visits, we carefully avoided mentioning or asking about his new family situation, but that did not abate our anxiety as he was our youngest brother, and we watched out for each other.

One weekend, when I visited Sham and we picked up Raj, Sham told us that our aunt, who was our mom's younger sister who used to live in Nairobi, was now living in a town called East Ham after they had to leave Kenya during the exodus of Indians. My uncle had been writing to Sham to visit them for dinner, so we went to visit them. After we ate a delicious Indian dinner cooked by my aunt and met our cousins, we sat down to relax on couches in the living room to talk more with my uncle over post-dinner tea and sweetmeats served by my aunt.

My uncle was a medium-built man in his forties with wavy black hair, graying on the sides, and wore steel-rimmed spectacles. He was an accountant working for a British Jewish father-and-son clothing manufacturing company. During our chat in our native Punjabi, he asked Raj where he lived, and Raj gave a minimal curt reply that he was renting a room. However, when Sham elaborated that he was renting at a house owned by an Indian widow who had a teenage daughter, the uncle grinned and told Raj bluntly, "She wants to make you a *Karjamai.*" The actual word in Hindi, the language commonly spoken in northern India, was *Gharjamai* and since Punjabi had many cognate words from Hindi, it was *Karjamai* in Punjabi. The word and its implications had a very negative connotation in the Indian society because it referred to a husband living with his wife's family, and even if he was working, the man was supposed to be supporting his wife and family independently and not live with them. *Karjamai* implied he was dependent on the welfare of the wife's family and not worthy of respect, irrespective of what he contributed. Like the final straw that broke the camel's back, Raj was now convinced his present situation was untenable.

However, Sham provided him with an alternative place to live, so Raj reluctantly moved into a room on the third floor of another five-bedroom, three-story house in Chelsea, a borough of London, owned by another Indian widow from Guyana who was an absentee landlord as she lived elsewhere, and all the rooms were rented to single tenants. To further incentivize him to move, Sham gave him a cheap, small Morris Mini car that an English colleague at work who was migrating to Australia had sold him for a few pounds. Sham hardly used the car as it was cheaper and easier to take the bus to work with no parking problems. Sham and our uncle's prescience was confirmed when Raj told the widow with the daughter he planned to move. She was extremely distraught, broke down, and beseeched him to stay, telling him in Hindi when he was out of the door with his suitcase, "We thought you were ours."

Chapter 5

The Revenant

Raj loved to drive the Mini as it was small, compact, hardly used any gas, and was easy to repair. He parked it at a deserted side street close to his housing complex. Mini Cooper, Morris Mini, and its various models were the most commonly used cars in England in those days because of their fuel economy and spaciousness inside. Driving was like a hobby and relaxation for him so much so that he insisted he would pick me up on Fridays from Cambridge and then drop me back off on Sunday evenings while I stayed with him for the weekend. I reluctantly agreed as it seemed like a lot of work driving back and forth for a weekend, but not to Raj. Our new routine was Raj would pick me up after six o'clock on Friday from Cambridge, I would stay with him for the weekend, and he would drive me back to Cambridge on Sunday evening.

The bond between us brothers was astounding and unique, and when we got together, we talked a lot and often freely because we trusted each other. We would tell each other personal stuff—our innermost feelings that we wouldn't tell anyone else. One Friday evening, when we were passing through a small town to get to London, we were so deeply engrossed in conversation and looking straight that we failed to see a lady with a baby stroller start to cross on the zebra crossing on the opposing side of the street. As we passed over the zebra crossing at moderate speed, luckily the lady was paying attention and stopped the stroller in the middle between the streets. If she had continued, we would have crashed into the stroller with disastrous consequences. We realized what we had done as we saw her stopped in the middle of the crossing, and Raj pulled the car to the side of the street further down. A police car, also a Mini Minor stationed across the street pulled up behind us, and the policeman, called a bobby in England, came to ask Raj for his driver's license. I profusely apologized and took responsibility as the bobby politely asked if we realized what would have happened if the lady had not stopped as she had the right of way. We told him we were in total agreement with him and were sorry and wanted to apologize to the lady, but she had already left. Raj did not have a driver's license of his own and was using Sham's. However, the bobby did not know the difference as a driver's license in those days had no photo of the driver. He gave Raj a ticket with a small fine. When I got back to Cambridge, I wrote a letter to the court clerk whose name was stated on the ticket as to our deepest apologies and if he could rescind the fine as we were students living on the edge with no money to spare. Then I thought I better pass this letter by some law students I knew as I was not a good letter writer, and Trinity Hall was well known for law. When I reached the law student's room, he had two other law students visiting him whom I also knew and told him the details of my problem and handed him the letter to see if it was okay or if it should be changed. They read the letter and had a hearty laugh and wrote a much better legal type of letter for me. I thanked them and mailed in the letter—and I was surprised that the court official rescinded the fine.

One weekend, we were driving to London when bingo—Raj told me he had seen Norbert. So much for his bravado and insistence that A-level physics, chemistry, and biology were useless subjects as far as medical schools were concerned. It was like Norbert had returned to our radar screens as a revenant.

Raj went to the university gym to shower on breaks. When he had come out from them one day, he had passed by the empty cafeteria and had seen Norbert sweeping the floor. At first, he could not believe it, and then when their gazes had met, Norbert had promptly turned his face away, ignoring him and looking down. Raj did not know Norbert well except from his visits to our home two years ago. This proved my second hypothesis—he had been expelled from the medical school and was doing a job appropriate for his existing skills.

It was then I told Raj about what had really transpired between us, what I had done for him, and the gall he had to send me a letter to solve biochemistry experiment problems for him. As I narrated, I saw Raj was expressionless and kept looking straight driving as if he knew about it. Then Raj divulged to me a similar tale: He'd taken the A-level exam in pure and applied math for the Sikh student, Gajinder Singh, or GS, whom the English student in our class had asked why he wore a turban. Raj said he had been bribed by an invitation to dinner, and all he had gotten was old food cooked by someone at his home. Raj had been desperate for Indian food and had taken up the offer. For that cheap meal as the bribe, he had reluctantly taken the exam at another center—just as I had done for Norbert—and had gotten him a grade A in pure and applied mathematics as GS kept cajoling him that he had landed a job offer, but the employer had wanted him to pass his A-level math and bring the certificate. The irony was GS had bragged to other students later how he had gotten a grade A and had never even thanked Raj for it. I told him it had been the same with Norbert.

As we relieved our guilt to each other, we realized we were two students with our heads in the books and had been taken advantage of by two street-smart ungrateful, sly crooks from the third world. We had little idea how the streets worked. I was glad that at least one crook had paid the price for his deeds. He would have been better off staying at his anatomy lab job. It bothered me that England was an advanced country, yet there was no mechanism to prevent one person from taking exams for another at A-levels, a crucial step to enter a university.

Even in my third-world home country of Tanzania, I wouldn't have been able to do so as we took our exams at the school we studied under the close supervision of tutors who knew us. However, I harbored deep guilt that in this very competitive field, where the deluge of applicants overwhelmed the number of admission openings, I had denied another worthy candidate a place at Middlesex Medical School because of what I had done in desperation.

Chapter 6

Goodbye to Tanzania

The problem faced by the Indians in Kenya caught up with them in Tanzania, whose government passed new laws that implicitly created conditions that made it impossible for Indians without Tanzanian citizenship to continue being employed or run their own business in the country. It was called Africanization, instead of Tanzanization, that really stipulated preference be given to the natives of the country, and Indians were not natives even if they were born there. Private enterprise was replaced with socialism; if you had a property with ten apartments, then you could keep only one unit to live in, and the rest were expropriated by the government. Factories and banks were nationalized. Indians there were desperate to emigrate, except their escape venues were limited or closed.

My dad had repeatedly applied over the years to all the various high commissions, including those of Canada and Australia, to immigrate to without success. He had also tried the United States Embassy in Dar es Salaam without luck. Because desperation knows no bounds, he wrote a letter to the President of the United States, Richard Nixon, and sent it for mailing to my oldest brother, Ram, who was studying in Los Angeles on a student visa, supporting himself working part time. Ram counseled it was a stupid idea because the President of the United States was the most powerful man on the planet and was very busy and had no time to read a letter from an aspiring immigrant from a third-world country and sat on it. Eventually, with Dad's pleadings, there was no harm in sending it, and Ram mailed the letter to the president at his address as the White House, Washington DC.

Voila! Dad received an airmail letter from the White House. As expected, the president never read the letter, but some staff member did and the response read that President Nixon acknowledged the receipt of his letter and that his office had notified the US Embassy in Dar es Salaam to entertain an application from Dad. This was a bizarre episode, and Dad ran to the US Embassy with the letter. They gave him an application that he submitted with a certificate of accountancy that he had earned after years of correspondence course accounting studies with a chartered accounting school in London. That qualified him for an immigrant visa, which he and my mom received as green cards, and both departed for America in the early part of 1972 with a stopover in London.

Dad and Mom packed two suitcases and said goodbye to Tanzania and took a flight to the US that landed at the Heathrow International Airport near London for a connecting flight. Raj and I were at the airport to meet them. However, the British immigration officer refused them entry outside the immigration control, fearing they could bolt and simply seek asylum in Great Britain because they were British passport holders and citizens who now had to obtain a special entry voucher in their home country first. They were told to wait in a room where another immigration officer questioned them as Dad pleaded with him that he simply wanted to see us as he had not seen us in years, had a valid US green card, and had no intention of breaking any laws and stay in Great Britain. The officer was not convinced and came to see us waiting for them in the waiting area of the immigration control.

He was a young man in his thirties with a round face and asked us if we had some proof that we were the kids of the detained parents.

Raj handed him an airmail letter from Dad written a few weeks before arriving. The airmail letter was a blue page with a stamp and airmail label, and it folded into a small envelope so the letter part was hidden. The officer read the letter, which had stated some instructions for Raj that if an immigration officer questioned him, he should state that they had no intention to stay in England illegally. The officer was surprised and also impressed that we communicated with our parents in English.

Raj got antsy as the interview progressed and that made me nervous that he could sink the deal, though what he was saying was true, but we had to be cautious how we presented it. He said that my parents did not want to stay here even if the officer allowed them as they had immigrant visas for America.

At this time, I thought of using reverse psychology—to tell the officer what he wanted to hear instead of what we wanted to say. I intervened and told the officer that we understood he was doing his job and trying to help us because he could simply refuse my parents' entry as he would be held accountable if they bolted after admission. I told him that we were very grateful to England for our education and that we fully understood that England was a crowded country, and therefore immigration was a serious and sensitive subject as I had discussed this frankly with some of my English colleagues, and I understood they did not want any more people migrating here. I showed him mine and Raj's Tanzanian passports that showed we were on student visas that had to be renewed annually, and we would leave when we were done with our studies and as such my parents could not stay here as we could not either. I offered him to hold our passports until my parents boarded their connecting flight that evening. He waved a hand indicating the offer was unnecessary and allowed my parents to depart immigration control. This was another example of the efficient British bureaucracy. The immigration officer had strict standing orders not to allow any East-African Asian with a British passport entry unless they had a valid voucher yet he showed flexibility and leadership in evaluating the circumstances of our case. A similar third-world bureaucrat would have very likely refused entry, no matter what the circumstances were, as they followed the book.

We all sat in the airport lounge, and I thanked our parents for all the sacrifices they had made for us and apologized for all the problems we had caused, especially to finance our education here. Dad said it was their duty. When they were departing for their connecting flight, we told them we would join them when we were done with our education here and help them, as they were aging. Raj and I realized that we would not go back to Tanzania when we graduated as we had no family there anymore but would now go to America to be with our parents. My dream of practicing medicine in Tanzania in my own private office and owning a big house and ranch with servants was now a pipe dream.

In the summer of 1972, my parents, who were now living with my oldest brother in Los Angeles, sponsored us for US immigrant visas. I went to the US Embassy located on Grosvenor Square in London and had the required chest X-ray and blood tests done there and some days later received a letter from the embassy and picked up a large brown sealed envelope that I would hand to the immigration officer at my first port of arrival in the US.

My dad had found a job with a transportation company in Los Angeles as an accountant and lived with my mom in a rented two-bedroom apartment in Monterey Park. Dad sent us two airline tickets, and we took a flight on a 747 jetliner and arrived at the Los Angeles International Airport where the immigration officer opened the envelope and handed each of us the green card inside and kept the rest of the papers from the embassy. We stayed there with them, enjoying Mom's homecooked meals and played with our three-year-old nephew, Sunil, our oldest brother Ram's son whom Mom babysat. He was a mischievous kid who kept Mom busy while she tried to cook. We returned to London toward the end of the summer of 1972 to continue our studies.

Chapter 7

London Clinicals

After three years at Cambridge, in May of 1972, the university conferred on me a Bachelor of Arts degree, even though I did not study any art subject. I'd completed the preclinical part of medicine, and the final part, called clinicals, would last three more years, comprising of clerkships or rotations at teaching hospitals in various branches of medicine, like internal medicine, surgery, obstetrics, gynecology, pediatrics, psychiatry, ophthalmology, and cardiology, learning by observation, tutorials by teaching staff, and practice under supervision. Medical clinicals were done at large teaching hospitals where there was an abundance of patients to learn from.

As Cambridge was a small town, which limited clinical material for training, the medical school only had a limited facility for specialization for medical graduates at its main hospital there, Addenbrooke's Hospital. All the medical students had to spend three years in London medical schools to complete their clinicals as London was a large city with a large population and several large teaching hospitals. This meant the minimum number of years a Cambridge medical student spent to obtain a medical degree was six, the same as at the medical schools at Oxford and University of Edinburg, the other top medical schools in the UK in those days, because all required an additional year of research.

At London and other medical schools, the total numbers of years for a medical degree were four and a half—one and a half years for the preclinical studies and three for the clinicals. Medical students from Oxford also went to London medical schools for clinicals as Oxford was a small city like Cambridge. There was no problem enrolling for clinicals at any London medical school for students from Cambridge or Oxford as the admission was almost guaranteed and the medical schools reserved a certain number of spots for them.

I enrolled at Westminster Medical School, which does not exist anymore, located close to the House of Parliament and its Big Ben clock. I rented a room at the International Students House (ISH), located south of Regent's Park across from the tube station of Great Portland Street. The room was on the second floor and overlooked the entrance of the four-story property, the street, and the tube station. Rooms were relatively cheap for the location as it was run by a charitable volunteer organization, but you could stay there only for one year. I took a bus in the morning that went past the House of Parliament to a stop close to the medical school. ISH had some British students but was mostly comprised of international students from all over the world and was a very lively place with a spacious cafeteria that served breakfast, lunch, and dinner for low prices and was also a convenient place to meet students from other countries. It had various entertainment facilities like a large TV hall with chairs like in a movie theater, an indoor sports gym to play table tennis and badminton, a large discotheque hall, an evening bar, a library for studying, and a large relaxing room with large windows and comfortable couches on the second floor on the side facing Regent's Park.

At the beginning of September 1972, I started my medical clinicals at Westminster Hospital, the main hospital of Westminster Medical School. Each medical student wore a short white coat with wide square side pockets and a small plastic name tag pinned in front near the collar. I carried a stethoscope curled up in one pocket and a small reflex hammer in the other. The reflex hammer consisted of a triangular red rubber piece attached to a metal handle and was used to test for tendon reflexes in diagnosing neurological disorders. There was a small front pocket on the coat where I kept a pen for writing and a small penlight to look into patient's throats and test pupillary reflexes as part of the physical exam. The medical teaching staff, housemen, and registrars wore long white coats to differentiate themselves from the medical students, who were at the bottom of the medical hierarchy totem pole and the least respected, if at all, by the nursing staff.

My first introductory clerkship was in general medicine with four other students, and we learned the basics of taking a proper detailed medical history from a patient; performing a physical examination; formulating a differential diagnosis, or what diseases could account for the history and the physical findings; and ordering appropriate tests to find the real cause of the problem and treat it. The attendant claimed we could diagnose almost eighty percent of diseases by a detailed history and physical examination. One of my first invasive procedures was to help the houseman, called an intern in America, take blood samples from patients on the floor, fill different colored tubes depending on the types of tests ordered, label the tubes, and place them in a plastic basket for lab pick up. The most common blood tests ordered initially were for hemoglobin, blood count, electrolytes, and liver and kidney function.

The medical wards were spacious with patient beds lined up on either side of the wall and a nursing station in the middle of a sprawling rectangular hall so one nurse could watch many patients. There were curtains that slid on overhead rods that went around a few feet along the periphery of the bed to give privacy to the patient when they were examined but were kept open for the initial history-taking part.

After about two months of introduction in general medicine, five of us went to general surgery under the preceptorship of Professor Harold Ellis, the professor of surgery for three months. This was my most memorable rotation as the professor was a brilliant surgeon in his mid-forties who loved to teach. I bought the book that he had coauthored with Professor Roy Calne, now Professor Sir Roy Calne, called the *Lecture Notes on General Surgery*, and he taught us the proper and methodical way to take a surgical history and to do a physical examination. He had two strict rules, one for the patient and one for the student. Any patient who wanted to see him—many were famous people and members of the parliament and government ministers who wanted him to treat them as he was one of the best in his field— must first be seen by one of his medical students who would take a full history and perform a full physical examination. There were no exceptions to this rule, even if you were the prime minister. All the high and mighty meekly accepted this caveat. The professor was a moral man of impeccable integrity and fully dedicated to his craft and to the National Health Service (NHS) and did not play games like some other professors who performed surgery on a private basis, often on rich foreign clientele for high reimbursement at Harley Clinic while drawing their NHS salaries.

All the students under him had to do a rectal examination as part of the patient's abdominal exam and for a good reason, as one-third of cancers of the colon, a common cancer in England, were found in the rectum and could be caught early by doing so. It could also detect prostate cancer. A rectal exam was the most painful, unpleasant, and embarrassing part of an examination both for the patient and the new timid student. But to learn the difference between the normal and the abnormal, and if even one cancer like a rectal ulcer or polyp was discovered early, it could mean the difference between life and death for the patient. Not only was it the most hated part, but it also was worse if you were a male student and the patient was a female or vice versa; then you felt even more embarrassed to ask them for their permission to do so. However, Professor Ellis told us that the British patient was very compliant and cooperative, and he was right on that point as in all my clinical years, I never came across any patient who refused to cooperate.

A case in point as to how strict Professor Ellis was about a proper complete history and physical examination occurred when the only female student in our group presented her patient who was a prominent government minister. The professor's routine was that all the students met in his office after they had completed histories and physicals on their patients who were in separate private rooms. He would lead them to the first room where the relevant student presented his case to all the remaining four students and the professor. When the female student presented her case, she left out the rectal exam findings. Everyone became quiet as they knew what was coming next. The professor waited for a few moments and looked at her and asked, "What did you find on the rectal exam?" The lady looked embarrassed, red in the face, and didn't say a word. The professor turned to the patient, a prominent government minister, seated at the edge of the examination couch, and told him, "Miss Kegan will examine your bowels," and walked out of the room as we meekly followed suit. No one in our group ever avoided that part of the exam thereafter. The same problem with rectal exams afflicted male students when it came to the breast exams of female patients that had to be done. We had to compare each quadrant of one breast with the other breast using the flat of a hand to feel for any lumps or differences.

Some mornings, we spent time in the operating room with Professor Ellis. We observed the anesthetist, anesthesiologist in America, put the surgical patient lying on the operating table to sleep in a separate room adjoining the operating room and then wheel them into the operating room as we followed him. He then connected the patient to the anesthesia machine.

We were always learning, like in the case of one abdominal surgery. The nurse introduced us to a Foley catheter used to drain the bladder and told us not to forget to replace the prepuce back to its original position after retracting it for placement, otherwise "the penis will fall off," an implausible claim to ensure we would not forget it.

The professor wanted absolute respect for the patient being operated on and did not like when negative comments were made. One morning, he was operating to excise the whole colon of a five-year-old Indian boy with a heart-wrenching history of unremitting ulcerative colitis and failed medical treatments. When the abdomen was opened, the colon was swollen and inflamed like an over-distended bicycle tire tube and full of blood. The anesthetist, who was also the chief of anesthesia, made a derogatory comment, saying that it was due to the boy eating curry. The professor, while concentrating on the operation and without looking up, deftly deflected this faux pas by narrating how some of his friends had recently gone to an Indian restaurant, and they all raved about how delicious the curry was, and he planned to go there himself and try it soon. The anesthetist, red in the face as seen around the side of his surgical mask, stooped his head down under the drapes, separating him from the surgical field and never looked up or said another word till the end of the case. If someone knew real diplomacy, it was the professor. In the next three decades, curry would become the most favorite food of the British to rival the iconic fish and chips, and in 2001, Foreign Secretary Robin Cook would declare Chicken Tikka Masala to be "a true British national dish."

Professor Ellis worked very hard and operated on weekends or any day to help a patient. One anecdotal story was about an injured coal miner he came to examine at three a.m. in his pajamas, and the patient asked if he was the night shift. "No," he said, "I'm the day shift."

He had two housemen for his surgical ward patients; each worked a twenty-four-hour shift. You needed extraordinary credentials to be hired by the professor to be his houseman as he expected them to work as hard as he did, and once they completed their housemanship, they could virtually get into any surgery or other residency. The houseman was the lowest person in the medical graduate's hierarchy as he had recently graduated from medical school and admitted all the patients to the floor for the consultant surgeon. One of his housemen was an Indian who told me that he was born in Nigeria, and I learned a lot from him as he would tell me which patients had interesting histories and physical signs to learn from. I told him I knew someone from Nigeria once, without elaborating of course, and I wondered if Norbert had gotten the idea for his convoluted story about my adoption by Nigerian parents because there were Indians living in Nigeria, like most other parts of Africa, as this houseman told me.

During my surgery rotation, I realized the envy and internal tensions that existed in the medical and surgical hierarchies. Professor Ellis was the professor and head of the surgery department that he had established at the Westminster Medical School in the early sixties as he had proven himself with his skills, research, dedication, and hard work. His closest rival was a smart English surgeon, next in rank in the surgery department, Assistant Professor Christopher Wastel, who mainly specialized in gastrointestinal surgery, especially for duodenal ulcers, a common surgical condition of those days. He was always envious of Professor Ellis for obvious reasons. We went on rounds with Wastel at a smaller hospital in the medical school chain where he performed most of his surgeries, and one day, he could not help taking a cheap potshot at the professor when he told us at one of his teaching rounds, with almost ten students standing in front of him, that Professor Ellis performed elective surgery on Christmas because he was Jewish. Someone behind quietly whispered that was why he was the professor. Ostensibly, Wastel, red in the face, had heard that and demanded to know who said it, but it was all hush and quiet. Professor Ellis is now ninety-two and teaches anatomy at King's College Medical School in London.

After the surgery clerkship, we moved back to internal medicine clerkship for another three months. We were always learning about new medical problems, their symptoms, and their treatments with frequent rounds and different medical professors and registrars, who took us to patients with interesting symptoms. We then sat around the instructor in a group, and he would question us about the case, like why the patient's pulse was slow and how we would treat it. If no one could answer, then he would explain. The stress was always on a thorough history and a physical examination.

We visited a heavy patient who had been admitted with a heart attack the night before, and he was questioned by the medical registrar about what he had experienced. He stated that he had gotten a sudden, severe mid-chest pain and tightness with difficulty breathing, like an elephant had a foot on his chest, and he felt like he was going to die. He had been admitted pale and perspiring profusely, but intravenous pain medication had made him feel better. After the round and examining the patient's heart, the registrar took us to a private conference room to discuss the case. He told us that after administering oxygen with a soft mask, the patient had been given a dose of intravenous heroin, or diamorphine, to alleviate the pain that simply caused more stress on the damaged heart. He said it was superior to morphine, the usual drug commonly used for such cases, in that it was stronger and did not have the side effect of nausea or vomiting caused by morphine. He explained a common feeling of "impending doom" in cases of heart attacks, as the patient had stated he thought he was going to die. That helped to distinguish it from other causes of similar pain like an ulcer. Then he narrated the known causes of heart disease in those days, using his fingers one by one to enumerate—smoking; a diet rich in saturated fats like red meats; a sedentary lifestyle; obesity, though many thin people also got them; and high blood pressure. In those days, it was not known, or commonly suspected, that another real culprit was sugar and other factors were also discovered later.

I noticed that the registrar was somewhat obese, and it made me realize that if we were to impart advice to patients, especially about lifestyle changes, then we must first follow them ourselves because the patients were not stupid and would see through our hypocrisy, like a doctor who smoked yet advised patients against smoking. It made me realize the importance of preventive medicine—an ounce of prevention was better than a pound of cure, and it gave me the idea to take advantage of the new knowledge I was acquiring to take good care of my own body, at least for those medical conditions that could be prevented, and treat my body as a gift of nature to be preserved for the long haul.

We were always encouraged to read patients' charts or ask the houseman about patients with interesting medical problems and then go and see the patients and examine them for any signs or symptoms. The patients were always helpful and cooperative. They were in bed the whole day and were happy to see a visitor. I visited one patient in a private room, a lady in her fifties, to examine her enlarged liver and other signs of liver failure because she was dying of liver cancer that was caused by cirrhosis, which in turn was caused by heavy drinking. I read her history in her chart, and after introducing myself and getting some more history from her, I looked for signs of liver failure. Her abdomen was bulging somewhat from fluid accumulating, and her liver was hard, irregular, enlarged, and rough from the cirrhosis. After the exam, I talked to her for a while about her drinking habits. She said that during the WWII, she worked as one of the secretaries for Sir Winston Churchill, who drank heavily, and his cabinet was well stocked with alcohol, especially whiskey, so she helped herself when he was not around and became an alcoholic because of her access to alcohol that otherwise would have been impossible during the war. She was paying the price of her folly and lamented and wondered why heavy drinking had not affected Sir Winston. I told her I had no idea and that different drugs, here alcohol, could affect each person differently, like the fact that not all smokers got lung cancer. Then I added that maybe Sir Winston had a tough liver that destroyed alcohol rapidly. I was not sure if she knew the gravity and incurability of her condition, as in those days, patients with cancer were not told they had cancer, even when on their deathbed.

After the medical clerkship, we moved to do gynecology clinicals for three months. Gynecology primarily dealt with the health and diseases of the female reproductive system. To teach us an integral part of gynecology, how to do an internal examination, commonly called a vaginal examination, we were taken to the operating room where all the students, six in all, had to do the exam in turn after the gynecology registrar did it on a patient under anesthesia with her legs up in stirrups awaiting a gynecological procedure, often a common procedure called dilatation and curettage, or D&C, to scrape the uterus. It was after that you did an exam on patients in the office setting under supervision. The rationale of so many students doing a vaginal exam on an unconscious patient confounded me, and I wondered if the patent was fully informed and signed consent to allow this, though the general hospital surgical consent stated that, but I was not sure if the patients read all the wording or if they just signed it. I wondered if the medical school could just pay women volunteers for this purpose because an unconscious patient was relaxed from the anesthesia and that was not a realistic setting for such exams done in conscious patients in an office setting.

Most of the patients were first seen by a medical student who took down a detailed gynecological and obstetric history and presented the case to the gynecology professor or the registrar who took further history to fill up any gaps and did an internal exam, telling the student his findings, like an ovarian cyst and its size, and what to feel for. Then the student did so under his supervision. One strict rule was a female nurse was always present during the examination. This made the patient feel comfortable and also the nurse ensured nothing was done that was not within the scope of accepted standards.

The gynecology rotation was to prepare us for the next important clerkship, obstetrics, or the branch of medicine that dealt with pregnancy, childbirth, and the postpartum period after childbirth.

Chapter 8

The House of Midwives

Before the Cambridge medical students went to London to start their clinicals, the medical school gave each of us a booklet with a hard gray cover that had instructions with specifications about all the medical clerkships they had to complete. The ophthalmology clerkship required six weeks of training in the ophthalmology department, and the general surgery required six months. When all the clerkships were completed in three years, the booklet with all the blank lines filled in and signed by the respective directors of the departments was to be submitted to the Cambridge Faculty of Medicine, which then certified that the student had completed his requisites in clinical medicine and now could take the final clinical medical and surgical examination to graduate as a physician, or a medical graduate, who could then practice medicine within confines of a teaching hospital under the preceptorship of a consultant physician.

Obstetrics was an onerous clinical clerkship because it required certification that the student had delivered thirty babies, an ostensibly large number. Most physicians in the UK in those days became general practitioners and would likely have to deliver babies, so the medical school wanted to make sure they were proficient in deliveries as the safety of the mother and the baby depended on it. In a teaching hospital, even though they are large, there weren't that many deliveries to satisfy such a number because if there were fifty students that meant fifteen hundred deliveries were needed in three months. Where do you go to deliver so many babies?

To solve this conundrum, my London medical school, the Westminster Medical School, sent some students to other hospitals in the suburbs of London with busy obstetrics services. I ended up at Queen Mary's Hospital in Roehampton. For two months, I was sent with two other students to a smaller sister hospital, located a few miles from Queen Mary's that was primarily a training facility for midwives and specialization in obstetrics for a few physicians. Queen Mary's gave us a house with four rooms that was close to the midwives' training hospital, but I still needed to take a bus to get there as walking would take considerable time.

Many babies in the UK were delivered by midwives who were nurse-specialists in pregnancy, delivery of babies for uncomplicated pregnancies, and postpartum care of the mother and the baby. While most babies were delivered in hospitals, a significant number were delivered at homes based on the mother's preference. At this smaller peripheral hospital, the only patients were pregnant women who came to deliver, and almost all the deliveries were done by midwife students who were nurses specializing to become midwives. Over fifty percent were Chinese nurses from Singapore and Hong Kong where most of the deliveries were also done by midwives. They came to Great Britain for their training because of its great practical training programs in this field. It was a symbiotic relationship as it filled up the training spots as there was a dearth of British nurses to fill them, and the overseas nurses were in great demand back home when they returned after graduating as midwives because of their British degrees. Some stayed back to work for the NHS, which was chronically short of qualified medical staff.

One such person, Sister Shu, a midwife supervisor responsible for my training, was a thin, handsome spinster in her early thirties. She wore the traditional nursing paper hat on her well-groomed hair, a blue and white striped dress up to her knees, and a white apron in front. A nursing supervisor was addressed as "Sister" because before nursing became a separate profession, deliveries and medical care were often rendered by nuns. Sister Shu called me to her office located at a corner near some delivery rooms on my first day for a brief interview and explained to me the training procedures and rules and told me to first watch a delivery by a midwife student delivering under her supervision. That happened soon that afternoon as there was no shortage of deliveries here as the family practice doctors, called general practitioners or GPs, also sent their patients here for deliveries. Most did not really deliver them personally as that was done by the midwife students under supervision by the sisters, and occasionally they made a perfunctory visit to simply watch in their office suits and ties and comment as necessary.

One such patient having her third baby was admitted in active labor having regular contractions and was intermittently self-administering some nitrous oxide, a mild gaseous anesthetic, through a black rubber mask at the start of the contractions. The GP, Sister Shu, and I watched as her legs were up in stirrups and the student midwife was hovering near her to deliver the baby. Sister Shu did an internal exam after putting on gloves and said she was fully dilated and ready to push. With each contraction, as Shu felt the abdomen with her hand, the mom was asked to push. We could see the crown of the baby's head visible at the dilating vaginal opening, which regressed after the contraction was over. With further contractions, the crown was visible at all times and eventually, the head popped out. With further encouragement to the mother to push during the contractions, the whole baby was delivered by the student and the umbilical cord was cut with scissors and clamped. The baby was cleaned, clothed, and handed to the happy mother to hold on her chest. The placenta was delivered within the next twenty minutes as the happy mother held her cute baby, now wrapped in a warm blanket, over her chest.

After that first encounter, I rarely saw Sister Shu as most of the teaching was done by other senior midwife students and experienced midwives. My daily routine was to take full care of a pregnant mother admitted in the morning in labor, usually having her first baby because their labor was usually long, often lasting eight hours or more.

I would take and document a gynecological and obstetric history, examine the mother's pregnant abdomen, and do the initial internal examination after the midwife had done so I could estimate the dilatation correctly. The dilatation was estimated by spreading the index and the middle finger like a V at the edges of the dilating circular cervix opening, feel its rims across the diameter, and estimate the length, with each fingertip length being one centimeter. A full dilatation was ten centimeters. There were other parameters used to gauge the progress of labor, like the baby's station, the position of the crown of the head in relation to the ischial spines, the bones on the side of the lower part of the mother's pelvis, that could be felt during the internal exam. A zero station was when the crown was at the level of the ischial spines.

To listen to the baby's heartbeats and count the heart rate, I was taught to use a stethoscope called a Pinard stethoscope, a hollow cone with its top cut out and a flat circular part, like a metal washer, at the round opening where the ear could rest. It was about eight inches long and made of aluminum and worked like an ear trumpet that amplified sound. To use it, I first palpated the mom's abdomen to find the baby's round head, usually found at the lower part of the abdomen, as the baby's upper back was a few inches above that. I placed the round horn part of the fetal stethoscope at the position on the upper back as the heart was under it and gently pressed my ear onto the flat top and changed the pressure applied or the position of the stethoscope till I could hear the amplified baby's heartbeats. It took some practice getting used to listening to fetal tones. Then I took the mother's heart rate at the wrist and documented both on a flow sheet attached to a clipboard. That was to make sure the fetal heart rate was not confused with the mom's heartbeat as sometimes the stethoscope picked the mom's abdominal aortic pulse, confusing the issue. I took the heart rates after the contraction was over to make sure the fetal heart rate did not slow down abnormally, which could mean the baby was in trouble, like not getting enough oxygen from cord strangulation. I noticed that some experienced obstetricians simply used their regular stethoscope to listen to the fetal heartbeats on the mom's abdomen.

Mothers in labor were tough to bear the pains of contractions. One mother could not stand the pain and was so out of control that the anesthetist was called. He sat her up at the side of the bed, inserted a large needle in her low back followed by a catheter, taped it to her back, injected some anesthetic through it, and the mother calmed down.

After delivery, the mothers were admitted to a postpartum hospital nearby to recover and bond with their babies. The midwife students learned to take care of the babies and instructed the mothers in the baby's care and feeding. One evening, I went to see a mom as part of the postpartum visit and to check on her baby that I had delivered. On my way, a thought struck me about midwives, like an epiphany.

Midwives also dealt with the sexual health of women, and as I walked toward the postpartum hospital along a clear path cutting across an expansive lush green lawn, I wondered that with such a dearth of men in this place, who were as rare here as a full moon, what views did these young women, many good looking and pretty, hold about sex and men? Were they puritanical, permissive, or "normal," depending on my definition? With a lack of sexual experience, my definition was a puritanical woman would not have sex until married, a permissive woman would agree right away, like a man in a woman's body, and a "normal" woman would want an established a relationship first and perhaps want love. It was a mystery to me as none of them had behaved abnormally to me in any way so far. They were just nice, polite, and helpful—more so than nurses at the large sprawling medical centers. Then I thought I was conjecturing too much and that they were probably just "normal" by my definition— wanting a relationship and to likely be in love first before having sex. But I wondered how that was possible with such a skewed male-to-female ratio.

To solve this mystery and my deep curiosity, I felt I had to get to know some of them. At this juncture, the midwives reminded me of what Sir Winston Churchill had said about Russia in 1939, something like "a riddle, wrapped in a mystery, inside an enigma, but perhaps there is a key." With *Russia* replaced by *midwife*, after a month in this place, I discovered some of the midwife students' quirky sexual predilections and peccadillos and the "key" or the likely reasons for such behaviors. To my surprise, I would discover that they did not fit into any of my three conjectured categories.

When I went up the several steps of the brick cottage hospital at the end of the pathway, I asked a petit, somewhat plain-looking Chinese midwife student hurrying down the steps, apparently leaving for the evening, where I could find my patient. Instead of just telling me, she turned back and walked me to the patient who had just finished breastfeeding her baby. I thanked the student, and she left with a quick smile and no words. After I talked to the patient for a few minutes about how she was doing, examined the abdomen to feel the size of the shrinking uterus, and inquired about the baby and feeding, I left to document my findings in her chart at the nursing station.

When I left the building, the midwife student was waiting outside at the bottom of the front steps, looking at me, but I wasn't sure if she was waiting for another nurse friend who might be leaving for the evening. I stopped to thank her again for going the extra distance to take me to the patient and asked her name, and she said Jun, but it sounded like the name of the month, June. We talked for a while, and she told me she was from Hong Kong, and I told her about my background, and then we strolled down the pathway toward the main hospital as I thought she was going there. She was surprisingly talkative and friendly. We reached a cute two-story cottage-style brick house, and she stopped and said she lived there. I told her that I had to take a bus back to my dorm house that was a few miles away. We chatted some more when a pretty midwife student, taller than Jun with shoulder-length hair, emerged from the house and walked toward us. Jun introduced her as Lin, who was from Singapore. Jun asked me if I was in a hurry, and I said definitely not, and she invited me in.

The house had an expansive living room, almost a hall, on the ground floor with a dining room with a long wooden table and chairs to the left of the entry and to the right was a kitchen. In the rear were stairs that Jun said led to six bedrooms on the second floor where they lived, and each midwife was assigned their own a private room. She said her room adjoined with Lin's and the significance of this comment would become apparent to me later. Jun asked me if I wanted to eat with them as all midwife students cooked their own meals in the kitchen, and they had food left over from the day before. With no place to eat around the area, it was always a challenge to find food so occasionally I went to eat at the main Queen Mary's Hospital that had a staff cafeteria. I was apologetic that I did not want to take their food, but Jun insisted it was no problem as they always made more than needed and I was welcome to share with them. I accepted her gracious offer and hospitality as I was starving. We sat at the table in the side dining room, and they left for a short while and returned with three bowls of warmed vegetable fried rice and noodles. The homemade meals were delicious, and I complimented them on being such excellent cooks. They said they had to cook as that was the only way they could make Chinese food they liked, and it saved on the cost.

After we finished eating, they took the dishes back to the kitchen and on return asked me if I wanted to go to the adjoining living room to talk some more and relax. Again, I loved the offer, and I sat in the living room, Jun and Lin sitting on one sofa and I on a small couch facing them across a small coffee table. We talked some more, and I found that while Jun was a chatty type, Lin was reticent and did not say much. However, one thing became clear; they were close friends.

It was getting late as the bus service ceased after nine o'clock at night, and I told them that I had to leave as I was worried about missing the last bus. However, Jun said I need not worry about that as I could stay there. That took me by surprise because the couch was too small for me to sleep on. I looked around confused, looking at where I could sleep and staring at the lush carpet. Jun saw my confusion, smiled, and told me I would not sleep on the carpet but in Lin's room! I looked more confused, thinking she was teasing, and looked at Lin for her reaction, and there was a slight smile as if she did not mind the comment. Why would Jun be offering me, who just met them this evening, to sleep in her best friend's room? Then she said she meant I could sleep on the floor with a comforter as a pad in her room. I was even more confused because here I was a young guy full of testosterone, and here was a young girl, and if I slept in her room, even on the floor, it could lead to fireworks. I made the excuse that I had to get some papers from my room at the dorm house when I returned the next day so I had to leave. They did not seem to mind, and I thanked them and bid them goodnight, telling them we would all meet again. Jun said she was off the next day. I went to the deserted bus stop that was on the main road across from the back part of the house and waited almost half an hour without any sign of the bus and got worried that the bus service had stopped for the night as it was already nine o'clock. I felt I should have accepted Jun's offer and started hesitantly walking toward the house. Halfway there, I heard the roar of a speeding bus and ran back to catch it.

The next morning, I returned and found that there was no one in labor so Sister Shu said I could have the day off. I went to the house of the midwives to see if Jun wanted to go out to London to see some sites with me as I had not done that for a long time. I entered the main hall after opening the heavy wooden entry door of the house and saw her friend Lin coming down the stairs at the rear in street clothes. I asked her if Jun was around and where I could find her as she said she had the day off. Lin said she went to work to cover for a friend and asked if she could give her any message from me. I said I was bored and hoped to ask her to go out for some sightseeing in London. Lin said Jun had a boyfriend so I looked a little disappointed and said sorry as she had never mentioned that the day before, but then Lin said she was off and would like to go to London for sightseeing. I readily agreed, and she went to her room and returned with a camera to take pictures. Then Lin gave me some more details about the boyfriend and said his name was Chen and that he was basically a Chinese version of me and occasionally stayed over at night with Jun, like she was rubbing in the point that he was really her boyfriend.

It was a cold day in October of 1973. I had my tricolor Trinity Hall scarf around my neck and wore my brown jacket, and Lin wore a shorter brown furry coat. We took several buses and trains and reached central London and walked around to various tourist spots like the Piccadilly Circus, the Buckingham Palace, and the Trafalgar Square where there were many tourists milling around taking pictures. Lin took my picture with her camera and then she gave her camera to a tourist to take a picture of both of us together. After a long day, it was dark when we reached Queen Mary's Hospital and took another bus that would drop me off at my house and Lin a few miles to her place. I disembarked at the bus stop next to my dorm house after thanking her for a wonderful day and went into the dark house as my other two colleagues were rarely home and often stayed at Queen Mary's Hospital where there were many rooms for medical students and on-call staff physicians. However, when I closed the door behind me, I saw the bus had not yet left but paid no attention to it.

I was exhausted from all the walking and changed into my night cotton pajamas and got under the thick blanket of my bed to warm up and soon fell asleep. Then I thought I heard the door of the house open and close gently but had difficulty opening my eyes from drowsiness and thought I was dreaming and fell asleep again, thinking that one of my colleagues had returned unexpectedly. Again, I thought I was dreaming when another body slipped under the blanket next to me and untied my pajama string and started massaging me with a soft, warm hand. It felt good and that woke me up. The body next to me was naked and warm and soon our lips were locked, and it was on top of me. I had fallen asleep later, and when I woke up in the morning, I was alone.

When I went to the midwives' hospital that morning, I was assigned to a real nice young English lady having her first baby in a side delivery room. By now, I was doing deliveries on my own and often there was no one to supervise as everyone was busy or they saw I was competent. I monitored the mom the whole day, and when six o'clock in the evening came around, she was fully dilated. I asked her to start pushing with her contractions. She was one tough lady who never complained about the painful contractions because she was so thrilled at the final result. I saw the baby's head stuck and cut an episiotomy after administering some xylocaine and the baby's head then popped out after some more contractions. After I handed the baby to the mom for feeding, the placenta popped out easily, and I closed the episiotomy. When I handed her the baby, she said she felt as if she were the first woman to have a baby. The husband never came, as this was common. Her fortitude in those difficult ten hours convinced me that women were much stronger than men—maybe not in physical strength but in most other respects, especially tolerating pain. *Would I be able to carry a baby for nine months and go through all this? No way,* I thought. After a while, a midwife student came and helped me clean up, and we took the mom to a postpartum room, and the student took the baby to the nursery.

Then I walked down the path to the house of the midwives to see Lin, and when I entered the house, Jun was in the living room and stood there almost glaring at me, as if annoyed at me and did not respond to my greeting. I worried now that Lin told her about our tryst the day before, but why would that bother Jun who already had a boyfriend who occasionally slept overnight with her according to Lin?

"Chen is not my boyfriend," she blurted out, looking at me sternly.

"But Lin said he was your boyfriend because I had come to ask you if you wanted to go to London with me for sightseeing."

"He was long ago. Seven years ago—but we are just friends now."

"Lin said he stays overnight with you. That is not my business."

"He does. At night his penis gets hard like a rock, but he does not want to have sex. He says he is too used to me and I feel the same."

This frank admission of the nature of their relationship surprised me. It appeared Lin had exaggerated their relationship to dampen my interest in Jun. I was now apologetic and said, "I'm sorry and apologize for any misunderstanding. I did not know that."

"I'll accept your apology and believe you it if you stay with me tonight. But don't just lie there if your organ gets hard. Don't let it go to waste."

"You won't have to worry about that. I'm not Chen. I haven't known you for seven years."

Now she smiled.

Again, surprised at this blunt, no-nonsense approach and barrage from Jun, it was obvious what she wanted, and I was happy to oblige and dutifully followed her up to her room upstairs. There was a long hallway upstairs with rooms on either side. Jun's room was at the far end to the left of the hallway, and when we passed the room before hers, she said it was Lin's room.

We must have been asleep for many hours, and it was later in the night when I woke up and felt frisky again and grabbed her, but she said I should go to Lin's room. This again surprised me as I thought she was happy I was with her, but she wanted me to go over to Lin. So, I went to Lin's room, opened the door, and slipped under her blanket for the rest of the night, and Lin took care of my friskiness. Lin was rough, and I felt sore in the back and had long bruise lines but accepted it as a cost of getting pleasure.

The next day was a Saturday, and I met Chen for the first time, and as Lin had said, he was like my Chinese doppelganger. He was a kind of quiet and friendly guy and did not seem to be bothered that I was with his friend Jun. I was still trying to figure out the relationship between Jun and Lin as it seemed they were joined at the hip, almost always together.

The following Saturday morning, Chen came with another poker-faced skinny Chinese boy, about five-eight, who, like a mute, hardly spoke anything, and his face was flat with a flat nose like a chimpanzee's. If there was any doubt in my mind that humans had evolved from apes or chimpanzee-like creatures like they had taught us at the Cambridge medical school, this guy laid my doubts to rest. Chen introduced him to me as Raja. That baffled me as I told him Raja was an Indian name, as my younger brother's name was Raj, and we called him Raja, or "king" in Punjabi. Chen jested that maybe he was an Indian in his previous life. Raja remained unamused and silent.

Later, Jun talked to Chen and invited me to accompany them to the local public fresh produce market to buy fresh vegetables and groceries to cook lunch. I was happy to go and insisted that I would like to pay for some of it as I was the beneficiary of their cooking, and Jun happily accepted my offer. Chen, Jun, and I went to the market, but Lin and Raja stayed behind. At first, we were busy chatting and did not think anything about it. A day later, Jun told me that Lin had told her when we left for the market, she had slept with Raja.

Some days later, Chen came over and stayed overnight with Jun. The next day, Jun told me that at night, he had gotten a hard on and so she had told him to go over to Lin's room to relieve himself, which he had never done before because she had never asked him to do so. After a while, he had returned, had shaken his head, and had said he had felt mauled by a tiger as Lin had been so rough he had red bruises on his glutei. Chen had vowed it was his first and last time with Lin—in bed. I told Jun I had had a milder experience of Lin's nail abrasiveness when she had sent me over. I found it amusing that Lin told everything to Jun who relayed it to me to complete the circle. There were no secrets here. It seemed Jun was Lin's mentor, or spiritual guru.

Then Jun said Lin had a boyfriend in Singapore and when she left, they had a pact to write one love letter to each other every week to keep their relationship steamy, and they had complied with the pact up to date for the year she had been in England. She showed me a thick stack of love letters from the boyfriend on a dresser in Lin's room. That confused me even more as Lin already had Chen, Raja, and me under her skirt yet she was in love with her boyfriend back home. Jun explained that to Lin, we were simply bed-proxies for her homeboy thousands of miles away and that she felt she was with him when she was in bed with another!

One day, I finished early at around three o'clock in the afternoon and sat at a desk in Jun's room, studying our obstetrics and gynecology textbook to keep current with what we were supposed to know. No one locked their doors here, day or night. You could simply walk in, even if occasionally the door was closed; no questions were asked, and no one was offended. Half an hour later, Jun and Lin walked in holding hands, and Jun said they were bored and wanted to have a threesome with me—something I had never heard of or imagined what it really meant. Lin remained quiet and pensive. These girls never ceased to amaze me with their antics.

I thought they were kidding, so I joked, "Ok, let's fuck."

Jun was taken aback and retorted, "Now, now, we are not those kinds of girls."

"Oh, no! I meant you are good girls. I'm a bad boy."

Before I stood up, the quiet Lin had already disrobed and lay on the bed and soon Jun, with her skinny shorter body, did the same and lay next to her. This was the first time I saw Lin's stupendous body in the daylight. It was during this tryst that I would find out some of Jun's quirks and her game plan because unlike Lin, she was not a particularly sexual person.

The threesome started with Jun, but soon she told me to go over to Lin as it became obvious Jun liked watching the two of us in action as if it were a game with two players, and she was the audience.

Jun then stood to the side of the bed, giving a running commentary. What their final game plan soon became obvious. After we were done and were talking, Lin, still in bed, told me, like an order, "Make me a baby." Jun said that Lin's maternal instinct was taking over and was very strong, and she wanted a baby. I refused as I did not want to get anyone pregnant.

One take away lesson I had learned from my gynecology rotation was to use protection to protect myself and the partner, not only to prevent pregnancy but to prevent infections. Jun then protested I should not use protection because Chen did not use it and told me he used the interruption method. I was confused about why they had not asked him to do the honors before I came around. It was obvious that the midwife students, delivering and taking care of the babies, became enamored to them and wanted to have their own. I was determined not to get anyone pregnant out of wedlock, and I was definitely not ready for prime time when it was a challenge just to pay for my bus fare to my dorm house. However, she just wanted me to make a baby for her and wanted nothing else from me.

But we were now like a small happy family of three—four when Chen showed up. However, I discerned some annoyance on the part of Jun and Lin for using protection. Then one day, Lin demanded of me, like a blunt ultimatum, "Can you bring more boys here?"

The only boy I could think of was my brother Sham, but this place was far, and I called him and told him that some girls wanted to be his friends. He came over after work on a Friday evening, and I left him there and went back to my dorm room, glad to be on my own for a change. Interestingly, Jun did not say anything about what transpired, probably because we were brothers, but from what I gathered from Sham, Jun had played the same game of making him vacillate between her and Lin at night. He left by Saturday morning.

One weekday evening, Jun proposed that all four of us, Jun, Lin, Chen, and I, go to another town at a house where several midwife students, including her friend Zhen, lived. We changed some trains to this town and arrived at the house and went into the kitchen where two midwife students were talking. One of them, who I assumed was Zhen, looked pleasantly surprised and greeted Jun.

Zhen, wearing a thin, loose evening silk gown, stood straight and was an astoundingly gorgeous girl with porcelain-smooth skin, a firm body with full cheeks, good-sized breasts like half coconuts, and lush lips. I wondered if she was in the wrong profession and should really be a high-prized model, or even an escort girl, instead of learning to deliver babies. She was the most beautiful midwife student I had seen so far. It was like, "Lady, are you lost? What are you doing here? This is the wrong place and the wrong line of work for you."

While Jun and Lin talked with her, I talked with the other midwife student, and Chen stayed quiet. Then we all went to Zhen's room as the three girls kept chatting animatedly, and when it was time to leave, Zhen asked Chen to stay. This baffled me as she had just met Chen. *What a lucky guy*, I thought, but sheepishly, Chen declined the offer. However, Zhen was persistent and kept cajoling him to stay like, "Please, you must stay," and refusing to take no for an answer. While they kept haggling with the poor, or should I say lucky, Chen, it was no dice, and I wished she would have asked me as I would have accepted immediately with gusto, but no such luck. I thought it might be because I was not Chinese. I wondered if Chen was being polite and didn't want to offend Jun by staying, but that seemed highly unlikely based on their relationship as just friends and how Jun had shoved him to Lin's room at night for a quickie.

Soon Jun was leading the way out, somewhat annoyed, as Zhen, in a final desperate attempt, pressed ahead repeatedly with her pleas to Chen to stay while he politely refused. I got an idea and stayed in the room while they all left toward the house entry door. I grabbed a pencil on the small table next to her bed in the room and quickly jotted down Zhen's phone number printed on a round part on her rotatory dial telephone on the desk. With the prized number in my front shirt pocket, I soon left the house with the rest as Zhen closed the door behind us, apparently disappointed Chen had let her down.

When we all returned, I excused myself and went to a hospital phone, pulled out the piece of paper from my pocket, and called Zhen, even though we had not even exchanged a word when I was there because of her inordinate obsession with Chen. Then I thought that she must be furious with Chen for letting her down and would seek revenge by allowing me to come over. So, I hesitantly called and told her I had just been to her place and asked her if I could come over—thinking I had nothing to lose except a no. Surprisingly, she said yes without hesitation, and I asked for directions. I was thrilled with excitement and rushed to the train station.

I was now twenty-four years old, and in a short span of a month, these two midwife students, Jun and Lin, though ostensibly younger than me but way ahead of their time, had transformed me from a growing boy into a man. My testosterone level was surging—I could feel it—and now came the ultimate temptation, like the forbidden fruit, in the form of the model-like Zhen who had no hesitation in accepting my request to come over. It was like I was mining for a gold nugget in the river and suddenly hit the mother lode.

When I reached the house where Zhen lived with other midwife students, I entered the unlocked front door and went straight to Zhen's room around the corner from the entry hallway. Zhen was standing near the bed, and I greeted her. She did not respond to it, and I went close to her and asked her if I could kiss her as I did not really know how to get the ball rolling. She said no politely, and that confused me as she had readily agreed for me to come over and had tried so hard to have Chen stay. So, I said, "Sorry, I did not mean to offend you," as I started rubbing her upper arm gently, and she started purring like she was getting excited. Then suddenly she said, "You don't ask. You just do it." I thought I was being polite and gentlemanly in seeking permission first, but to my surprise, she didn't want this gentlemanly foreplay stuff and wanted me to go into action immediately. Soon she was in her bed after removing her gown and flinging it to the side on the floor.

The young lady had the most stupendous picture-perfect body, and soon two bodies were on the bed as I had discarded my jacket, shirt, and everything else. However, she had the same golden rule that I subscribed to—that the mate use protection. Zhen in bed was loud and noisy—not just producing any noise, but a noise so loud it was like screaming, like someone being tortured and punished with excitement, which excited me even more but also worried me that everyone in the house and beyond could hear it—that loud. But she didn't seem to care. There were other midwives living in the house. Would they not come to check? When I was done, she said she was just getting started, and it seemed she had forgotten that nature had restricted the ability of the male species to certain time limits of performance after they reached their peak and needed a break. So, the only way I could think of to continue and satisfy her was to use the appendages similar to the real organ that nature had bestowed me.

I grabbed the plastic container of white body lotion cream on her table and used the lotion as lubricant and continued the action. The screaming got louder, so loud that I worried the police would break in anytime and arrest me. It was for so long my arm was tired and I sweat, but the lady could continue for the whole night. Eventually, tired, I stopped and went to take a bath as I was perspiring from the hard physical labor with my arm ready to fall off. The hallway was dark when I left the room, and all was quiet as if no one seemed to be disturbed by all the ruckus. With the hot and cold water taps of the bathtub fully opened and the gushing water, I slid into the bathtub and bathed myself with a soap bar. When I returned after drying myself with a towel and entered the room, Zhen, lying on the bed, blasted me. "Why did you make so much noise in the bath?" *Wow!* She sounded like the pot calling the kettle black.

A week later, Zhen showed up at the house of the midwives later in the afternoon when I was studying at Jun's table while Jun and Lin were at work. After the way she cajoled Chen to stay overnight, it didn't bother me at all if she divulged to the others our tryst as they all wanted the same thing. In this place, no one cared who did whom and exclusivity and jealousy were alien words.

"You gave me monilia," she accused me. Monilia was a vaginal infection caused by a fungus that looks like white curd.

"I don't have monilia. I used the raincoat you demanded, and I always do," I shot back, offended at this accusation.

"I went to see a gynecologist."

"So, the gynecologist made the diagnosis?"

"No, I told her that. Asked her to prescribe me nystatin." Nystatin was a drug used to treat monilia.

"Did she examine you to confirm your diagnosis?"

"No. I refused to be examined by a woman. She gave in after I insisted it was monilia. She prescribed nystatin."

Now that answered my question why most of the gynecologists were men as ostensibly many women did not want to be examined by other women in those days.

"Then why did you not see a male gynecologist because you need confirmation it was monilia before treating it."

"Can't do that."

I was astounded at this reasoning and said, "Look, you never had monilia. You wanted hand action, and I used the white cream on your table for lubrication. You saw that leaking out and assumed it was monilia because both look like a white cream."

"Oh! That makes sense. It disappeared before I used nystatin. After a bath."

I was glad the misunderstanding was cleared and felt reassured we were back in business. Then she pointed her index finger at me and confided, "I really appreciate the finger."

We heard the front main entry door open as Jun and Lin had returned from work. After dinner and a lot of chit-chat, it was bedtime, and Zhen decided to stay over. Jun, who had another antic up her sleeve, decided Lin should sleep in Jun's room while Zhen and I sleep in Lin's room!

Zhen raised no objection to such a proposition. As we headed to Lin's room next door, I heard Lin whisper to Jun that Zhen was noisy at night, like the news had spread. Evidently, they wanted to hear her out. We entered Lin's room and closed the door, and as I approached Zhen who was already in bed, she politely asked me to sleep on the floor as she could not help screaming and this was the wrong venue. However, Zhen did not return to the house after that night, and Jun and Lin were disappointed their game plan had failed as there was pin-drop silence in our room that night.

The situation started to get dicey for me. There was a party the midwives had one Friday evening in the main entry hall of the house where various midwife students and some midwife sisters were chatting. They were all dressed in their nice clothes. However, the party was conspicuous in what it lacked—men. However, they were all having a great time mingling around and chatting animatedly, and I saw Sister Shu and another lady chatting together at one corner across the stairs that led upstairs to the living quarters. I had recently noticed at work that when I occasionally bumped into Sister Shu and greeted or addressed her as "Sister," as I had been instructed to do, she looked annoyed like I was being rude. So, what would be a better way to make amends, for whatever was bothering her about me, then to meet her at this friendly social party? When I approached the two ladies and again greeted her as "Sister," she did not seem to be amused and told me in my ear, "You've got to stop calling me 'Sister' if you want to get physical with me." I was stunned as I'd never thought like that about her and that that was the real reason for her hostile response whenever I called her "Sister" on the hospital floors. Luckily, I saw Jun walking toward me looking upset that I was talking to Shu. She glared at Shu, who she hated, then furiously grabbed my hand and led me up the stairs to the living quarters where some other students were talking in the hallway and told me not to talk with Shu. I was worried and confused as the last person I wanted to make enemies with was my boss. The situation would soon worsen.

Jun was capricious. Two new midwife students from Hong Kong moved into two rooms at the far end of the hallway. They looked like young female dolls, and Jun asked me to go and "do them." I balked, worried things were out of hand, but I didn't want to offend Jun with an outright refusal. However, Jun tried to force the issue.

Once a week, I had to be on night call and had to stay at a nearby house with a room upstairs with on-call male registrars and a night nurse stationed at the front entry office. One call night, I had retired to the room and later heard some commotion downstairs but ignored it. Later, the night nurse told me she had refused entry to four girls who had wanted to visit me as this was prohibited and two had been dressed skimpily. Their description matched the two "dolls." The next day, Jun told me, "We came to visit you." I was able to deduce Jun's game plan and was worried about further implications, and my fears were realized when I took a bath in the bathroom with a large bathtub in the middle of the hallway where the midwife students lived on the second floor. When I came out, the matron of the midwifery school was heading toward me as our gazes met. She was an older English lady, and I was uncertain what I should do but stopped. The matron looked serious but did not say anything and climbed down the stairs to her right. When I went to Jun's room, she was irate and blasted me that I shouldn't be taking a bath here at this time as the matron was here. This was never a problem before as the matron never visited the place, and it happened after the ruckus when I was on call. Apparently, the night nurse had informed her superiors.

It became apparent to me that this facility had echoes of its origin—a nunnery—when men had been banned entry where the nuns had lived as nuns were supposed to be chaste. No wonder history was rife with tales of men visiting such places furtively, under the connivance of the nuns, to avoid detection by the more kosher mother superiors. My real fear was the certification of all my deliveries to the head of the obstetrics at Queen Mary's Hospital had to be submitted by the matron, and I could be in trouble after what the matron had seen. They were gracious to accept medical students, and I could jeopardize that for others in the future.

So, I asked Jun, "Can we all just be friends? Like guy friends. Like you and Chen are."

Jun agreed but seemed annoyed by this proposition, and I wondered if there would be some backlash or even retaliation. I worried that with her unpredictable nature, where it was her way or the highway, I would pay the price, but my two months at this school of midwives would end in a couple of weeks, and then I had to do one more month at Queen Mary's Hospital. I had already done a lot of deliveries, often on my own, and I felt very comfortable with my abilities to do normal deliveries. The further deliveries at Queen Mary's would be like extra icing on the cake.

On Friday of that week, I went to Jun's room in the evening to study, and a while later, Jun and Lin came in well dressed and asked me if I wanted to go dancing with them to a discotheque. I politely declined the offer as I really had to study, and they left without saying anything. I left the premises later to return to my dorm room, and the following day when I visited them, Jun told me that Lin had brought back a random guy she had danced with to her room and he had stayed overnight. He was a chubby English fellow who often started showing up in the evenings, and his focus was on Lin.

My two months at the midwives' school soon ended and I vacated my room at the house where I lived with two other medical students, and all of us all got rooms at the main Queen Mary's Hospital to complete our remaining month in obstetrics. I visited Jun and Lin infrequently as they were much further from Queen Mary's now. At Queen Mary's, we were supervised more closely and had many rounds in the wards with the obstetrics professors where we visited pregnant women admitted for various complications of pregnancy like severe preeclampsia or high blood pressure and anemia. About five of us would stand around the bed with the patient. The professor would question her and ask us questions to test our knowledge of the pregnancy-related problems the patient suffered from. Then he would examine the pregnant abdomen and ask us more questions as to our estimate of the baby's age, and he would demonstrate. We were also taught by obstetric registrars who supervised us with deliveries, and we watched them deal with complicated pregnancies like breech delivery where the baby came feet first.

Medical students had individual rooms along a hallway on the ground floor, and I was comfortable in my new designated room. One afternoon, another student knocked on my door to announce I had visitors. When I came out, I saw Jun and Lin heading down the hallway toward me, smiling. Once inside my room, Jun complained that my brother Sham had borrowed her blue leather suitcase with straps a while back and had not returned it. She needed it as they would soon be completing their studies and would return home to Singapore and Hong Kong. I apologized and promised to get it back for her.

Sham lived far from Roehampton where I was, and it was another two weeks before I could leave on a weekend to see him in Woolwich as I had to stay in the hospital on alternate weekends for deliveries. When I met him, he said that he had talked to Jun over the phone, and they had some altercation as she was furious he had not returned the suitcase. We both left to deliver the suitcase and to apologize to her in person, but when we reached her residence, it was deserted, and the rooms were locked so we left the suitcase' outside her door with a note of apology.

The following week, I was done with my three months of obstetrics and had delivered the required thirty deliveries and got my gray log book from Cambridge certified by the director of obstetrics at Queen Mary's Hospital. Sham and I returned to see Jun and Lin again the following weekend to offer our apologies in person for the suitcase, but they were gone, and I felt deep contrition that it had ended badly because of a misunderstanding over a delayed suitcase return and felt I should have been more proactive and faster in returning the suitcase when Jun first complained about it. Now, they had ostensibly gone back home, and I would return to my temporary home at the ISH.

Chapter 9

The Medical Graduate

At the end of 1973, after my three-month stint at Queen Mary's Hospital and the midwives' school, I returned to my room at the ISH on Great Portland Street in London, but my lease was ending because of my residency time limit. The head of the charitable organization that ran the house, Mr. Patterson, was a tall Englishman in his sixties with thick white hair who was a retired provincial commissioner from East Africa during the colonial rule and made occasional rounds of the place in the afternoons. He had agreed to consider my request for a lease extension for another year favorably as I was in medical school. ISH discouraged long-term stays as it was an affordable place for international students to stay, often on vacation. I did not see any problem as I was a quiet resident whose only occasional visitors in the evening were my two brothers. His only encounter with Sham and Raj was when they were climbing the broad winding stairs to the lounge on the second floor that overlooked the beautiful Regent's Park. Mr. Patterson was waddling down and asked Sham, "You live here?" Sham, in his zestful way, replied, "No. We are here just to watch the girls." The elderly gentleman was not amused.

My room was located on the second floor of the sprawling four-story white building that had a tall rectangular window with two panes.

The upper one was fixed, and the lower one opened up and down for a quick exit in case of a fire. The window overlooked Great Portland Street with a bus stop and a tube station across the street. An expansive horizontal flat roof, like a broad ledge, ran along the bottom of the wall of the second-floor rooms facing the street so you could get out of your open window and walk over it, but that was prohibited by the property's rules and regulations, and I had never seen anyone do that as it invaded another tenant's privacy. My small gay Spartan room had a closet to the right of the wooden entry door and a sofa bed along the wall next to it with a small desk and a chair across the bed along the opposite wall close to the window. The window curtain was open during the day time, and I occasionally enjoyed watching the outside hustle and bustle of the buses and people coming to and leaving ISH. The room's heating system consisted of hot water flowing through coils of three-foot vertical metal pipes located against the wall below the window and had two pipes on either lower edge holding it upright connected to the central water heating system pipes under the floor. The hot water flowing in the pipes radiated heat to the room, and when it was freezing outside, the first thing I did on entering the room was to grab the hot heater directly to warm my frozen hands. The room did not have a phone but had a buzzer system whereby the porter at the entry could call you in for a message, like a visitor's arrival, and the room was cleaned daily by some elderly Spanish maids.

I took a bus to the medical school in the morning at eight-thirty as in the past, and the house of midwives was now in the early stages of becoming a distant memory as I was busy at the medical school, studying in my room on returning in the afternoon. One cold afternoon, I returned from the medical school and went past the entry porter's glass booth to my left on the first floor manned by an aging Indian student and took a left through the expansive lobby to the wooden mailboxes located on a wall across the stairs to the upper three residential floors. After picking my mail, I climbed the stairs to the second-floor landing and made a right into the main carpeted hallway with a wall telephone. I went past the entry door to the restrooms and stall showers and reached my room located above the porter's lodge. As I fumbled for my room key in my pants' pocket, I heard the room buzzer, but by the time I retrieved the key and entered, the buzzer was quiet, so I hurried back to the wall phone to call the porter and inquired the reason for his call.

"You had a visitor. I told her you were not in," he said in an Indian accent.

"But I'm here," I said.

"You did not answer the buzzer," he responded.

"Did she give her name?" I was curious because I did not have a girlfriend or knew of any girl who would have liked to visit me.

"No. When I asked her to leave a message, she said never mind and left."

"How did she look?"

"A tall, beautiful oriental model. I was surprised she wanted to see someone like you."

His sarcastic remark reflected his animus toward me because he was a married graduate student who looked older than his age with gray hairs on the sideburns. When Sham had first visited me, he had addressed him as *Dadaji,* which meant "respected grandpa" in Hindi, and I had loudly laughed as he had fumed.

With a quick, old Indian saying, "Beauty is in the eyes of the beholder," I hung up the phone and rushed down the stairs as there was only one such person I knew who fit that description, but I'd never told her where I lived, and she lived far from ISH. When I reached the front glass entry door and looked ahead across the cement path that led straight to the road, I saw the familiar figure of a lady waiting to cross the street—it was Zhen. I rushed out and yelled her name. She turned around. I noticed that the lower part of her two-piece thin silk gown was wet, and she was wearing black high-heel sandals like pumps.

When we walked back, I had forgotten some of Zhen's quirks. For instance, she had said, in public, "Don't touch the merchandise and keep your distance," like you would with a queen, as she moved her hand away when I tried holding it, she walked faster in front of me past the entry. Then I wondered why she would travel so far and change several trains to see an ordinary kind of guy like me.

I was in for a surprise and would soon discover what made this elegant lady tick.

Zhen said it had been raining when she had taken the train from Bromley and that had wet her gown. She said that Jun had told her I lived here and both Jun and Lin had gone back to Hong Kong and Singapore respectively. We entered my room, and I switched on the light even though it was daytime and went ahead and pulled the upper window pan down to seal shut the window and locked it with its semi-circular metal latch because I had no doubt why Zhen was here, and it was definitely not just to talk.

I pulled down the window curtain for complete privacy, adjusting it to make sure there were no gaps for a peeping tom. I had forgotten Zhen's other quirk that was opposite of her public one, like a Dr. Jackal and Dr. Hyde personality. In private, she could not wait for physical action, and the rougher, the better. I was performing my privacy securing measures as fast as I could when Zhen, unbeknownst to me, had undressed and placed her wet gown over the heater next to me to dry. As I turned around, she was already on the bed with her stupendous firm body and large half-coconut-sized breasts, motioning to me with her open arms, like pulling waves toward her.

Of course, I was excited just as I had been the first time when I went to her place and as she was my guest, my aim was to please the guest with whatever I could. Soon I was undressed and went over for action. It was then I remembered Zhen's third quirk—loud vocalizations to express her pleasure. In no time, the room was reverberating with her loud screams like she was being tortured and lashed. At this stage, I did not care as it excited me. It was going on for many, many minutes and getting louder by the second when I heard people outside the window. I heard the student who lived in the room before mine talking outside the window to the one who lived on the opposite side, and he was trying hard to find an opening to peek in. I was glad I had sealed all the gaps with the curtain. At this stage, Zhen was in a different world and probably did not even know that someone was outside, or cared, and I did not care either as I was hyper-excited with all the action. A while later, I had some concern as one of the guys tried to open the window, and I was glad I had locked it. Then I vaguely heard one say someone was being tortured inside, though it was hard to hear over the inordinate din emanating from Zhen, and I still did not really care because they were just jealous. So, to make them even more jealous, I continued, and eventually, they left as the talking outside had stopped.

A fiery feast ends when the fuel that drives it runs out and the tank needs refilling, which can take some time. The round ended after over an hour as I used all the human ingenuity and supplemental body tools possible to satisfy the insatiable lady. I got up to take a break and walked to the window to carefully peep out from the side of the curtain to see if the voyeurs outside had left, and they had. When I turned around, Zhen had moved up to a sitting position on the sofa bed, looking relaxed and satiated, and started giving me a chronology of her trysts with men.

"He had really good control. Used many positions. Real rough man. Good. And another one lifted me all over. On the table, chair, floor. Wanted to take me to the kitchen. Also, against the closet. And that muscular guy lifted me. Straddled me. Did me standing."

I found this amusing, as this was real intimate stuff most people, particularly women, would rather keep secret, especially from other men. She must have gone through many with full details, and there had to be a climax that came. She lifted her forearms in front with two index fingers about eight inches apart to demonstrate and said, "The Nigerian had a penis this long."

I interjected and jested, "Was his name Norbert?"

"I don't ask names."

"I also once had a Nigerian friend called Norbert. He shafted me but not the way your Nigerian did to you. I didn't feel good after what he did to me."

She looked confused and asked, "You also do men?"

"No. A figure of speech. It's a long story and I'd rather forget it."

Zhen was an equal-opportunity screwer and did not care who the dude was as long as he had a protected piston and could perform well. Bored, but somewhat astounded at this loose bragging, I said, "You want to walk around so I can show you this place?" Her gown on the heater was dry, and I handed it to her. We dressed up and went to the lobby and up the winding stairs to the expansive second-floor lounge facing the Regent's Park. It was bustling with students, some seated on the couches along the rows of tall vertical rectangular windows facing the park. As we strolled on the plush carpet, I noticed Zhen had a roving eye for men, always in search for that next performer who would take her to a higher level of ecstasy.

Halfway through the row of two couches across a coffee table, Zhen stopped. Right in front of us, her prying eyes focused a North African guy in his twenties with a smooth-skinned clean-shaven face and a pointed nose, like a beak, and an Afro hairdo. The light-skinned African sat in the middle of the sofa with his legs spread wide apart in a V-shape, exposing the contours of his heavy artillery and balls in his crotch through his tight, gray silk pants. His arms were spread out like an eagle's wings on the top of the sofa. He was wearing a thin gray wool sweater with a round neck collar and a gray silk jacket over it, all matching the pants, with pointed tip black boots. While we looked at him, he looked toward us, but not at our faces, at my crotch. I quickly glanced at my crotch and saw my fly was open, so I quickly zipped it shut and a small smile appeared on his face like he was telepathing me, *You owe me for that, mate.* In my hurry to dress up in my room, I'd forgotten to zip the fly.

Zhen whispered in my ear, "Can you introduce me to him?"

"I don't know him."

"That's okay. Man to man, you talk to him."

"Let us sit down at that couch, and I'll explain."

I led her to a vacant couch further down, and I saw the Afro-do guy had shifted his gaze to some other guys who had reached the landing near the stairs, and this gave me an idea, with his inordinate attention to my crotch. We took a seat, and I said, "He is not your type."

"What do you mean not my type?"

"He is gay. He is only interested in me." I guess I didn't want this guy to do Zhen.

"No. I don't believe that."

We went on and on, in circles, and I realized that Zhen was persistent when she had latched on to a guy, just as she had repeatedly cajoled Chen to stay overnight when we had first visited her. Eventually, I said I needed to go back to my room and study. Zhen said she wanted to enjoy the outside view of the park for a while even though it was getting dark. I told her she could return to my room when she was done but guessed she wouldn't as with her beauty, she would have no trouble finding another mate. That was the last time I ever saw her.

The next day, there was a note in my mailbox asking me to see Mr. Patterson, the head of the ISH, urgently in his office. There, he berated me for the prolonged loud disturbance that occurred in my room the previous afternoon and narrated the several complaints he had received, two from my neighbors and a third from the Indian porter at the front door. Because of this ruckus, there was no doubt the answer to my lease renewal, and I had to vacate the premises within a week and look for other digs. As a parting shot, he admonished I was lucky he was not declaring me a persona non grata at ISH.

After that, I went to my medical school's administration office, and the secretary sent me to see the matron at the medical school's dormitory called the Brabazon House. After a ten-minute walk through various streets, I reached the four-story brick building and met with the English matron who was a heavy-set spinster in her sixties with short graying hair who looked like a peasant woman. She gave me a small gay room with a bed, a narrow adjoining leather lounge chair, and a wooden table and chair facing a tall window on the fourth floor, which looked onto other properties.

I vacated my room at ISH with a heavy heart as it was a lively place and now my brothers would have no incentive to go there during the evenings. I moved into the Brabazon House, a quiet house located at 5 Moreton Street, London SW1 at the end of 1973. It was rent free as the Westminster Medical School owned the property, and I assumed it was included in the fees that were paid by the Inner London Education Authority for most students. One positive outcome was I did not have to take a bus in the morning as I just walked to the medical school in the morning, often with some of my colleagues who also lived at the house.

At the start of 1974, I started a three-month rotation in psychiatry, and we also went to other hospitals with active psychiatric services affiliated with Westminster Medical School. We were taught to take long, detailed personal histories running into several pages from patients with various psychiatric ailments like depression, mania, anxiety, and schizophrenia. After interviewing a patient and writing down the history at the same time, I would present my case to the psychiatry registrar or the consultant psychiatrist. I found it confounding that psychiatry registrars smoked a lot while discussing the long patient histories and analyzing the symptoms and diagnoses at conference tables. It set a bad example for the patients, but in those days, the health hazards of smoking were not widely appreciated.

There were three students in my psychiatry rotation group, and a chubby Indian psychiatry consultant took us all in his car one day to a mental sanatorium where there were many patients with chronic, or burnt-out, schizophrenia, as he called it. We stayed there in a room designated for visitors for a few days and interviewed many patients, mostly living in their own mental world of elaborate and fantastic delusions, especially of grandeur, that they firmly believed in and were content sitting outside in the garden living in their mental fantasies. One said when he had walked along a street and had seen the traffic light turn red, he had known he was the incarnation of Hannibal. The consultant told us there was no treatment for such long-standing cases, but it was easier to treat acute cases of schizophrenia with drugs called phenothiazines, which eliminated the acute delusions, like the voices they heard. This was an incapacitating and very serious condition in which the patient lost contact with reality and could turn violent. He mentioned a case of a registrar having been kicked in the face by an agitated patient during an interview when the patient had claimed the registrar a devil. Many patients with schizophrenia were also depressed, and the consultant told us that while a depressed person could also hear voices and be misdiagnosed as schizophrenic, in depression, the voices come from inside or within, while in schizo-phrenia, they are from outside, and if the voices referred to the patient in the third person, especially denigrating, that was pathognomonic of schizophrenia. He cautioned the voices had to be heard in clear consciousness and not in dreams or during sleep.

I studied our thick paperback psychiatry textbook to read about the psychiatric diseases we encountered afflicting the patients we saw in the outpatient clinics. Curiously, I read a small section in the book titled nymphomania, which described a woman with obsessive sexual interactions, and its male counterpart description, satyromania, and wondered if Zhen was a nymphomaniac. When in private, I discreetly passed my experience with Zhen to the consultant. He said that these conditions could be construed as an exaggeration of what one calls "normal" like at one end of a spectrum, and he offered some cautionary parting words of wisdom as I left: "A relationship simply based on sex will not last."

After psychiatry, I went to other specialty rotations like ophthal-mology, ear, nose, and throat, orthopedics, cardiology, and pediatrics. Ophthalmology was mainly taught in an outpatient clinic at the hospital, and I learned to examine patients' eyes with an ophthalmoscope to view their retinas at the back of the eyeballs and look at the optic nerve, the only nerve one could view directly in the intact body. Our chief was a famous consultant ophthalmic surgeon called Patrick D. Trevor-Roper, whose textbook, *Lecture Notes in Ophthalmology*, I bought and studied. I had started wearing hard contact lenses that had just been invented to replace glasses as my vision was changing. I panicked as I started seeing halos around outside lights at night and read in the lecture notes that that was a symptom of glaucoma, or high pressure in the eyes. It was interesting and unfortunate that as a medical student, the worst possible diagnosis popped up instead of the less severe, common causes first as the most likely reason for the symptoms. The first thing I did was see Trevor-Roper, who was always around in the sprawling clinic. He had a slightly bulging belly and wore light wired glasses with the bottom half of lenses for reading. I told him my problem, and he looked at me intently above the half-lenses and reassured me I did not have glaucoma and told me it was due to my hard lenses causing edema, or swelling, of my cornea, and that I should stop wearing them. He told one of his ophthalmology registrars to check my eye pressure, which turned out to be normal. The halos disappeared after a while as I stopped wearing the lenses. The soft lenses that replaced them were not invented yet.

After six months in residence, the matron at Brabazon House called me and took me to the largest student room that had just been vacated by a student who graduated. It was more than twice the size of my present one and located on the first floor near the entrance of the building with a full street view from its large windows. She told me she was rewarding me for keeping my room the cleanest of all. Whenever I left my room in the morning for the medical school, I always made my bed and kept the room very neat and tidy as a matter of habit since I was at Cambridge. The matron obviously used to sneak into all the rooms to see how the students kept them.

One day, I was heading to the medical school in the morning and met another student whom I had not seen before and introduced myself to him, and we chatted as we walked. He was a medical student from the United States doing a month of externship at our medical school. I was curious and asked him why he came to England to do an externship if the United States was the world's most advanced country in medicine. His immediate response was that there was too much specialization in the United States and too much emphasis on tests because of their great resources, while here, more stress was on a detailed history and physical examination to diagnose medical problems. For example, he said, in the US, if you had a cough, you would be sent for a chest X-ray. Here, you would take a detailed history and perform a full physical exam, including listening to the lung sounds and tapping the chest and so on. He was right as I rarely saw any chest X-ray ordered. I opined it was because of the limited resources of the health system in Great Britain as all were covered by the system. After his month was over, he wanted to travel to other parts of Great Britain and left his suitcase with me as he had vacated his room, and I was glad to hold it for him till he returned after a week.

One of my last clinical rotations was in pediatrics at the Westminster Children's Hospital, a branch of our main hospital and also walking distance from Brabazon House. I went to a lot of outpatient clinics there, including child psychiatry clinics. I took the child's history from the accompanying parent and then presented it to the pediatric registrar or consultant. Once a week, I had to stay overnight at one of the hospital's call room in case of an emergency in the ER. I was called by the nursing supervisor to be with the ER physician to learn from emergency cases arriving in the ER at night.

In June of 1975, after completion of my three years of clinical medicine in London, all the Cambridge medical students of my class returned to take their final clinical exams at the Addenbrooke's Hospital in Cambridge to get their medical degree. For the most important part of the exam, we saw patients with various medical and surgical problems who had volunteered to participate, and we didn't know anything about them and had to take a history, do a physical exam within certain allocated time limits, twenty minutes for a long surgical case and one hour for a long medical case, and then present the case to the examining professor. We could not write down anything.

For the long medical case, I got an old lady with severe rheumatoid arthritis with multiple complications and an extensive medical history. For the long surgical case, I got a seventy-year-old man who had difficulty swallowing, and because of his age, I had to consider cancer of the esophagus as one of the possible causes high on my list of differential diagnoses. After I presented the case and my physical findings and told the examiner what the various causes of the symptoms could be, he asked what tests I would order to confirm my likely diagnosis. He provided the test results. I asked for a barium-swallow for the patient, and the professor grabbed an X-ray from a folder and clipped it on the X-ray view box next to the bed, asking me to interpret the findings for him.

For the short medical and surgery cases, we had patients who were sitting in a circle in a large room on beds, and we got five minutes to see each patient and demonstrate the physical signs the questions on a card next to the bed asked for. One of the patient's card asked to examine his eyes. His pupils were small, and they did not react to my small flashlight, so I diagnosed him with Argyll Robertson pupils, usually found in patients with old neuro-syphilis or diabetic neuropathy. Other patients had heart murmurs and other physical findings like cranial nerve palsies. For the clinical examination in obstetrics, for which twenty minutes were allowed before the obstetrics professor came, I got a pregnant lady who was sitting comfortably on a bed with her knees bent. After getting a full history from her about her pregnancy, I found on abdominal examination of the pregnant uterus that her baby was upside down, or breech presentation, and presented the case. At the end of my examination in front of the professor, he tried to trick me and asked how I could be sure there was no second baby in the uterus. I told him that the abdomen, in the case of twins, was much larger, and I could not feel a second head or hear a second baby's heartbeat. He seemed satisfied with my interpretation.

After passing the clinical exams in early July of 1975, I was conferred the degrees bachelor of medicine and bachelor of surgery and now could practice medicine as a houseman. However, the actual graduating ceremony was held at the Senate House, an elegant old Cambridge building with a huge brown entry door and walls with large rectangular windows on August 2, 1975. Each graduating student had to wear a square academic black cap and a gown and walk down the central aisle starting at the door and with parents, friends, and well-wishers sitting on benches on either side of the aisle. I felt exhilaration when I climbed up the steps of the podium to get my certificates after my name was called out. Most of the British graduating students had their parents and friends in attendance. My brother Raj and an Indian friend of his named Shah were present for me. After the ceremony, we went to Trinity Hall as all the newly minted medical graduates went to their respective colleges with their parents and friends to celebrate. I held my two medical graduate certificates in my hand—one for a bachelor of medicine and one for a bachelor of surgery. Raj took a photo of me standing on the bridge over River Cam where it flowed behind Trinity Hall. I took off my cap for the photo.

I was free to practice medicine within the confines of a teaching hospital as a houseman under the supervision of a consultant physician or surgeon, as the case may be, and the registrars. However, I could not practice outside these parameters until I got my general medical license after completing one year of housemanship—six months in surgery and six months in medicine. As a houseman, you lived in the hospital, as the name implied, because you could be called at any time for an emergency or to a patient with an acute medical problem that needed immediate attention like seizures.

Chapter 10

The Houseman

I couldn't wait to start practicing after six years of medical school and earn some money as soon as possible. I saw my opportunity in an early-start housemanship at the beginning of July 1975 for six months with Mr. Lawson, a pediatric surgery consultant and head of the pediatric surgery department at the Westminster Children's Hospital where I did my pediatric clerkship for three months. My base salary was about two hundred and fifty pounds per month. It was a walking distance from its namesake main hospital where I did many of my other clerkships as a student. I also had a unique opportunity to earn overtime as an added attraction because there were two houseman and each alternated taking the night calls, but both had to work in the daytime because of the large number of patients on the floor, in admissions, and in the ER if a patient needed surgery. There was minimal competition for these two spots because pediatrics was an unattractive specialty in those days, and this housemanship started immediately after graduation, instead of August, and most medical graduates wanted some vacation time to unwind. My focus now was to get my full general medical license and earn money.

As a surgical houseman, I worked twenty-four-hour shifts on alternate days with another houseman, so we hardly saw each other.

However, we alternated working for a whole weekend. We were given free rooms to stay at in a quiet corner of the hospital, and the meals were free for the medical staff only at a nearby hospital cafeteria. The hours as a houseman were long, and the pay was low, but I made more than other housemen at the main hospital because of the overtime hours I worked. I saved most of it as I hardly had any expenses, except on my day off, when I occasionally walked to a nearby restaurant to eat my favorite food, the iconic British fish and chips, or sporadically baked cod, chips, and ketchup. I was excited to be earning money and even called the Inner London Education Authority and asked them if I could start repaying them the grant money they had spent to educate me. They politely refused the offer and stated that the taxes deducted from my paycheck went to the government and that contributed to their budget to help other students, so I was indirectly repaying my grant through my taxes. My weekly pay on Fridays came in a small sealed brown envelope with my name on it and contained the regular weekly salary and the overtime in cash. It was then I really appreciated the value of money as it was compensation for the long hours I spent at work, and I deposited most of it in my bank savings account.

The ages of the patients I looked after ranged from babies to about twelve. On the days I worked, all the patients for scheduled surgery, including those from the ER, were admitted by me. I took the history from their parents in an outpatient clinic while charting it, did a physical examination in front of the parents, documented the findings, had them sign a surgical consent, and then wrote preoperative orders for the nurses before admitting the kids to the floor with their medical records chart.

Once a couple came and the dad was a surgical registrar at another hospital. He demanded that only the consultant pediatric surgeon, Mr. Lawson, not the surgical registrar, operate on his kid and wanted that documented in the consent. I told him that it shouldn't be a problem, and I would relay the message to the consultant who was in surgery. I told him that I was only a houseman who did the basics, and he should realize that. "I'm sure you know that as you were a houseman once." He pondered on that statement and nodded in agreement. To lighten the situation, as his wife looked annoyed at his behavior, I said, "One thing I can guarantee right now. I won't be the one operating." He was embarrassed and said, "Oh, no! I didn't mean it that way."

I also learned diagnosing and treatment of various surgical problems by attending the outpatient clinics of the two general pediatric consultant surgeons whose patients I admitted and those of the two ear, nose, and throat, or ENT, consulting surgeons. Most of the common surgeries they performed were tonsillectomies, inserting ear tubes for drainage, and adenoidectomies. The two ENT consultant surgeons, while on the NHS payroll and time, also conducted a profitable side business of operating on their private patients, mostly from the Middle East and Saudi Arabia, whose governments paid for the full cost at the Harley Street Clinic, a famous private medical center in London. One of them, a beefy mustachioed surgeon, would occasionally use me to assist him with his surgeries there on my days off and would always promise to pay me five pounds but never did; I found such greed and cheapness confounding.

A surgeon was addressed as "Mr." in England as hundreds of years ago one became a surgeon after apprenticing with another surgeon, who was not a medical doctor. Later, that changed when they had to get a medical degree first, they were called "Dr." and that changed to "Mr." after they completed their surgery registrarship or residency—to address a surgeon there as "Dr." could be insulting! The surgeries in the operating room were performed by the pediatric surgical registrars or residents, occasionally under the supervision of the consultant surgeon, who did the difficult cases himself with the registrar's assistance.

One day we were waiting in surgery for a twelve-year-old kid scheduled for an elective right inguinal hernia repair. The team and the surgeon were getting impatient at the inordinate delay. When I called upstairs, the nurse in charge of the surgery floor said that no one was willing to shave his right groin area. Shaving was usually done on the floor by a nurse prior to sending the patient to surgery, and the nursing supervisor insisted one of us should do it, but she would not give me a reason, or even a hint, why no nurse wanted to do it. This was highly unusual and had not been a problem in the past. I had not seen the kid as he had been admitted by the other houseman a day earlier. Since I was the houseman for the case now, I went back to the floor to the charge nurse's office, but she was evasive when I asked her what the problem was with shaving the kid's groin; instead, she simply handed me the equipment on her desk to shave the kid—a shaving razor and shaving cream in a plastic dish and a small white towel.

When I entered the room where the kid lay on the gurney, I was shocked that his abdomen and private parts were unnecessarily exposed. He lay staring at the ceiling and then turned his head to me as I entered. For his age, he had an inordinately long penis, longer than many adults. The well-endowed poor kid was paying the price for his hormonal precociousness, which was not his fault. I shaved his right groin where the hernia was, covered him with a blanket and pushed the gurney to the elevator to take him to the surgery suite as all the nurses avoided him like the plague, even to help me with the gurney. I failed to fathom such behavior as he was just a patient and still a kid. I guess this was a children's hospital, and they expected everything to be kid-sized. All I gathered later was that the student nurse sent to shave him had run out of the room shrieking after seeing his big organ. However, I did not dare complain as the nurses were the backbone of the healthcare delivery system, and if they did not want to do something, the safest route was to accept it meekly and humbly, even thank them for giving you the honor to do it, and then do it yourself and forego complaining as they could gang up on you and make your life utterly miserable.

There was a heart-wrenching sight in one large room with numerous rows of neatly arranged baby cribs and newborn babies lying on their abdomens because they had a large reddish bulbous swelling, like a small thick sausage on their low back through which you could see the nerves. Here, the bony canal or the spinal canal that covers the spinal cord was not fully formed, leaving a defect and a fluid-filled sac. It was tragic as there was no effective means of diagnosing this condition early in pregnancy in those days and these kids had difficulty walking or were paralyzed when they grew up. Surgery was performed to excise the bulbous sac and close the opening. These kids had other complications like bladder and bowel difficulties and incontinence. These newborns needed to be fed so an IV had to be started that was possible to insert on their tiny scalp veins. This was a challenging task as I could not place the baby on his or her back to access to a scalp vein.

Nights were relatively quiet. Occasionally, I was called for a problem with a kid, like a high fever, and needed urgent antibiotics, so I would call the night charge nurse, who would open the small hospital pharmacy for me. I would find the medication needed as they were stored in alphabetic order by the name of the medication. However, there were tragic cases like the eight-year-old kid brought to the ER screaming with both his ulna and radius sticking out, and I called several places like his school headmaster from the wall phone in the ER, searching for his parents. The hospital had a strict policy that we obtain the parent's consent before any surgical procedure or invasive treatment could be done on a kid.

Then there was the tragic case of a Jamaican father who brought his five-year-old son with a distended and rigid abdomen at four in the morning on a Monday. He said the kid's abdominal pain started three days prior. From the history and physical, I diagnosed the kid had a ruptured appendix that had infected his entire abdomen causing peritonitis, a serious, potentially lethal condition. I called the nursing supervisor and told her that the kid needed immediate surgery and to call the surgical registrar. In the meantime, I desperately searched for a vein in the kid's arms and legs and could not see or find any as he was so dry and hardly responsive. In surgery, the anesthetist could not find a vein either and so put him to sleep with an anesthetic gas through a mask and then the surgical registrar made an incision near his ankle to find a vein to insert a catheter directly into it so that fluids, antibiotics, and other anesthetics could be administered. The child's abdomen was full of pus, and the kid died despite all our efforts. All deaths are tragic, but especially one of a child to their parents. The dad wailed and cursed himself for not bringing the kid in earlier.

During the six months of my surgical housemanship, I searched for advertisements in a national medical journal for a six-month medical housemanship that I would need to complete to obtain a general medical license. One day, I saw such an advertisement from Poole General Hospital located in the port city of Poole on the south coast of England. I wrote to the consultant physician for whom the hospital was adverting and got a letter inviting me for an interview. I took the day off and had a senior medical student doing a pediatric rotation at my hospital to cover me for twenty-four hours as I was not sure when I would return from the interview and wanted to take the day off anyhow. I paid her five pounds, and she was thrilled at my generosity, but little did she know that I made good money with overtime. My net salary with overtime, after all the tax and health insurance deductions, was almost three hundred and fifty dollars a month and most it was saved as I had no housing or lodgings expenses.

I took a train to Poole in the morning and walked to the large coastal hospital. The interviews started at eleven in the morning to give the applicants time to reach Poole. At this prime location hospital, I guessed my chances of acceptance were low because one of the five interviewees was already a surgical houseman at the hospital as I discovered when we chatted in the waiting room for our turns to be interviewed. The consultant physician needed two housemen, and one had already been picked from a batch of five from another day's interviews. A few days later, I received a letter of acceptance.

I was not a real physician until I completed a six-month medical housemanship because I had to do most of the problem solving, treatments, and procedures on my own as I might be the only person available, especially at late hours. As a houseman, I wore a long white coat to distinguish myself from the medical students. The white coat had two large lower side pockets. In one, I carried a guide book of common medical procedures a houseman would need to perform and the doses of various drugs to treat various common ailments. In the other pocket, I carried a reflex hammer and a stethoscope. In the front upper pocket was a pen and a pen flashlight. The nurses now respected me and were very helpful, unlike when I was a student.

In early January of 1976, after completion of my six-month surgical housemanship at the end of December of 1975 and an enviable cache of fifteen hundred pounds in my savings account, I began my medical housemanship under the preceptorship of a medical consultant, Dr. Hindle, at the Poole General Hospital. Dr. Hindle was a genial man who wore a gray suit, a tie, and brown plastic-rimmed glasses. While he treated patients with all kinds of medical problems, the bulk of his patients had heart problems that often started with a heart attack.

Like most consultant physicians and surgeons, Dr. Hindle had two housemen, and my fellow houseman was a great jovial guy who liked to be called B, short for his actual name, Babulal. His dad was Indian and his mom was English, and he was born in Edinburgh, Scotland. We alternated night calls, every twenty-four hours and weekends, but each of us worked till five in the evening when not on call, as there were many patients. We worked under a medical registrar, Richard, a handsome Englishman with wavy blond hair.

As Dr. Hindle's houseman, I got firsthand experience of the devastation, pain, suffering, and death wrought on the patients and their families from heart disease that you would never imagine existed in the general public. Heart disease was the most common killer and cause of morbidity in Great Britain. It reminded me of my butler at Trinity Hall who died of a heart attack. The medical term was

myocardial infarction, MI, or death of the heart muscle from interruption of its blood supply. Most heart attack patients arrived in the
hospital's emergency room by ambulance, and the ER doctor called
us for their admittance to the six-bed coronary care unit, or the CCU.
Many just waited in the ER as there was no room in the CCU until we
moved the most stable ones from the CCU to the adjoining floor.

Like initiation by fire, on my second day, I was on a ward on the
fourth floor discussing management of a case with Richard for his
guidance when an urgent overhead announcement came to rush to
the ER. We rushed down the steps to the ER located on the first floor
close to the hospital entrance for easy access by ambulances. The
paramedics were performing a cardiopulmonary resuscitation, or
CPR, on the victim as his lifeless body lay on a table in the ER. The
CPR consisted of chest compressions at the rate of about one hundred
times a minute, or thirty compressions, followed by two breaths, given
through an ambu bag, consisting of a plastic face mask attached to a
football-shaped bag that was preferred to mouth-to-mouth resuscitation. We took over and that was my first actual performance of CPR of
the numerous I would have to perform in the following months. After
half an hour of intense resuscitation that including several electrical
shocks to the heart with a defibrillator and injecting various drugs to
stimulate the heart, there was no response and the EKG stayed flat.
The man had a massive infarct and did not respond. At only forty-two,
he was pronounced dead. I went to a small private waiting room near
the ER where the man's wife was waiting to give her the grim news
that her husband was dead on arrival despite the heroic efforts by the
ambulance personnel during transportation to the hospital and our
efforts for half an hour. She wailed, repeating that she had two small
children. That saddened me deeply as I tried my best to comfort her
with words and offered to have the nurse give her valium, an anti-anx-
iety and calming drug commonly used then. She calmed down and
said she would be okay. I realized that in Great Britain, there was a
good social and government safety net for her and her children.

I shuddered to think of the consequences for a mother if this happened in Tanzania or another third-world country. She would be left destitute or dependent on other family members.

The coronary care unit was a well-lit room with six beds, three on each side wall with wide entry doors for quick entry and egress of patients and equipment. In the center of the room was a work and monitoring station where we sat to do our paperwork for the patients' charts. There were six patients who had acute myocardial infarctions and were monitored continuously with an EKG to detect any heart rhythm changes that may need immediate treatment as the damaged heart was irritable. The patients were in sitting positions to reduce strain on the heart.

Every morning starting at eight, I met B at the CCU, and we went through the patients' charts to make sure all the lab work and tests were current. All patients got an EKG done in the morning and occasionally a chest X-ray if there was suspicion of heart failure from the symptoms and physical examination to see if any fluid accumulation was present at the base of the lungs. The EKG showed if there had been any change in the heart rhythm or further extension of the muscle damage. To get a chest X-ray, the X-ray technician wheeled her portable machine into the CCU and placed the X-ray plate behind the sitting patient and positioned her portable machine near the bed and adjusted its X-ray box that fired the X-rays directly at the chest. We all left the room at that time to reduce the risk of repeated exposure to X-rays.

Twice a week, on Monday and Friday, starting at nine in the morning, we had grand medical rounds with our consultant and boss, Dr. Hindle, and his medical registrar, Richard. We were accompanied by the nursing supervisor, the most important person of the coterie, because of her in-depth knowledge of the patients. Our rounds started in the coronary care unit, and then we proceeded to the adjoining room where the patients from the CCU, after their five-day standard bed-rest period, were discharged to. We visited each patient, and the houseman who had originally admitted the patient and continued with the management plan presented the case. If it was a newly admitted patient by me, who Dr. Hindle had not seen yet, then I gave a detailed initial admission history, physical exam findings, results of any lab tests, and treatment so far. Dr. Hindle then did a brief physical examination, usually of the heart and lungs, listening with his stethoscope, and occasionally asked the patient some additional questions and gave his opinion and recommended any additional tests and treatments to improve the patient's care. For example, he recommended I change the antibiotic to amoxicillin, a new broad-spectrum antibiotic on the market, for a patient with bronchitis as it was more effective and had to be administered only three times daily compared with the older generation antibiotic, ampicillin, which was administered four times daily.

In the CCU, I dealt with many problems resulting from heart attacks. Some patients got abnormal heart rhythms as the heart became irritable from the damage. This had to be treated with intravenous medications, like lidocaine, to reverse it and prevent cardiac arrest. Some rhythm problems were resistant to anti-arrhythmia drugs so the anesthetist was called to sedate the patient, and Richard would perform a cardioversion, or a shock to the heart by placing two pedals across the upper chest and pressing buttons on the pedals that sent an electrical shock across the heart to clear the abnormal rhythm. Occasionally, a newly admitted patient never had a chance to urinate with morphine given for severe chest pains, and I had to catheterize them in the CCU. It was amazing that I had seen only one catheterization in the operating room as a medical student, and I had to do it on my own as a houseman, just like many other procedures.

The patients who were discharged from the CCU to the adjoining post-CCU room had cardiac rehabilitation in the form of gradual mobilization, like short walks, but were still in high danger. You always knew who had a cardiac arrest as you heard a few obstructed breathing sounds, like loud snoring, and then quietness as the cardiac arrest was followed by respiratory arrest. This occasionally happened during our medical rounds. The patient had to be on a hard surface, and we flattened the bed and placed a hard plastic plate under the patient after a quick check of loss of pulse, apart from the absence of breathing, to confirm the diagnosis of a cardiac arrest. CPR was started with chest compressions as a red crash cart with the emergency medications for the heart was available nearby in the room. Despite immediate CPR, the outcome was often poor, and most died. The bed was cordoned off with curtains so other patients around could not see the depressing sight and the body, covered fully with a white blanket, was hauled away in the bed, leaving an empty space until another clean bed was placed there. All the neighboring patients were quiet and ostensibly sullen long after a death, wondering if they would be the next one.

The most depressing area was the Intensive Care Unit, a large room where several of the patients with massive heart attacks lay, usually unconscious, with plastic endotracheal tubes in their throats connected to respirators breathing for them. The heart is a pump made of a special-ized muscle that pumps oxygenated blood to all parts of the body, including itself, and with extensive injury from a massive heart attack, it was unable to adequately perform this life-sustaining duty leading to low blood pressure and other complications, like inability to breathe, necessitating artificial respirations. The basic treatment was a contin-uous infusion of intravenous drugs, called vasopressors, to elevate the blood pressure. The prognosis was usually poor because of low blood pressure as I did not see anyone walk out of the hospital from this stage while I was there for six months. Some just sat on beds of the regular ward as cardiac cripples, dying of heart failure with barely enough blood output from the heart to keep them alive on medications like digoxin to strengthen the contractions of the heart. Heart transplants, done only at a few large medical centers, were in their infancy and were not an option as the numbers needing transplants vastly overwhelmed the supply of hearts available for transplants.

On most weekdays, we did faster medical rounds with Richard, visiting each patient, often without the nursing supervisors, going from ward to ward across the hospital. Once a week, in the morning,

I attended an outpatient clinic where patients came to see Dr. Hindle; some were new, and many were those needing follow-up care after their discharge from the hospital as inpatients. I learned a lot on these medical rounds and in the outpatient clinic in taking better care of the patients, diagnosing medical disorders, and treating diseases. Some patients had progressive diseases for which there was no effective treatment to slow the progression, like the forty-year-old lady who was wheelchair-bound from multiple sclerosis, a neurological disorder in which the body attacked myelin, the covering of its nerve fibers in the brain and spinal cord, with antibodies, as if they were foreign tissues, resulting in progressive paralysis and loss of sensation and vision as messages from the brain could not fully reach their target organs via the damaged nerves. However, the weekly course of injections of ACTH, or adrenocorticotropic hormone, acted as a placebo, and the patient felt better when asked on subsequent visits. ACTH was the hormone that the brain's pituitary gland produced naturally to stimulate the production of cortisol, an anti-inflammatory hormone from the adrenal glands in the body. The disease itself had stages of progression and regression, so it was difficult to know if the injections helped, but the long-term outlook was grim.

After the rounds and ordering new tests as recommended by Richard or Dr. Hindle during the rounds, B and I always had lunch together at the hospital cafeteria. Our favorite dish was a freshly made omelet made by the cook.

My life as a medical houseman never had a dull moment. I was always busy on the wards, checking patients' blood works and other tests to confirm diagnoses and institute treatments, referring to my pocket medical guidebook about correct doses of medications to prescribe and consulting with Richard. I wrote prescriptions in the patients' chart on a special prescription page. I performed on my own all the procedures I had only observed as a medical student, like the patient who I suspected had meningitis. I had him curl at the edge of his bed for a spinal tap to take a sample of his spinal fluid under sterile conditions and send it to the lab to test for the presence of any bacteria and sensitivity to antibiotics.

On my alternate night calls, I was busy dealing with acute problems of patients on different floors as there was a skeletal staff to help. Emergencies varied, like the elderly man with severe shortness of breath due to fluid accumulating around his lungs. I sat him on the side of the bed and got a tray to prepare a small area of the chest with a bactericidal solution and inserted a needle through it into the chest to drain enough fluid so he could breathe. There were others, like one person dying of advanced lung cancer and was severely short of breath. I placed him on oxygen and administered some morphine for comfort and anxiety. There were occasionally patients who got grand mal seizures, and it was a challenge to start an IV in a seizing patient to stop the seizures quickly. Some heart patients discharged on the floor got severe rhythm problems resulting in shortness of breath, and I would take my portable EKG machine to get a continuous EKG and give appropriate IV medication, like beta blockers, to slow down the heart. In my six months, I learned a lot and became very confident in my ability to manage patients with various medical disorders. I worked hard as a houseman and could be up a whole night when on call, but I was young and energetic, and it did not bother me because I would need all I learned when I would be practicing on my own.

At the end of June of 1976, after completing twelve months of housemanship, I received my medical license, or the certificate of full registration as a medical practitioner, from the General Medical Council of Great Britain, the licensing body for physicians and surgeons. The certificate had a letter E after the date of the certificate for a graduate of a medical school in England. With the certificate in my folder, I vacated my room at the Poole General Hospital and walked to the Poole train station with all my meager possessions, mainly clothes and medical books, in a small suitcase and took a train to London. After changing several trains and buses, I reached the Heathrow International Airport near London to catch a flight to the United States, to be with my parents, in a 747-passenger jumbo jet, the workhorse of international flights of those days. After checking in at the airline counter with my airline ticket and passport, I was ready to board the plane. However, I was filled with emotion as it was exactly nine years ago that I had arrived at the Gatwick International Airport near London with the ambition to become a medical doctor, and now, I had come full circle and achieved my objective.

I mentally thanked Great Britain and its people for their largesse in the educational opportunity I got and giving me a chance to prove myself and achieve my goal, and I thanked God that the British ruled East Africa and India. Before entering the jet bridge, I casually and deliberately dropped my boarding pass, and with one hand, touched the floor to thank the British soil and then picked up the pass, transiently glanced back at the passengers behind me who were probably wondering what I was doing, and moved on and boarded the plane.

MATRICULATION AT TRINITY HALL, CAMBRIDGE.
SEPTEMBER 9th, 1969

A group photo of all the undergraduate students matriculating at the college in 1969 was taken in front of the main dining hall facing River Cam. I'm standing in the second row from the bottom, second from left. My friend and fellow medical student, Mark Drayton, is standing in the third row from the bottom, fifth from the left. Note the colleges were segregated by sex in those days and there were only men at Trinity Hall. Out of the twenty-five Cambridge Colleges, only one was a ladies college, Girton College.

Dear Ashok

Congratulations, you got a first, — a truly magnificent result! I confess I was a little cynical when you told me you had done well, — please forgive me!

DJCove

A NOTE FROM MY DESIGNATED TUTOR/ADVISOR, Dr. D.J. COVE. MAY 1970

This was the note left in my mailbox at the Porter's Lodge, Trinity Hall, Cambridge, at the end of May 1970, by Dr. D. J. Cove, the designated tutor/advisor for the six medical students at Trinity Hall, Cambridge, congratulating me on getting a FIRST, or Grade 1, in the first year-end medical school exams at the University of Cambridge Faculty of Medicine. When I mailed it to my dad in Tanzania, he returned it after adding "Dear Ashok" at the top of the note to identify me as the recipient, though it was a personal note from the tutor. It was part of my outside-of-the-box, far-fetched plan to get a FIRST at the end of the first year medical school exams in the hope it would forestall my expulsion from the medical school for my lack of financing and defaulting college account. My theory was that the medical school was less likely to expel me for the unpaid medical school bills if I outperformed in the exams.

THE COUNTY HALL, LONDON, SE1
Telephone 01-928 5000 ext 8866/~~1441~~/~~1747~~
Ref: EO/HE 8/ /

MAJOR COUNTY AWARDS and FURTHER EDUCATION GRANTS

Final/~~Provisional~~ Assessment 1969/70

Dear Sir/~~Madam~~,

The Authority will make you an award for full-time study leading to

B. A Medicine at *Trinity Hall Cambridge*

28-5-70

for a period of *5/6 years* commencing *October 1969.*

Student number

428663

The value of the award will be approved fees plus a grant calculated as follows:

	£	s	d
Standard maintenance grant (home, college or lodgings rate)	L *395*	*0*	*0*
Additional .... weeks.....days at £7.0s.0d/£4.0s.6d per week			

This section applies only to Independent students — see 'student status' at top of form.

Dependants — spouse

— children

Two homes grant

Mature student grant

	£	s	d
TOTAL GRANT	*395*	*0*	*0*
Less			
Parental contribution	*160*	*0*	*0*
Student's contribution			
TOTAL CONTRIBUTION	*160*	*0*	*0*
TOTAL PAYABLE/~~EXCESS OF CONTRIBUTION OVER TOTAL GRANT~~ (see enclosed letter)	*235*	*0*	*0*

The award is subject to the Authority's regulations and rules (summarised in the enclosed booklet) and any changes and additions thereto and is made on the understanding that if you fail to start the course or if you leave college before the end of the course the Authority reserves the right to claim repayment of all or a proportion of the grant already paid to you as it deems fit. Acceptance of the award implies acceptance of these conditions.

You should read the booklet for details of how your grant will be paid, of additional grants for which you may be eligible, and for other general information about your award. I enclose a form for claiming excess travelling expenses.

To expedite a reply to any enquiry about your grant you should quote the reference and student number (both shown above) and your college.

MR. A. K SHARMA
Bolton House
Wychfield, Huntington,
Cambridge

W. J. Houghton
Education Officer

SAVED BY THE INNER LONDON EDUCATION AUTHORITY'S LARGESS. MAY 1970

This letter, dated May 28th, 1970, from the Inner London Education Authority, awarding me a grant for six years of medical school, which I received at the end of my first year of medical school, rescued me from abandoning medical school due to lack of funds. It was the result of long-distance unremitting efforts by my dad in Tanzania.

BACHELOR OF ARTS DEGREE. JUNE, 1972

I'm standing in front of the Senate House, Cambridge, where I was conferred the degree of Bachelor of Arts, even though all the subjects I had studied so far in my three years there could be considered as science (anatomy, physiology biochemistry, pathology, pharmacology, research in the role of diet in atherogenesis) subjects. I guess science and arts were equivalent, as both fundamentally explored and described the world around us.

TRAFALGAR SQUARE, CENTRAL LONDON. SIGHTSEEING AROUND CENTRAL LONDON. OCTOBER, 1973

At Trafalgar Square, a famous London tourist haunt, with a midwife student from the House of Midwives. I still wore my Trinity Hall tri-color scarf during cold weather.

GRADUATED FROM MEDICAL SCHOOL. JULY 1975

I graduated from Cambridge Medical School on July 2nd, 1975. However, the graduation ceremony was held on August 2nd, 1975. For the graduation, we had to wear a black gown, a white cape, a white bowtie and a black hat. After the graduation ceremony held at the Senate House, I'm standing here on a bridge over River Cam flowing behind Trinity Hall, with my two medical graduation certificates in hand. The certificates were for Bachelor of Medicine and Bachelor of Surgery.

UNIVERSITY OF CAMBRIDGE

I hereby certify that

ASHOK KUMAR SHARMA

of   Trinity Hall

in the University of Cambridge was admitted to

the Degree of BACHELOR of SURGERY

on   2   July   1975

Witness my hand this   18th   day of   July

one thousand nine hundred and   seventy-five

Registrary of the University

Registrary's Clerk

BACHELOR OF SURGERY CERTIFICATE FROM CAMBRIDGE.
JULY, 1975

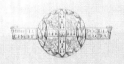

UNIVERSITY OF CAMBRIDGE

I hereby certify that

ASHOK KUMAR SHARMA

of   Trinity Hall

in the University of Cambridge was at a full

Congregation holden in the Senate House on

2 August 1975 admitted to the Degree of

BACHELOR of MEDICINE

Witness my hand this second day of August

one thousand nine hundred and seventy-five

R. S. *Waddington*

Registrary of the University

Registrary's Clerk

BACHELOR OF MEDICINE CERTIFICATE FROM CAMBRIDGE.
AUGUST, 1975

CERTIFICATE OF FULL REGISTRATION
AS A MEDICAL PRACTITIONER
(PRINCIPAL LIST)

Registration No.: 2239431   Date of Certificate: 24 June 1976

 I HEREBY CERTIFY that the person named below has to-day been fully registered under the Medical Acts in the Principal List of the Register of Medical Practitioners:—

SHARMA, Ashok Kumar *8 Jul 1975, 24 June 1976 E
16 Wellwood Rd, Goodmayes, Essex
MBBS 1975 Camb

 The particulars shown above comprise the name, date of full registration, address, and qualifications of the practitioner to whom this certificate relates. If two dates are shown, the first date (distinguished by an asterisk) is that of *provisional* registration.
 A letter E after the date of registration indicates that the practitioner was registered by the Registrar of the Branch Council for England and Wales. C or F indicates that the practitioner was registered as a Commonwealth or as a foreign practitioner, as the case may be.

MR Draper

REGISTRAR

NOTE

 This certificate affords evidence of registration in the Principal List on the date stated. Evidence that the practitioner continues to be registered in the Principal List in subsequent years will be afforded by the inclusion of the practitioner's name as fully registered in the Medical Register which is published annually by the Council, and reference should thereafter be made to the CURRENT Medical Register for evidence of the continued registration of the practitioner in the Principal List.

MY MEDICAL LICENSE. JUNE, 1976

 My certificate of full registration as a medical practitioner from the General Medical Council of Great Britain, awarded after completing twelve months of housemanship in June of 1976. The letter E after the date on the certificate indicates the practitioner is a graduate of a medical school in England. The date of the medical graduation is to the left of the certificate date.

Printed in Great Britain
by Amazon

76676777R00170